新基点 (New Benchmark) 全国高职高专院校商务英语系列规划教材
NEW BENCHMARK

英 美 概 况

（第三版）

An Outline of the UK and the USA

（Third Edition）

主　编：刘夏青　刘白玉
副主编：包　芳　顿小慧　王春玲
编　委：（以拼音为序）
包　芳　顿小慧　扈　珺　刘白玉
刘璐丝　刘夏青　刘　雪　矫永芹
潘　凌　王春玲　张军燕

对外经济贸易大学出版社
中国·北京

图书在版编目（CIP）数据

英美概况 / 刘夏青，刘白玉主编. —3 版. —北京：对外经济贸易大学出版社，2019.8 (2023. 5 重印)

新基点（New Benchmark）全国高职高专院校商务英语系列规划教材

ISBN 978-7-5663-2078-0

Ⅰ. ①英… Ⅱ. ①刘… ②刘… Ⅲ. ①英语–阅读教学–高等职业教育–教材 ②英国–概况–英文 ③美国–概况–英文 Ⅳ. ①H319.4：K

中国版本图书馆 CIP 数据核字（2019）第 176024 号

英美概况（第三版）

An Outline of the UK and the USA（Third Edition）

刘夏青 刘白玉 主编

责任编辑：董 黛

助理编辑：郭玉红

对 外 经 济 贸 易 大 学 出 版 社

北京市朝阳区惠新东街 10 号 邮政编码：100029

邮购电话：010 – 64492338 发行部电话：010 – 64492342

网址：http://www.uibep.com E-mail：uibep@126.com

北京时代华都印刷有限公司印装 新华书店经销

成品尺寸：185mm×260mm 18.25 印张 422 千字

2019 年 8 月北京第 3 版 2023年 5 月第 3 次印刷

ISBN 978-7-5663-2078-0

印数：4 501 – 5 700 册 定价：39.00 元

出版说明

“新基点（New Benchmark）全国高职高专院校商务英语系列规划教材”是对外经济贸易大学出版社联合全国重点职业学院的骨干教师推出的一套全新的商务英语系列教材。本套教材适用于全国高职高专院校英语专业商务/应用/外贸英语方向以及财经类专业的学生。

目前高职教育提出了“工学结合、项目为中心、案例驱动教学、边讲边练”为核心的理念。本套教材就是贯彻这个理念，着眼于提高学生实际操作能力和就业能力的目的，采取模块化、多案例、互动式、重实训的编写方式，让学生在理论够用的基础上，在实训环节上有所突破。

我国高职高专教育的培养目标是以能力培养和技术应用为本位, 其基础理论教学以应用为目的、够用为尺度、就业为导向；教材强调应用性和适用性，符合高职高专教育的特点，既能满足学科教育又能满足职业资格教育的“双证书”（毕业证和技术等级证）教学的需要。本套教材编写始终贯彻商务英语教学的基本思路：将英语听说读写译技能与商务知识有机融合，使学生在提高英语语言技能的同时了解有关商务知识，并练就“两条腿走路”的本领，培养以商务知识为底蕴、语言技能为依托的新时代复合型、实用型人才。

本套教材包括《商务英语综合教程》（1–4 册）、《商务英语听说》（1–2 册）、《商务英语口语》（1–2 册）、《国际商务报刊选读》《商务英语写作》《商务英语翻译》《国际商务函电》《国际商务谈判》《国际商务制单》《国际商务英语模拟实训教程》《商务礼仪》《英语应用文》《跨文化交际》《英美概况》《旅游英语》《酒店英语》《物流英语》《财经英语》《文秘英语》《会计英语》《餐饮与服务英语》《劳动与社会保障英语》等。本套教材不是封闭的，而是随着教学模式、课程设置和课时的变化，不断推陈出新。

本套教材的作者不仅具有丰富的商务英语教学经验，而且具有本专业中级以上职称、企业第一线工作经历、主持或参与过多项应用技术研究。这是本套教材编写质量的重要保证。

此外，本套教材配有教师用书或课件等立体化教学资源，供教师教学参考（见书末赠送课件说明）。

对外经济贸易大学出版社

2014 年 7 月

第三版前言

《英美概况（第二版）》于 2015 年出版至今已四年有余。四年多以来，国际形势风云变幻，英国脱欧、美国总统大选、德国总统大选、法国总统大选、中共十九大召开、美联储持续加息、叙利亚战争、中美贸易战……所有这些都影响着世界格局，也影响着英国和美国的政治、经济、文化、军事等。本书第二版承蒙全国高校广大师生喜爱，多次重印。为了给广大师生提供最新的资讯信息和教学资料，特对此书进行更新与完善。

第三版教材秉承了第一版和第二版教材的特色：语言规范，理论系统，技巧实用，内容完整，教辅齐全。同时，第三版教材对部分内容进行了更新修订。修订的内容主要如下：（1）对排版、内容等方面存在的纰漏和差错进行了订正；（2）对有关章节的背景资料、常用例句和课后习题进行了更新；（3）对有关章节教材内容和条目进行了调整和修改；（4）对教材配套教学课件、试题进行了修改和补充。

本教材由刘夏青和刘白玉担任主编并负责统稿工作。具体编写分工为：刘雪（概要）、张军燕（历史）、王春玲（政治）、顿小慧&矫永芹（经济）、顿小慧（军事）、刘夏青&刘璐丝（文化与教育）、包芳（宗教），包芳&潘凌（文学艺术）、刘白玉（保持乐观）、扈珺（附录）、矫永芹（试题）。

第三版教材的修订得到了对外经济贸易大学出版社的全力支持和鼎力相助，在此表示衷心的感谢！在本教材修订编写过程中，我们参阅了国内外多位专家学者的著作，也参考了同行的相关教材和资料，在此向他们表示崇高的敬意和真诚的感谢！

由于编者水平所限，书中错漏和不妥之处在所难免，恳请专家、同行及读者继续赐教。

刘夏青　刘白玉

2019 年 3 月 12 日于烟台黄海之滨

第二版前言

《英美概况（第一版）》于2010年出版后，因其语言通俗易懂、内容新颖、趣味性强而深受广大师生喜爱，多次重印。但四年多来世界发生了很大变化，尤其是英美两国的政治、经济和军事。为了给广大师生提供最近的成果，有必要对此书进行修订。

新修订的教材体例保持了原版的风貌，只是对部分内容进行了更新，使其更符合英美国家现实。譬如，英国现任首相是卡梅伦，2013年英国的GDP为2.522万亿美元，人口是6 410万；美国的GDP则为16.8万亿美元，人口是3.161亿。另外，概要、历史、政治、经济、军事、文化与教育、宗教、文学艺术等内容也作了更新。

参加本书修订的教师及参编部分如下：刘雪&部寒（概要）、张军燕&宋艳梅（历史）、王春玲&王莉&王晓琳（政治）、韩小宁&刘白玉（经济）、顿小慧&王建波（军事）、刘夏青&刘璐丝（文化与教育）、包芳（宗教）、包芳&顾征（文学艺术）。“保持乐观”部分由刘白玉编写，“附录”部分由扈珺编写。

本教材在再版的过程中继续得到对外经济贸易大学出版社和资深编辑李丽老师的鼎力支持，再次表示衷心感谢。同时也特别感谢包芳和韩小宁两位老师认真细致的校对。

水平所限，书中错误在所难免，切望读者继续赐教。

刘白玉

2014年7月于烟台黄海之滨

第一版前言

随着经济的发展，我国对外交往活动日益增多，越来越多的国内机构和企业与国外相关企业开展了交流与合作。在这样一个全球化的背景下，商务英语人才不仅要懂得基本的专业知识，更要深入了解国外的文化，《英美概况》正是基于上述前提应运而生。

本教材根据《高职高专教育英语课程教学基本要求》编写，在编写过程中力图符合英语教师及学生的实际需要和实际水平，做到语言通俗易懂、内容新颖、趣味性强。

本教材分为两大部分：英国部分和美国部分。每部分各分为八章，介绍了英、美两国的历史、政治、经济、教育、宗教及文学艺术等方面的基本知识，有助于学习者了解英美的价值观念及生活方式，加深对语言和文化的理解，增强对文化差异的敏感性，达到扩大知识面、巩固和提高英语水平的目的。

英语语言规范是英语教材的基础，为保证学生学到原汁原味的英语，我们的资料全部选自英美书籍、报纸、杂志和网站。大学不仅要教书，而且要育人。我们在每章中穿插了：名人名言——名人的力量是无穷的；欢乐时刻——幽默是金；保持乐观——永远保持积极向上的人生观，使我们的大学生在具备“高智商”的同时也具备“高情商”。其中，“保持乐观”由刘白玉编写。

参加本书编写的其他教师及其分工如下（按照每部分中八章的内容分）：刘雪（概要），张军燕（历史），王晓琳&王春玲（英国部分政治），王莉（美国部分政治），韩小宁&顿小慧（经济、军事），刘夏青（文化与教育），包芳（宗教、文学艺术）。附录部分由扈珺编写。

本教材既可供高职高专英语专业的学生使用，也可作为全校选修课用书供非英语专业的学生使用，同时也可供英语本科专业学生及其他英语爱好者参考使用。

本教材另配PPT课件和5套试题，并提供全部练习答案，使用者可查看书后的“课件赠送说明”，以便获取。

本教材在编写过程中得到了对外经济贸易大学出版社及其编辑李丽老师的大力支持，对此表示深深的谢意。同时也特别感谢刘夏青、韩小宁两位老师，她们不辞辛劳，参与教材的定稿校正。

由于时间仓促，再加上编者水平有限，书中难免有错漏之处，恳请专家和读者批评指正。

刘白玉

2010年3月于烟台黄海之滨

Contents

Part One
The United Kingdom

Chapter 1

Brief Introduction to the United Kingdom

Histories make men wise; poems witty; the mathematics subtle; natural philosophy deep; moral grave; logic and rhetoric able to contend.

—Francis Bacon, British philosopher

1. Brief Introduction

The United Kingdom of Great Britain and Northern Ireland (commonly known as the United Kingdom, the UK, or Britain) is a **sovereign** state located off the northwestern coast of the continental Europe. It is an island country, spanning a group of islands including Great Britain, the northeastern part of Ireland, and many small islands. Northern Ireland is the only part of the UK with a land border, sharing it with the Republic of Ireland. Apart from this land border, the UK is surrounded by the Atlantic Ocean, the North Sea, the English Channel and the Irish Sea. The largest island, Great Britain, is linked to France by the Channel Tunnel[1].

Countries of the United Kingdom are a term used to describe England, Northern Ireland, Scotland, and Wales: these four together form the sovereign state of the United Kingdom of Great Britain and Northern Ireland. While "countries" is the term commonly used to describe them, because of a lack of a formal British constitution, and owing to a **complicated** history of the formation of the United Kingdom, no official name exists and various terms are used. England, Northern Ireland, Scotland and Wales however are not formal **subdivision**s of the United Kingdom.

The Parliament of the United Kingdom and Her Majesty's Government in the United Kingdom deal with all reserved matters for Northern Ireland and Scotland and all non-transferred matters for Wales, but not in general with matters that have been devolved to the Northern Ireland Assembly, the Scottish Parliament and the Welsh Assembly. England remains the full responsibility of the Parliament of the United Kingdom, which is centralized in London. As a sovereign state, the United Kingdom as a whole is the **entity** which is used in intergovernmental organizations, and as the representative member state within the European Union and the United Nations, as well as under international law; England, Northern Ireland,

Scotland and Wales are not listed on the International Organization for Standardization (ISO) list of countries.

The Channel Islands and the Isle of Man[2] are British islands, but are not under the **jurisdiction** of the United Kingdom. Ireland is a separate republic; although part of the geographical British Isles, it is not a part of the UK. English, Northern Irish, Scottish and Welsh nationals are all British citizens without **distinction**. (Irish nationality laws entitle those born in Northern Ireland also to citizenship of the Republic.)

2. Location and Area

2.1 Location

The United Kingdom, consisting of Great Britain (England, Wales, and Scotland） and Northern Ireland, is twice the size of America's New York State. England, in the southeast part of the British Isles, is separated from Scotland on the north by the granite Cheviot Hills[3]; from them the Pennine chain of uplands extends south through the center of England, reaching its highest point in the Lake District in the northwest. To the west along the border of Wales—a land of steep hills and valleys—are the Cambrian Mountains[4], while the Cotswolds[5], a range of hills in Gloucestershire[6], extend into the surrounding shires.

Important rivers flowing into the North Sea are the Thames, Humber, Tees, and Tyne. In the west are the Severn[7] and Wye[8], which empty into the Bristol Channel[9] and are **navigable**, as are the Mersey[10] and Ribble[11].

2.2 Area

The total area of the United Kingdom is approximately 248,532 square kilometers (95,960 sq mi) comprising of the island of Great Britain, the northeastern one-sixth of the island of Ireland (Northern Ireland) and other smaller islands. It lies between the North Atlantic Ocean and the North Sea, coming within 35 kilometers (22 mi) of the northwest coast of France, from which it is separated by the English Channel. The United Kingdom lies between latitudes 49° and 59°N (the Shetland Islands reach to nearly 61°N), and longitudes 9°W to 2°E.

3. Climate

The United Kingdom has a **temperate** climate, with plentiful rainfall all year round. The temperature varies with the seasons but seldom drops below −11℃ or rises above 35℃. The prevailing wind is from the southwest, bearing frequent spells of mild and wet weather from the Atlantic Ocean. Eastern parts are most **sheltered** from this wind and are therefore the driest. Atlantic currents, warmed by the Gulf Stream, bring mild winters, especially in the west, where winters are wet, especially over high ground. Summers are warmest in the southeast of England, being closest to the European mainland, and coolest in the north. Snowfall can occur in winter and early spring, though it rarely settles to great depth away from high ground.

The climate of the United Kingdom is classified as a mid-latitude oceanic climate, with warm summers, cool winters and plentiful precipitation throughout the year. However, a **plausible** argument can be made that some parts of south-east England (for example, Essex) actually have a **semi-arid** climate by virtue of having less than 500mm average **annual** rainfall. The principal factors that influence the country's climate include its northerly **latitude**, the close **proximity** to the Atlantic Ocean, and the warming of the surrounding waters by the Gulf Stream. The weather can be **notoriously** changeable from one day to the next but temperature variations throughout the year are relatively small.

The boundary of **convergence** between the warm tropical air and the cold polar air lies over the United Kingdom. In this area, the large temperature variation creates instability and this is a major factor that influences the often unsettled weather the country experiences, where many types of weather can be experienced in a single day.

Regional climates in the United Kingdom are influenced by the Atlantic Ocean and latitude. Northern Ireland, Wales and western parts of England and Scotland, being closest to the Atlantic, are generally the mildest, wettest and windiest regions of the UK, and temperature ranges here are seldom extreme. Eastern areas are drier, cooler, and less windy and also experience the greatest daily and seasonal temperature variations. Northern areas are generally cooler and wetter and have a smaller temperature range than southern areas. Though the UK is mostly under the influence of the **maritime** tropical **air mass** from the southwest, different regions are more **susceptible** than others when different air masses affect the country: Northern Ireland and the west of Scotland are the most exposed to the maritime polar air mass which brings cool moist air; the east of Scotland and northeast England are more exposed to the continental polar air mass which brings cold dry air; the south and southeast of England are more exposed to the continental tropical air mass which brings warm dry air; Wales and the southwest of England are most exposed to the maritime tropical air mass which brings warm moist air.

4. Topography

The physical geography of the UK varies greatly. The geography of England consists of lowland terrain, with mountainous terrain north-west of the Tees-Exe line including the Cumbrian Mountains[12] of the Lake District, the Pennines[13] and limestone hills of the Peak District[14], Exmoor[15] and Dartmoor[16]. The geography of Scotland is distinguished by the Highland Boundary Fault[17]—a geological rock **fracture**—which **traverses** the Scottish mainland from Helensburgh[18] to Stonehaven[19]. The fault-line separates the two distinctively different regions of the Highlands to the north and west and the lowlands to the south and east. The geography of Wales is mostly mountainous, though south Wales is less mountainous than north and mid Wales. The geography of Ireland includes the Mourne Mountains[20] as well as Lough Neagh[21], at 388 square kilometers (150 sq mi), the largest body of water in the UK and Ireland.

The overall **geomorphology** of the UK was shaped by the combined forces of **tectonics** and climate change, in particular **glaciation**.

The exact centre of the island of Great Britain is disputed. Depending upon how it is calculated. It can be either Haltwhistle[22] in Northumberland[23], or Dunsop Bridge[24] in Lancashire[25].

England accounts for just over half of the total area of the UK, covering 130,279 square kilometers (50,301 sq mi). Most of the country consists of lowland terrain, with mountainous **terrain** north-west of the Tees-Exe line[26] including the Cumbrian Mountains of the Lake District, the Pennines and limestone hills of the Peak District, Exmoor and Dartmoor. The main rivers and **estuaries** are the Thames, Severn and the Humber. England's highest mountain is Scafell Pike[27], which is in the Lake District 978 meters (3,209 ft) high. England has a number of large towns and cities, including six of the top 50 Larger Urban Zones[28] in the European Union.

Scotland accounts for just under a third of the total area of the UK, covering 77,933 square kilometers (30,090 sq mi), including nearly eight hundred islands, mainly west and north of the mainland, notably the Hebrides[29], Orkney Islands[30] and Shetland Islands[31]. The topography of Scotland is distinguished by the Highland Boundary Fault—a geological rock fracture—which traverses the Scottish mainland from Helensburgh to Stonehaven. The fault-line separates two distinctively different regions, namely the Highlands to the north and west and the lowlands to the south and east. The more **rugged** Highland region contains the majority of Scotland's mountainous terrain, including Ben Nevis[32], which at 1,345 meters (4,413 ft) is the highest point in the British Isles. Lowland areas, especially the narrow waist of land between the Firth of Clyde[33] and the Firth of Forth[34] known as the Central Belt[35], are flatter and home to most of the population including Glasgow, Scotland's largest city, and Edinburgh, the capital and political centre of the country.

Wales accounts for less than a tenth of the total area of the UK, covering 20,779 square kilometers (8,023 sq mi). Wales is mostly mountainous, though south Wales is less mountainous than north and mid Wales. The main population and industrial areas are in south Wales, consisting of the coastal cities of Cardiff[36] (the capital and political and economic centre), Swansea[37] and Newport and the South Wales Valleys to their north. The highest mountains in Wales are in Snowdonia, and include Snowdon[38], which at 1,085 meters (3,560 ft) is the highest peak in Wales. The 14 (or possibly 15) Welsh mountains over 914 meters (3,000 ft) high are known collectively as the Welsh 3000s. Wales has over 2,700 kilometers (1,680 mi) of coastline. There are several islands off the Welsh mainland, the largest of which is Anglesey[39] in the northwest.

Northern Ireland accounts for just 14,130 square kilometers (5,460 sq mi) and is mostly hilly. It includes Lough Neagh, at 392 square kilometers (151 sq mi), the largest body of water in the UK and Ireland. The highest peak in Northern Ireland is Slieve Donard[40] at 850 meters (2,790 ft) in the Mourne Mountains.

5. Rivers and Lakes

5.1 The Longest River

The River Severn (Welsh: Afon Hafren, Latin: Sabrina) is the longest river in Great Britain, at 354 kilometers (220 mi). It rises at an altitude of 610 meters (2,001 ft) on Plynlimon near Llanidloes, Powys, in the Cambrian Mountains of mid Wales. It then flows through Shropshire, Worcestershire and Gloucestershire, with the county towns of Shrewsbury, Worcester, and Gloucester on its banks. With an average discharge of $107m^3/s$ at Apperley, Gloucestershire, the Severn is England's greatest river in terms of water flow.

The river is usually considered to become the Severn Estuary after the Second Severn Crossing between Severn Beach, South Gloucestershire and Sudbrook, Monmouthshire. The river then discharges into the Bristol Channel which in turn discharges into the Celtic Sea[41] and the wider Atlantic Ocean. The Severn's drainage basin area is 11,420 square kilometers (4,409 sq mi), excluding the River Wye and Bristol Avon which flow into the Bristol Channel. The major tributaries to the Severn are the Vyrnwy, Teme, Warwickshire Avon and Stour.

5.2 The River Thames

The river Thames is a major river flowing through southern England. While best known because its lower reaches flow through central London, the river flows through several other towns and cities, including Oxford, Reading and Windsor.

The river gives its name to several administrative or political names: The Thames Valley, a region of England centered around the river between Oxford and West London, the Thames Gateway, the area centered around the tidal Thames[42], and the Thames Estuary to the east of London.

The river Thames is the second longest river in the United Kingdom and the longest river entirely in England, rising at Thames Head in Gloucestershire, and flowing into the North Sea at the Thames Estuary. It has a special significance in flowing through London, the capital of the United Kingdom, although London only includes a short part of its course. The river is tidal in London with a rise and fall of 7 meters (23 ft) and becomes non-**tidal** at Teddington Lock. The **catchment** area covers a large part of south-eastern and western England and the river is fed by many tributaries. The river contains over 80 islands, having both seawater and freshwater stretches support a variety of wildlife.

5.3 Lough Neagh

Lough Neagh, sometimes Loch Neagh, from Irish, is a freshwater lake in Northern Ireland.

With an area of 392 square kilometers (151 sq mi), it is the largest lake in the British Isles and ranks among the forty largest lakes of Europe. Located 32 kilometers (20 mi) to the west of Belfast, it is approximately 30 kilometers (18 mi) long and 15 kilometers (9 mi) wide. It is very shallow around the **margin**s and the average depth in the main body of the lake is about 9 meters (30 ft); although at its deepest the Lough is about 25 meters (82 ft) deep.

Although the Lough is used for a variety of recreational and commercial activities, it is exposed and tends to get extremely rough very quickly in windy conditions. It is also used as a source of fresh water by Northern Ireland Water. Plans to increase the amount of water drawn from the Lough, through a new water treatment works at Hog Park Point, have long been planned but are yet to materialize.

6. Mountains and Hills

The ten tallest mountains in the UK are all found in Scotland. The highest peaks in each part of the UK are:

Ben Nevis (Aonach Mòr, 1,345 meters) in Scotland; Snowdon (Snowdonia, 1,085 meters) in Wales; Scafell Pike (Cumbrian Mountains, 978 meters) in England; and Slieve Donard (Mourne Mountains, 850 meters) in Northern Ireland.

Ben Nevis

Ben Nevis is the highest mountain in the British Isles. It is located at the western end of the Grampian Mountains in the Lochaber area of the Scottish Highlands, close to the town of Fort William.

As is common for many Scottish mountains, it is known both to locals and visitors as, simply, the Ben. It attracts an estimated 100,000 ascents a year, around three-quarters of which are made using the well-constructed Pony Track from Glen Nevis on the south side of the mountain. For climbers and mountaineers the main attraction lies in the 700-meter (2,300 ft) high cliffs of the north face; among the highest cliffs in the United Kingdom, they harbor some classic scrambles and rock climbs of all difficulties, and are one of the principal locations in the UK for ice climbing.

The summit, at 1,345 meters (4,413 ft) above sea level, features the ruins of an observatory, which was permanently staffed between 1883 and 1904. The meteorological data collected during this period are still important for understanding Scottish mountain weather. C. T. R. Wilson was inspired to invent the cloud chamber after a period spent working at the observatory.

7. Population

7.1 Population

According to the 2011 census, the total population of the United Kingdom was around 63,182,000. It is the 21st-most populated country in the world. Its overall population density is 259 people per square kilometer (671 people per sq mi), with England having a significantly higher population density than Wales, Scotland and Northern Ireland. Almost one-third of the population lives in England's southeast, which is predominantly urban and suburban, with about 9 million in the capital city of London, the population density of which is just over 5,200 per square kilometer (13,468 per sq mi).

The United Kingdom's population is predominantly White British. Being located close to continental Europe, the countries that formed the United Kingdom were subject to many invasions and migrations from the continent, especially from Scandinavia, including Roman occupation for several centuries. Historically, British people were therefore thought to be descended mainly from the different ethnic stocks that settled there before the 11th century: pre-Celtic, Celtic, Anglo-Saxon, Viking and Norman. However, recent genetic testing has revealed that these migrations contributed very little to the British genepool, with around 80% of white British DNA coming from an ancestral population who settled in the British Isles 12,000 years ago.

The United Kingdom (UK) Office for National Statistics' 2016-based National Population Projections indicated that, if recent trends continue, the UK's population would increase by 3.6 million between mid-2016 and mid-2026. This represents an average annual growth rate of 0.5%. Over the same period, the population of England is projected to grow by 5.9%; for Wales, this figure is 3.1%, while for Scotland and Northern Ireland the figures are 3.2% and 4.2% respectively. These projections do not allow for any possible effects of the UK leaving the European Union.

7.2 Ethnic Groups

Historically, British people were thought to be descended from the varied ethnic stocks that settled there before the 11th century: the Celts, Romans, Anglo-Saxons, Norse and the Normans. However, recent genetic analysis indicates that around 80% of British DNA comes from an indigenous population who settled Britain around 12,000 years ago at the end of the last Ice Age, with **subsequent** invaders contributing very little to the gene pool. Since 1945, substantial immigration from Africa, the Caribbean and South Asia has been a **legacy** of ties **forge**d by the British Empire. Migration from new EU member states in Central and Eastern Europe since 2004 has resulted in growth in these population groups, but, as of 2008, the trend is reversing and many of these migrants are returning home, leaving the size of these groups unknown. As of 2001, 92.1% of the population identified themselves as White, leaving 7.9% of the UK population identifying themselves as mixed race or ethnic minority.

Ethnic diversity varies significantly across the UK. 30.4% of London's population and 37.4% of Leicester's[43] was estimated to be non-white as of June 2005, whereas less than 5% of the populations of North East England, Wales and the South West were from ethnic minorities according to the 2001 census. As of 2016, 31.4% of primary and 27.9% of secondary pupils at state schools in England were from ethnic minority families.

8. Languages

The UK does not **de jure** have an official language but the **predominant** spoken language is English, a West Germanic language descended from Old English which features a large number of borrowings from Old Norse[44], Norman French and Latin. Largely due to the British Empire, the English language has spread across the world, and become the international language of business as well as the most widely taught second language. Scots, a language descended from early northern Middle English, is recognized at European level. There are also four Celtic languages in use in the UK: Welsh, Irish Gaelic (generally just referred to as Irish), Scottish Gaelic and Cornish. In the 2001 Census over a fifth (21%) of the population of Wales said they could speak Welsh, an increase from the 1991 Census (18%). In addition, it is estimated that about 200,000 Welsh speakers live in England. The 2001 census in Northern Ireland showed that 167,487 (10.4%) people "had some knowledge of Irish", almost exclusively in the Catholic/nationalist population. Over 92,000 people in Scotland (just under 2% of the population) had some Gaelic language ability, including 72% of those living in the Outer Hebrides. The number of school children being taught in Welsh, Scottish Gaelic and Irish is increasing. Welsh and Scottish Gaelic are also spoken by small groups around the globe with some Scottish Gaelic still spoken in Nova Scotia, Canada and Welsh in Patagonia, Argentina.

Across the United Kingdom, it is generally compulsory for pupils to study a second language to some extent: up to the age of 14 in England, and up to the age of 16 in Scotland. French and German are the two most commonly taught second languages in England and Scotland. In Wales, all pupils up to age 16 are either taught in Welsh or taught Welsh as a second language.

Joyful Moment

When Was Rome Built?

Teacher: When was Rome built?
Tom: At night.
Teacher: Who told you that?
Tom: You did. You said Rome wasn't built in a day.

Notes

[1] Channel Tunnel 连接英法的英吉利海峡海底隧道
[2] Isle of Man 英国属地曼岛，首都道格拉斯
[3] Cheviot Hills 切维厄特丘陵，英国苏格兰和英格兰之间延伸 50 多公里的高地，以养羊业为主
[4] Cambrian Mountains 寒武山，地质年代中的寒武纪因此山得名
[5] Cotswolds 科茨沃尔德丘陵地带，位于英国西南部
[6] Gloucestershire 格洛斯特郡
[7] the Severn 塞文河，英国境内最长的河流
[8] the Wye 怀河，又为瓦伊河

[9] the Bristol Channel 布里斯托尔海峡，位于威尔士东南部
[10] the Mersey 莫西河，全长 110 公里
[11] the Ribble 里布尔河，全长 120 公里
[12] Cumbrian Mountains 坎布里亚山脉，在英国威尔士境内
[13] Pennines 奔宁山脉，从德比郡一直延伸到与苏格兰交界处，将英格兰北部地区分割为东西两侧
[14] the Peak District 英国峰区国家公园
[15] Exmoor 埃克斯穆尔国家公园，是英国的一处国家公园，位于西南英格兰的索美塞特郡西部和德文郡南部地区
[16] Dartmoor 达特穆尔，英格兰德文郡中部穆尔兰的一个地区，面积 368 平方英里（953 平方公里），是一个受保护的国家公园
[17] the Highland Boundary Fault 高地边界断层
[18] Helensburgh 海伦斯堡，苏格兰的一个镇
[19] Stonehaven 斯通黑文，位于苏格兰东北岸的阿伯丁郡
[20] Mourne Mountains 莫恩山脉
[21] Lough Neagh 内伊湖，英国北爱尔兰地区的一个淡水湖，欧洲西部第三大湖泊
[22] Haltwhistle 霍特威斯尔，英国传统集镇
[23] Northumberland 诺森伯兰郡
[24] Dunsop Bridge 英国的一个村庄，位于英国兰开夏郡
[25] Lancashire 兰开夏郡，位于英格兰西北部
[26] Tees-Exe line 蒂斯-埃克斯线，是一条假想的东北-西南线，起于蒂斯河，止于埃克斯河，可在大不列颠地图上绘制，大致将该岛分为低地和高地地区
[27] Scafell Pike 斯科菲峰，英格兰的最高峰
[28] Larger Urban Zones 欧洲都会城市排名
[29] Hebrides 赫布里底群岛，位于苏格兰西部
[30] Orkney Islands 奥克尼群岛，位于苏格兰以北，挪威以西
[31] Shetland Islands 设德兰群岛，苏格兰北部群岛
[32] Ben Nevis 本尼维斯山，英国最高山峰，海拔 1343 米，位于苏格兰西部，属格兰扁山脉
[33] Firth of Clyde 克莱德湾
[34] Firth of Forth 福斯湾
[35] the Central Belt 中央地带
[36] Cardiff 卡迪夫，威尔士首府
[37] Swansea 斯旺西，威尔士南部港口城市，西格拉摩根郡首府
[38] Snowdon 斯诺登山，英国威尔士北部的一座山
[39] Anglesey 安格尔西岛，威尔士西北爱尔兰海上的一座岛屿
[40] Slieve Donard 多纳德山
[41] Celtic Sea 凯尔特海

[42] Thames 泰晤士河
[43] Leicester 莱斯特郡
[44] Old Norse 古斯堪的纳维亚语

New Words

1. **sovereign** /'sɒvərɪn/ *adj.* independent of outside authority（国家）有主权的；完全独立的
—When did it become a sovereign country?
这个国家是什么时候成为主权国的？
2. **complicated** /'kɒmplɪkeɪtɪd/ *adj.* made up of intricate parts or aspects that are difficult to understand or analyze 复杂的
—Why does he have to wrap it all up in such a complicated language?
他为什么非得用这么晦涩的语言说话呢？
3. **subdivision** /'sʌbdɪˌvɪʒən/ *n.* a portion that is the result of subdividing 细分，一部分，分支
—Clan is a large citizens' organization based on kinship, constituting the largest political subdivision of an ancient Greek city-state.
宗族是一种基于亲戚关系的巨大的市民组织，它组成了古希腊城邦的最大的政治分支。
4. **entity** /'entɪti/ *n.* that which is perceived or known or inferred to have its own distinct existence (living or nonliving) 实体；存在；本质
—With bees one always talks about the colony as a single entity.
人们总是将蜜蜂这个群体作为一个单独的整体来谈论。
5. **jurisdiction** /ˌdʒʊərɪs'dɪkʃən/ *n.* (law) the right and power to interpret and apply the law 司法权，审判权，管辖权，控制权
—The court has no jurisdiction over foreign diplomats living in this country.
法院对居住在本国的外交官无裁判权。
6. **distinction** /dɪ'stɪŋkʃən/ *n.* a discrimination between things as different and distinct 差别，不同
—We should make a distinction between right and wrong.
我们应该分清是非。
7. **navigable** /'nævɪgəbəl/ *adj.* able to be sailed on or through safely 可航行的，可通船的，适于航行的
—With its engine broken, this great ship was not navigable.
这条大船的引擎坏了，无法再航行了。
8. **temperate** /'tempərət/ *adj.* (of weather or climate) free from extremes; mild; or characteristic of such weather or climate 温和的，适度的，有节制的
—Ninety percent of the country lies in the temperate zone.

这个国家百分之九十的地方都是温带。

9. **sheltered** /'ʃeltəd/ *adj.* kept away from（动词 shelter 的过去式和过去分词形式）受保护的；受庇护的

—These plants must be sheltered from direct sunlight.

这种植物必须遮起来，免受阳光直射。

10. **plausible** /'plɔːzəbəl/ *adj.* apparently reasonable and valid, and truthful 似真实合理的，似可信的

—He trotted out a most plausible story, but most of us were inclined to doubt the truth of it.

他提出了一个听起来很有道理的说法，但我们大多数人对此都持怀疑态度。

11. **semi-arid** /ˌsemi'ærɪd/ *adj.* 半干旱的

12. **annual** /'ænjuəl/ *adj.* occurring or payable every year 每年的，年度的，一年生的

—If you want to join, there's an entrance fee of $20 and an annual membership fee of $10.

入会须缴入会费 20 美元，年费 10 美元。

13. **latitude** /'lætɪtʃuːd/ *n.* 纬度，界限，自由选择权

—The latitude of the island is 30 degrees north.

这个岛的纬度是北纬三十度。

14. **proximity** /prɒk'sɪməti/ *n.* the region close around a person or thing 接近，亲近

15. **notoriously** /nəʊ'tɔːriəsli/ *adv.* to a notorious degree 臭名昭著地，众所周知地

—The innkeeper is a notoriously hard driving, whip-cracking perfectionist.

这个酒馆的老板出名地凶狠，不准手下人犯一点错误。

16. **convergence** /kən'vɜːdʒəns/ *n.* the occurrence of two or more things coming together 汇聚，汇合点，收敛

17. **maritime** /'mærɪtaɪm/ *adj.* relating to or involving ships or shipping or navigation or seamen 海的，海上的，海事的

—England was a great maritime power.

英国曾是海上的强国。

18. **air mass** *n.* 气团

19. **susceptible** /sə'septəbəl/ *adj.* easily impressed emotionally 易受外界影响的，易受感染的

—He's so susceptible that she easily gained his affection.

他易受感情影响，所以她很轻易就得到了他的爱。

20. **fracture** /'fræktʃə/ *n.* breaking or being broken (especially of a bone) 破裂，断裂；骨折

—Fracture of any part of the body can be very serious in old people.

老年人身体的任何部位发生骨折都有可能成为严重疾患。

21. **traverse** /trə'vɜːs/ *n.& v.* a horizontal beam that extends across something; to move across, over or through something 横木；横贯

—The railway traverses hundreds of miles of desert.

这条铁路贯穿数百英里的沙漠。

22. **geomorphology** /ˌdʒiːə(ʊ)mɔː'fɒlədʒɪ/ *n.* the branch of geology that studies the characteristics and configuration and evolution of rocks and land forms 地形学
23. **tectonics** /tek'tɒnɪks/ *n.* the science of architecture 构造学，构造地质学
—Structural geology and tectonics is an important branch of geology, which shows no prosperity in recent years.
构造地质学是地质学中的一个重要分支学科，近来显得不大景气。
24. **glaciation** /ˌgleɪsi'eɪʃən/ *n.* the condition of being covered with glaciers or masses of ice; the result of glacial action 冰河作用，冻结成冰
25. **terrain** /tə'reɪn/ *n.* a piece of ground having specific characteristics or military potential 地带，地域，地形
—A jeep is ideal for driving over rough terrain.
吉普车很适合在高低不平的路面上行驶.
26. **estuary** /'estʃuəri/ *n.* the wide part of a river where it nears the sea 河口，江口，海湾
—The river opens out suddenly into a broad estuary.
江面忽然开阔起来，形成一个宽广的河口。
27. **rugged** /'rʌgɪd/ *adj.* topographically very uneven 粗糙的，坚固的，崎岖的，高低不平的
—A postman pedals along a rugged path. Rain or shine, they bring the villagers news about the world beyond.
邮递员奔波在崎岖的山路上，他们风雨无阻，为村民们带去外面世界的信息。
28. **tidal** /'taɪdəl/ *adj.* of or relating to or caused by tides 潮的，有关潮水的；潮汐的；定时涨落的
—This trend of thought and society tidal current have deep traditional foundation and realism reason.
此思潮和社会潮流有着深远的传统基础和现实原因。
29. **catchment** /'kætʃmənt / *n.* a structure in which water is collected 流域；集水
—Buying a closes tool to know the catchment way of one's toilet is a very serious problem.
购买马桶了解自家卫生间的排水方式是个很重要的问题。
30. **margin** /'mɑːdʒɪn/ *n.* the boundary line or the area immediately inside the boundary 边缘；利润，余裕；页边的空白
—Could you use correction fluid to cover the letters on margin?
你能用涂改液涂去页边上的这些字母吗？
31. **subsequent** /'sʌbsɪkwənt/ *adj.* following in time or order 随后的，后来的
—He confessed to other crimes subsequent to the bank robbery.
他供认抢劫银行案后，又坦白了其他罪行。
32. **legacy** /'legəsi/ *n.* a gift of personal property by will 祖先传下来之物，遗赠物
—He left me a small legacy in a nuncupative will, as a token of his kindness to me.
他口头遗言上遗留给我一点遗产作为他对我关爱的表征。

33. **forge** /fɔːdʒ/ *vt.* come up with (an idea, plan, explanation, theory, or principle) after a mental effort 锻造，想出，伪造，构建

—They forged their manager's signature on the cheque.

他们在支票上伪造了经理的签名。

34. **de jure** /ˌdiːˈdʒʊri/ *adj.& adv.* by right; according to law [法]根据法律（的），权利上（的）

35. **predominant** /prɪˈdɒmɪnənt/ *adj.* having superior power and influence 卓越的；有力的；支配的；主要的；有影响的

—Will Chinese have become the predominant Internet language by 2025?

到 2025 年，汉语会成为占主导地位的网络语言吗？

Exercises

1. Choose the correct answer.

1) The longest river in England is ________.

A. River Thames B. River Tay C. River Bann D. River Tywi

2) The United Kingdom's population is predominantly ________.

A. Viking B. White British

C. Celtic D. Norman

3) Historically, British people were thought to be descended from the varied ethnic stocks that settled there before the ________.

A. 10th century B. 11th century

C. 12th century D. 13th century

4) There are also four Celtic languages in use in the UK, they are ________.

A. Welsh B. Irish Gaelic C. Scottish Gaelic D. Cornish

5) England accounts for just over ________ of the total area of the UK.

A. 1/2 B. 2/3 C. 2/5 D. 3/4

2. Decide whether the following statements are True or False.

1) The United Kingdom has a temperate climate, and it is very dry and cold all year round.

2) Scotland accounts for just over a third of the total area of the UK, covering 77,933 square kilometers (30,090 sq mi).

3) The River Thames is the second longest river in the United Kingdom and the longest river entirely in Scotland.

4) Across the United Kingdom, it is not necessary for pupils to study a second language.

5) Belfast is the capital of and the largest city in Northern Ireland, a constituent country of the United Kingdom.

3. Fill in the blanks according to the passage.

1) ________ of the United Kingdom and ________ in the United Kingdom deal with all reserved matters for Northern Ireland and Scotland and all non-transferred matters for

Wales.

2) ________ and ________ are the two most commonly taught second languages in England and Scotland.

3) The total area of the United Kingdom is approximately 248,532 square kilometers (95,960 sq mi) comprising of the island of Great Britain, the northeastern one-sixth of ________ and smaller islands.

4) In UK, the fault-line separates two distinctively different regions; namely the ________ to the north and west and the ________ to the south and east.

5) UK's overall population density is 259 people per square kilometer (671 people per sq mi), with ________ having a significantly higher population density than ________, ________ and ________.

4. Explain the following terms according to the passage.

1) location of the United Kingdom
2) the geographic features of Scotland
3) River Thames
4) Ben Nevis
5) Ethnic diversity of the United Kingdom

5. Answer the following questions according to the passage.

1) Please introduce the general features of UK's geography.
2) What are the characteristics of UK's climate?
3) Try to introduce the capital city of the United Kingdom.

6. Discussion.

1) Try to appreciate the British National Anthem "God Save the Queen".

God Save the Queen

God save our gracious Queen
Long live our noble Queen
God save the Queen
Send her victorious
Happy and glorious
Long to reign over us
God save the Queen

O Lord our God arise
Scatter her enemies
And make them fall
Confound their politics

Frustrate their knavish tricks
On Thee our hopes we fix
God save us all

Thy choicest gifts in store
On her be pleased to pour
Long may she reign
May she defend our laws
And ever give us cause
To sing with heart and voice
God save the Queen

2) Discuss the relation between the United Kingdom as an entity and its four subdivisions.

Stay Positive

1. Destiny is not a matter of chance; it is a matter of choice.
2. First say to yourself what you would be, and then do what you have to do.

Chapter 2

History of the United Kingdom

The people who get on in this world are the people who get up and look for circumstances they want, and if they cannot find them, they make them.

—George Bernard Shaw, British dramatist

1. Early Settlers

None of the pre-Roman inhabitants of Britain has survived, so its history, culture and way of life are known mainly through archaeological finds. Before the 1st century AD Britain was made up of many Celt[1] tribe kingdoms. So there is also a small amount of linguistic evidence, from river and hill names, which is covered in the articles on Pre-Celtic and Celtic.

Stonehenge（巨石阵）

It is believed that Stone Age[2] man migrated to Britain across the land bridge that then joined Britain to the rest of Europe. Around 6500 BC, the rising water levels cut Britain off from Europe and left these peoples to develop separately and largely untroubled by any large outside tribes or armies. Although Stone Age artifacts can be found all over Britain, the largest of their construction are found in southern England.

Later Iron Age[3] men, known as Celtic peoples, started to change their living habits. They stopped building burial mounds and stone circles, and stopped using the ancient sites like Stonehenge[4]. Instead, the Iron Age peoples took to farming in settled fields and to living in protected hill forts. Then farming land became important but agriculture progressed slowly as during the Stone Age, since the Celts primarily obtained food by hunting, fishing, weaving and, above all, fighting.

2. The Roman Invasion of Britain

In 55 BC the Roman general Julius Caesar[5] conquered France (at the time the country was called Gaul[6]). The Gauls fought hard against the Romans and had been helped by their friends in Britain. Caesar was upset by their assistance and decided to teach the Britons[7] a lesson. In 55 and 54 BC Julius Caesar came to Britain with a Roman Army. Both times the British warriors

Hadrian's Wall

and the bad British weather made his army give up and return to Gaul.

Ideas of invading Britain faded until Claudius[8] became Emperor in 41 AD. The Roman Army sailed from France across the English Channel and landed in Kent[9]. After the blooding battles the Romans gained the victory and they took the whole of modern England and Wales over the next forty years and periodically extended their control over much of lowland Scotland. Roman rule saw great cultural change, but obviously without any mass migration. It was Romans who brought Christianity to England first.

Before the Romans invaded, the Celts ruled Britain. The Celts were divided up into different tribes ruled by kings or chiefs who lived in hill forts. Until the Roman Conquest of Britain, Britain's British population was relatively stable, and by the time of Julius Caesar's first invasion, the British population of old Britain was speaking a Celtic language. In Celtic Britain there were no towns, no roads and most people were farmers who lived in houses made from wood.

After entering into Britain the Romans pushed north, and built the network of straight roads across the country, most of which can still be followed today. As they pushed north into Scotland, they decided to build a great wall, Hadrian's Wall[10], to control the frontier. It was started in 122 AD and you can still see large sections of Hadrian's Wall in England today. And the country appears to have enjoyed a period of peace. Around 300 AD the Roman Empire came under continuous attack by the wild groups in central Europe and some troops were withdrawn to help in that area. Northern Britain started to suffer attacks from the Scots[11] and Picts[12].

But it was not until 410 AD that the Roman Emperor Constantine finally removed the troops of Britain to defend the Rhine[13] frontier from attack. The cities of Britain were instructed to look to their own defense. The Romans never returned to Britain again. Then Britain was to slip into a 600-year-period of wars and separation. Since the later Angles[14] and Saxons[15] invasion, the Celts were pushed West, and the country was under almost continuous Viking[16] attack.

3. Anglo-Saxon Conquests

In the 5th and 6th centuries the Germanic Angle, Saxon, and Jute[17] tribes invaded Britain and they were known as the Anglo-Saxons. Historians are not sure why the Anglo-Saxons came to Britain. It may have been because their land often flooded and it was difficult to grow crops, so they were looking for new places to settle down and farm.

There is of course the whole legend of King Arthur[18] that is ascribed to this period. Arthur appears to have been a fictional, rather than historical figure. The new Anglo-Saxon invaders were not organized centrally, as the Romans had been, or as the Normans would be. They slowly colonized northwards and westwards, pushing the native Celts to the border of Britain. Roman

Britain was replaced by Anglo-Saxon Britain, with the Celtic peoples remaining in Cornwall, Wales and Scotland. And the Celtic language was also replaced by the language of Anglo-Saxon. They took control of most of Britain, although they never conquered Scotland, Wales and Cornwall. The modern culture of Britain originated from that of Anglo-Saxon.

4. Viking Challenge and the Rise of Wessex

The Viking people came from three countries of Scandinavia: Denmark, Norway and Sweden. They were also known as the Norse[19] people. Many Vikings were great travelers and sailed all over Europe and the northern Atlantic Ocean in their long ships. Some went as fierce pirate raiders: they stole treasure and attacked local people. But most Vikings who sailed overseas were simply searching for better land for their farms. The Viking Age began in the 8th century AD and lasted for 300 years.

The Vikings attacked Wessex[20] in 878, and the Saxon king, Alfred[21] (871-899) had to flee to the Somerset[22] marshes. However he was able to regroup and counter attack. His efforts and those later of his son and grandsons gradually pushed the Vikings northwards and eventually into the sea. By 955, Edgar[23], the grandson of Alfred the Great, ruled over a united England. Government became centralized, and the king ruled the whole country. A decade later the strongest Earl Harold[24], Earl of East Anglia, controlled Wessex and was in a powerful position. So when Edward the Confessor[25] died in 1066 without a male heir, Harold claimed the throne. His claim was disputed by William[26], Duke of Normandy, whose claim to the English throne was even slighter than Harold's, and this started the later Norman invasion.

5. Norman Conquest

The Norman Conquest of England took place in 1066. After Edward the Confessor died childless on January 5, 1066, he was succeeded by Harold, whose sister was married to Edward the Confessor. He claimed Edward the Confessor had chosen him the successor on his deathbed in the presence of the queen. Since Harold was a powerful lord in the country, he soon received the approval of the Witan[27], the decision making body who could decide who would be king. This was resented by William of Normandy[28] (a region in Northern France today, just across the English Channel). He was distantly related to Edward the Confessor and claimed that Edward the Confessor had promised him the throne of England on his death, which caused the invasion of Norman.

5.1 The Invasion of Norman (1066)

Duke William and his army crossed the English Channel and landed in England on September 28, 1066, and won the decisive victory at the battle of Hastings[29]. He was crowned William I in London on Christmas Day, 1066. For the next five years he faced a series of English rebellions in various parts of the country and a half-hearted Danish invasion, but he was able to overcome all resistance and establish an enduring regime.

William continued to build a lot of castles across the whole country in which the Tower of London[30] was built with the express aim of showing the inhabitants of London who was in charge now. The uniqueness of the Norman Conquest in British history is that it introduced England the feudalism and French language. The English nobility lost their lands, and the new landowners built castles like Windsor[31] that survive to this day. By the time William died in 1087 around 100 major castles had been built. The other major legacy of William's reign is the Domesday Book[32]. William wished to know the existing and potential value of his new kingdom. Surveyors were sent out across the whole country and their report was the massive Domesday Book which noted land down to individual landholdings.

The other Norman Kings were no easy-going persons, but they had little effect on posterity until Henry II[33] ascended to the throne in 1154. Since the Crown of Henry II the England entered the House of Plantagenet[34](1154-1399).

5.2 House of Plantagenet

The reign of Henry II represented a reversion in power back from the **barony** to the monarchical state in England; it was also to see a similar redistribution of legislative power from the Church, again to the **monarchical** state. This period also foretold a properly constituted legislation and a shift away from feudalism. After Henry II, English started running into problems, either with the Barons or the people. It was also during the reign of Henry II that the nature of England's relationship with the rest of Britain, and with the kings of France was defined. Henry II was the first English king to go into Ireland, and his attempts to partition Ireland were unsuccessful.

Henry's successor Richard I[35], "the Lion Heart" (also known as "the Absent King"), was preoccupied with foreign wars, taking part in the Third Crusade[36] and defending his French territories against Philip II[37] of France. His younger brother John（1199-1216）, who succeeded him, was not so fortunate. He suffered the loss of Normandy and numerous other French territories. He also managed to outrage the feudal nobility and leading Church figures. To the extent that in 1215, they led an armed rebellion and forced him to sign the Magna Carta[38], which imposed legal limits on the king's personal powers, stated that the king was not above the law, that he only ruled by the will of the people, represented by **Parliament**, and that if he broke his part of the contract, then the Parliament had the right to overthrow the king.

During the Middle Ages the Normans declined gradually. Between 1370 and 1413, kings were dethroned; peasants revolted in 1381 and the House of Lancaster seized the throne after the Wars of Roses[39] from 1455 to 1485. The Norman conquest brought an important change in English history for a number of reasons. The conquest linked England more closely with Continental Europe, and made Scandinavian influence less important. It created one of the most powerful monarchies in Europe. The conquest changed the English language and culture, and set the stage

for rivalry with France, which would continue (with breaks) until the 19th century. It also had important consequences for the rest of the British Isles, paving the way for further Norman invasions in Wales and Ireland, and the extensive penetration of the aristocracy of Scotland by Norman and other French-speaking families.

6. Tudor England (1485-1603)

In 1485 Henry Tudor of the House of Lancaster was crowned as Henry VII. Henry VII married into the House of York. This personal union ended the conflict, and a new famous dynasty, the Tudors, emerged, which subsequently ruled England and Wales for 116 years.

The Tudor[40] dynasty ruled England from 1485 to 1603 and oversaw the transition of England from a feudal country to a modern state. Their story includes some of the most dramatic and unforgettable events in European history. And they remain the most famous and **controversial** of royal families.

6.1 Henry VIII (1509-1547)

Henry VIII, son of Henry VII, who came to the throne in 1509, was a man who left his stamp on history. His six marriages in search of a male heir led to two daughters, named Mary and Elizabeth, and a son Edward, who died young. Henry's need for a divorce led to a conflict with the pope who refused to grant Henry one. He countered them by dissolving the Roman Catholic Church[41] in Britain, and was inspired by the Protestants[42] Reformation led by Martin Luther[43]. He set up the Church of England. Though his religious position was not at all Protestant, the resultant separation ultimately led to England distancing itself almost entirely from Rome.

Henry VIII and his wives

A Church of England with Henry at the head could then allow Henry to divorce his first wife Catherine of Aragon[44], a Spanish princess and the mother of his first daughter, Mary. Henry VIII's six wives went respectively divorced, beheaded, died, divorced, beheaded, and survived. He was a tyrant, and with complete ruthlessness he let nothing and nobody get in his way.

6.2 Mary I (1553-1558)

Henry VIII had three children who survived him, all of whom ascended to the Crown. The first to reign was Edward VI of England, the only son of Henry VIII. Although he followed Protestantism and was intelligent, he was only nine years old when he took the throne in 1547. When Edward VI lay dying of illness in 1553, Mary took the throne, crowned as Mary I. Mary was a total Catholic who had been influenced greatly by the Catholic King of Spain and Holy Roman Emperor, and she tried to reimpose Catholicism on the realm. There were 283 Protestants burnt at the stake in her reign. Her efforts as queen to restore Catholicism to England made her the most unpopular queen in British history and the means that she used to pursue her aims earned her the nickname "Bloody Mary"[45]. And the Spanish party of her husband, Philip II, caused much resentment around court. Mary lost Calais[46], the last English possession on the continent, and became increasingly unpopular (except among Catholics) as her reign wore on. When she died childless in 1558, her Protestant half-sister Elizabeth succeeded.

6.3 Elizabeth I (1558-1603）

Elizabeth's reign brought in one of the most glorious eras of British history. Exploration, colonization, victory in war, flourish of arts and growing world importance, all these factors characterized this period as the Elizabethan Age. But as with her sister, plots against the queen were mounted and the wars against Spain and in Ireland were expensive—she had debts of £400,000 when she died. Eventually there was all out war with Spain. Philip of Spain assembled the largest fleet the world had seen, and in 1588 it set sail to invade England. The smaller, more motive English ships attacked the Spanish Armada all the way up to the English Channel. But the Armada reached Calais and anchored. The English sent in fire ships (crammed with burning tar and gunpowder). This forced the Spanish to cut anchor and scatter, which weakened the strength of the Spain and offered a chance for England to defeat them. Spain was humiliated on the world stage.

Elizabeth I

A few months later came news of the defeat of the long running battle against the rebels in Ireland. But by now Elizabeth's health had declined, and she was dying without marriage for her whole life. The choice of successor was not so easy, as she was the last of Henry VIII's children and none of them had any children themselves. Elizabeth delayed making her choice of successor until she was on her death bed. Her successor would be James Stuart, King of Scotland, whose mother was executed as a traitor by Elizabeth.

7. The House of Stuart (1603-1714)

James I was born in 1566 to Mary, Queen of Scots and her second husband, Henry Stewart, Lord Darnley. He descended from the Tudors through Margaret, daughter of Henry VII: both Mary Queen of Scots and Henry Stewart were grandchildren of Margaret Tudor. The Catholic James ascended the Scottish throne after his mother in 1567, and the English throne after the death of Elizabeth I in 1603, as King James I of England, continuing to rule the Kingdom of England and the Kingdom of Scotland separately.

James I

After this, there was a Union of the Crowns under James VI & I who had become the senior claimant to all of the holdings of the extinct House of Tudor. Thus there were five Stuart monarchs who ruled England and Scotland as well as Ireland (although the Stuart era was interrupted from 1649-1660, as a result of the English Civil War). Additionally at the foundation of the Kingdom of Great Britain after the Acts of Union, which politically united England and Scotland, the first monarch was Anne of Great Britain. However, she died without issue and all the holdings passed to the House of Hanover[47], under the terms of the Act of Settlement 1701.

Religious dispute was the basis of an event that confirmed and fueled James' doubt: the Gunpowder Plot of November 5, 1605. Guy Fawkes and four other Catholics were caught attempting to blow up the House of Lords on a day in which the king was to open the session. The **conspirator**s were executed, but a fresh wave of anti-Catholic sentiments washed across England. James also disliked the Puritans who became excessive in their demands on the king, resulting in the first wave of English immigrants to North America. James, however, did manage to commission an *Authorized Version of the Bible*[48], printed in English in 1611. The relationship between king and parliament became steadily worse. What's more, under his faith of the "Divine Right" of King he just ruled as he pleased neglecting Parliament, which led to the misunderstanding of the English tradition of parliament liberty and finally caused the civil war during the reign of his son, Charles I.

7.1 English Civil War (1642-1649)

After the death of James in 1625, Charles I immediately came into conflict with parliament. He tried to rule without summoning parliament for 11 years, but eventually ran out of money, and summoned parliament in 1640.

Parliament was naturally outraged by his neglect of their rights. They refused him money, and the country split between supporters of the king and supporters of parliament. The former was called "Cavaliers[49]" and the latter "Roundheads[50]" under the command of Oliver Cromwell[51]. In 1649 Charles I was executed at Whitehall Gate in London.

Oliver Cromwell was given the title Lord Protector in 1653. It was the start of England's only period of **dictatorship** when Cromwell was unable to find anything to replace the monarchy, but to establish a republic Commonwealth. When he died in 1658 his son Richard succeeded him, but he was forced to abdicate within a year, and in 1660 Charles II was restored to the throne his father had died for, triggering the Restoration[52].

7.2 The Restoration (1660-1688) and the Glorious Revolution (1688-1689)

Cromwell's failure to put in place a workable alternative to the monarchy resulted in the country bringing back the **exile** monarchy Charles II, son of the beheaded Charles I. However it was still the succession that concerned the country. Charles II produced no legitimate heirs, and it was his Catholic brother James II who succeeded him in 1685. Britain had briefly been republic, led by Protestant, but it was now backing to the disastrous reign of Catholic James II, who upset the government by suspending the anti-Catholic laws, and arresting six bishops.

Leading politicians turned to James II's protestant daughter Mary and her husband William of Orange[53] and offered them the throne in 1688 on condition that they would respect the rights of parliament. The peaceful crown of them was proudly called "the Glorious Revolution" by British. James fled to Ireland, where he was eventually defeated in battle by William. James II's son and grandson both tried to retake the throne but failed. Anne, protestant daughter of James II succeeded William and Mary II in 1702. It can be argued that James's overthrow began modern English parliamentary democracy: never since has the monarch held absolute power, and the Bill of Rights passed in 1689 to limit the power of kings and being regarded as the second Magna Carta. The Bill of Rights[54] has become one of the most important documents in the political history of Britain.

William III and Mary II

7.3 Birth of the United Kingdom

During the reign of Anne, by passing an Act of Union, a unified sovereign state—the United Kingdom was established under the political union of the kingdoms of England, which included Wales and Scotland on May 1, 1707. The Union created the United Kingdom of Great Britain, which shared a single constitutional monarch and a single parliament at Westminster. A further Act of Union in 1800 added the Kingdom of Ireland to create the United Kingdom of Great Britain and Ireland. The English capital of London was adopted as the capital of the Union.

In 1714, the reign of Queen Anne ended. She was the last monarch of the House of Stuart and was succeeded by her German cousin, George I, of the House of Hanover, who was a descendant of the Stuarts through his maternal grandmother, daughter of James VI & I.

8. The Hanoverians (18th-19th Century)

The House of Hanover (the Hanoverians) was a Germanic royal dynasty. It succeeded the House of Stuart as monarchs of Great Britain and Ireland in 1714 and held that office until the death of Victoria in 1901. There were a lot of better qualified people available to be king of England, but unfortunately most of them were Catholic. George I was a German who did not speak a word of English, but was Protestant. So started the rule of the House of Hanover, under whom Britain achieved wealth and peace over the next century.

During George's reign, the powers of the monarchy diminished and Britain began a transition to the modern system of Cabinet[55] government led by a Prime Minister, which plays an important part in connecting the King and Parliament together. Towards the end of his reign, actual power was held by Sir Robert Walpole[56], Great Britain's first Prime Minister until 1742. He avoided the expense of war, and Britain prospered. George died on a trip to his native Hanover, where he was buried. The coming of George III to the throne in 1760 after the death of George II brought the first British-born king for 50 years. Those were exciting times, except the loss of the American Colonies. Britain won new territories in Canada and India, but lost the oldest settlement of all, with the declaration of independence by the American colonies in 1776 and the final surrender at Yorktown in 1781.

8.1 Industrial Revolution

During the late 18th and early 19th centuries, there was considerable social disorder as a largely **agrarian** society was transformed by technological advances and increasing mechanization, which was the Industrial Revolution. Much of the agricultural workforce was uprooted from the countryside and moved into large urban centers of production, as the steam-based production factories could weaken the traditional cottage industries, because of economies of scale and the increased output per worker made possible by the new technologies. The consequent saw dramatic increases in the rate of **infant mortality**, crime, and social deprivation.

At home the Industrial Revolution was developing fast. But in Europe, French power was manifesting itself following the French revolution in 1789. Four years later the Napoleonic[57] Wars started. There were a series of conflicts involving Napoleon's French Empire and changing sets of European allies and opposing **coalition**s that ran from 1803 to 1815. The Great Britain was also involved in the long loomed wars, which ended following Napoleon's final defeat at Waterloo[58] on June 18, 1815. Britain was the dominant power, and the defeat of Napoleon removed French dreams to rule the world.

8.2 Victorian Era (1837-1901)

It was an age of the glorious development of poems, science and artists against which Victoria came to the throne in 1837, when she was 18, to commence a reign that spanned 64 years. She became a symbol of her age. It was an age of steam and iron, and industries had well developed. The Great Exhibition of 1851 in Hyde Park[59] was a showcase for British achievements. Authors like Dickens[60] wrote novels. A new parliament building was constructed at Westminster[61].

Queen Victoria

The British Empire, like all empires, was acquired by force of arms. By 1900 Britain had the largest navy in the world, and used it to control an Empire "on which the sun never set". The British Empire in 1900 had covered Canada, Australia, India, large chunks of Africa, the Caribbean and the Far East. However by Victoria's death in 1901, Britain was being challenged militarily by Germany. During the war, the British Royal Family, under George V, son of Victoria, dissolved ties with its German relatives and changed its name to the current House of Windsor.

9. Two World Wars (1914-1945)

9.1 World War I (1914-1918)

The United Kingdom was one of the Allied Powers during World War I (1914-1918), and developed as a nation throughout the war in order to further its goal of defeating the Central

Powers[62]. The country's armed forces were reorganized and increased in size because of the introduction of forced **conscription** for the first time in the country's history. 750,000 Britons died in the next 4 years of warfare. This was the first war Britain had fought on European soil since Waterloo closed a century before.

It was only in 1918 that the Allies, with the Americans now in the war, began to make advances. A better battle plan and the use of the new tanks gave the Allies[63] the breakthrough that they had been seeking for years. Within three months the war was over. Altogether over 8 million soldiers on both sides had died. New weapons like tank, poison gas, and aircraft had entered wars. Cavalry[64] were no longer used. Air raids and U-boat[65] attacks on merchant ships brought war to the world. However, the war did not create a "land fit for heroes to live in" as the war time prime minister had promised. Britain was to enter an era of social change, economic recession and large scale unemployment.

9.2 Britain between the Wars

The period between the two World Wars was dominated by economic weakness known as the "Great Depression". The working class became unionized, and labor relations worsen. In the 1930s Britain was focused on the continuing high unemployment at home. Then there was the shock of the abdication of Edward VIII[66] who wished to marry an American divorcee in 1936. Few saw the threat of Hitler's rise to power in Germany. Germany was rearming at a frightening rate, but Britain had neither the inclination nor the money to follow Hitler's increased spending on armaments. Eventually Hitler's expansion went too far. The German invasion of Poland led Britain by treaty to declare war on Germany. In 1939, World War II started.

9.3 World War II and Rebuilding

The United Kingdom, along with the British Empire's crown colonies, especially British India, declared war on Nazi Germany in 1939, after the German invasion of Poland. Hostilities with Japan began in 1941, after it attacked British colonies in Asia. The Axis powers[67] were defeated by the Allies in 1945.

The end of World War II saw a landslide general election victory for the Labor Party. They were elected on a manifesto of greater social justice with left wing policies such as the creation of a National Health Service[68], an expansion of the provision of council housing and nationalization of the major industries. The UK at the time was poor, relying heavily on loans from the United States of America (which were finally paid off in February 2007) to rebuild its damaged infrastructure. **Rationing** and conscription dragged on into the post war years, and the country suffered one of the worst winters on record.

As the country headed into the 1950s, rebuilding continued and a number of immigrants from the remaining British Empire were invited to help the rebuilding effort. As the 1950s wore on, the UK had lost its place as a superpower and could no longer maintain its large empire. This led to **decolonization** and a withdrawal from almost all of its colonies by 1970. The 1950s and 1960s were, however, relatively prosperous times after the World War II, and saw the beginning of a modernization of the UK, with the construction of its first motorways for example.

9.4 Empire to Commonwealth

Britain's control over its Empire loosened during the interwar period. Nationalism strengthened in other parts of the Empire, particularly in India and in Egypt. Between 1867 and 1910, the UK had granted Australia, Canada, and New Zealand "**Dominion**" status, which means that they are near complete autonomy within the Empire. They became charter members of the Commonwealth of Nations[69], an informal but closely-knit association that succeeded the British Empire. The current Commonwealth of Nations was formally constituted by the London Declaration in 1949, which modernized the community, and established the member states as "free and equal". The symbol of this free association is Queen Elizabeth II, who is the Head of the Commonwealth. The Queen is head of state of 16 member states, known as the Commonwealth realms, while 32 other members are republics and five others have different monarchs. Member states have no legal obligations to one another. Instead, they are untied by English language, history, culture and their shared values of democracy, human rights and the rule of law.

Although often marked by economic and political nationalism, the Commonwealth offers the United Kingdom a voice in matters concerning many developing countries, and is a forum for those countries to raise concerns. Notable non-members of the Commonwealth are Ireland, the United States and the former Middle-Eastern colonies and **protectorate**s. In addition, the Commonwealth helps preserve many institutions deriving from British experience and models, such as Westminster-style parliamentary democracy, in those countries.

9.5 Growth of Modern Britain in the Late 20th Century

After the relative prosperity of the 1950s and 1960s, through the 1970s the UK began integration to the European Economic Community[70] but experienced extreme industrial conflicts and **stagflation** following a global economic downturn. As well as this, the conflict with the IRA[71], known as the Troubles[72], reached its peak in Northern Ireland[73]. A strict modernization of its economy began under the controversial leader Mrs Margaret Thatcher[74] during the 1980s, which saw a time of record unemployment as much of the country's manufacturing industries were closed but also a time of economic boom as stock markets became liberated and state-owned industries became privatized. This was also the time that the IRA took the issue of Northern Ireland to Great Britain, maintaining a **prolonged** bombing campaign on the island.

Elizabeth II

After the economic boom of the 1980s, a brief but severe recession occurred between 1991 and 1992 following the economic chaos of Black Wednesday[75] under the John Major[76] government. However the rest of the 1990s saw the beginning of a period of continuous economic growth that lasted over 16 years and was greatly expanded under the New Labor government of Tony Blair[77] following his landslide election victory in 1997. And in 2007 he was replaced by Gordon Brown[78].

10. The 21st Century

In the 2001 general election, the Labor Party won a second successive victory and the country's economic expansion continued greatly despite the effects of the September 11th attacks in the United States in 2001. On Thursday May 5, 2005 the Labor Party won the general election again and it's also Tony Blair's third consecutive term in office. However, the effects of the War on Terror following September 11th increased the threat of international terrorists plotting attacks against the UK. On July 7, 2005, a series of four bomb explosions struck London's public transport system. All four incidents were suicide bombings that killed 52 commuters in addition to the four bombers.

The year of 2007 saw the conclusion of the premiership of Tony Blair, followed by the premiership of Gordon Brown (from June 27, 2007). The year of 2007 also saw an election victory for the pro-independence Scottish National Party in the May elections.

In the wake of the economic crisis of 2008, the United Kingdom experienced negative economic growth throughout 2009. Causes were based upon the collapse of the housing market and rising oil prices which had increased fuel bills in households. The announcement in November 2008 that the economy shrank for the first time since late 1992 brought an end to 16 years of continuous economic growth.

On May 11, 2010, following the resignation of Gordon Brown as Prime Minister and on his recommendation, Elizabeth II invited Cameron to form a government. At age 43, Cameron became the youngest British Prime Minister since Lord Liverpool, who was appointed in 1812. In his first address outside 10 Downing Street, he announced his intention to form a coalition government, the first since the World War II, with the Liberal Democrats.

In 2014 he agreed the Scottish Government to hold a referendum on Scottish independence, with 55.3% of voters rejecting the independence proposal and opting to remain within the United Kingdom. When the Conservatives secured an unexpected majority in the 2015 general election he remained as Prime Minister, this time leading a Conservative-only government. To fulfill an election manifesto pledge, he introduced a referendum on the UK's continuing membership of the EU(a referendum of "Brexit") in 2016, and with 51.9% of voters in the United Kingdom voting to leave the European Union he resigned to make way for a new Prime Minister. On July 13, 2016 Theresa May was appointed Prime Minister by Queen Elizabeth II, becoming only the second female British Prime Minister after Margaret Thatcher.

The legal process of leaving the EU began on March 29, 2017, with the UK's invocation of Article 50 of the Treaty of Lisbon[79], stipulating that the negotiations to leave will last at least two years and that the UK remains a full member of the EU before March 29, 2019.

Joyful Moment

Whose Son Is the Greatest

The mothers of four priests got together and were discussing their sons. “My son is a monsignor,” said the first proud woman. “When he enters a room, people say, ‘Hello, Monsignor’.”

The second mother went on, “My son is a bishop. When he enters a room, people say, ‘Hello, Your Excellency’.”

“My son is a cardinal.” continued the next one. “When he enters a room, people say, ‘Hello, Your Eminence’.”

The fourth mother thought for a moment. “My son is six-foot-ten and weighs 300 pounds,” she said. “When he enters a room, people say, ‘Oh, my God’!”

Notes

[1] Celt 凯尔特人，现代凯尔特人指现代凯尔特语民族或地区的本族人或本地人，包括祖籍爱尔兰、苏格兰高地、马恩岛、威尔士的人
[2] Stone Age 石器时代，是考古学对早期人类历史分期的第一个时代
[3] Iron Age 铁器时代，它以能够冶铁和制造铁器为标志
[4] Stonehenge 巨石阵
[5] Julius Caesar 尤利乌斯 • 恺撒（公元前 100—44），罗马将军，政治家
[6] Gaul 高卢，欧洲一古老地区，包括现在的法国、比利时等国家
[7] Briton（罗马时期或以前的）布立吞人；大不列颠人；英国人
[8] Claudius 克劳狄，公元 41 年至 54 年任罗马皇帝，以公元 43 年入侵不列颠闻名
[9] Kent 肯特，英格兰东南海岸一郡，首府梅德斯通
[10] Hadrian’s Wall 哈德良长城，穿越英格兰北部的罗马防御屏障，长约 117.5 公里
[11] Scots 指公元 5 世纪从爱尔兰进入苏格兰的凯尔特人，现在用来指苏格兰人
[12] Picts 皮可特人
[13] Rhine 莱茵河，欧洲西部河流，源于瑞士阿尔卑斯山流经德国和荷兰注入北海
[14] Angles 盎格鲁人，日耳曼人的一支，公元 5 世纪时来到英格兰
[15] Saxons 撒克逊人
[16] Viking（8～11 世纪在西北欧许多地区进行劫掠或定居的）北欧海盗
[17] Jute 朱特人，日耳曼一部族成员
[18] King Arthur 亚瑟王，中世纪传说中的不列颠国王，圆桌骑士团的首领
[19] Norse 古代（或中世纪）挪威的，古代（或中世纪）斯堪的纳维亚的
[20] Wessex 韦塞克斯，西撒克逊人的王国，创建于公元 6 世纪
[21] Alfred 阿尔弗烈德，韦塞克斯国王（871—899），通称“阿尔弗烈德大帝”
[22] Somerset 萨默塞特郡，位于英格兰西南部，临布里斯托尔海峡

[23] Edgar 埃德加（公元 944—975），英格兰国王
[24] Harold 哈罗德二世，1066 年在位，英格兰最后一个盎格鲁–撒克逊国王
[25] Edward the Confessor “忏悔者”爱德华，盎格鲁–撒克逊王朝的君主
[26] William I 威廉一世，1066—1087 年在位
[27] Witan 盎格鲁–撒克逊时代的议会议员们；国王顾问
[28] Normandy 诺曼底，法国西北部一地区，北临英吉利海峡
[29] battle of Hastings 黑斯廷斯战役
[30] Tower of London 伦敦塔
[31] Windsor Castle 温莎城堡，位于英格兰东南部
[32] Domesday Book 末日审判书，又称“最终税册”，1086 年根据威廉一世的命令对英格兰土地情况的全面调查记录
[33] Henry II 亨利二世，1154—1189 年在位，第一位金雀花王朝国王
[34] the House of Plantagenet 金雀花王朝（1154—1485）
[35] Richard I 理查一世，1189—1199 年在位，人称“狮心王”
[36] Crusade 十字军东征，11、12 和 13 世纪欧洲天主教徒为了从穆斯林手中收复圣地而进行的一系列战争
[37] Philip II 腓力二世
[38] Magna Carta 大宪章，拉丁文，英文为 Great Charter
[39] Wars of Roses 玫瑰战争，指英国兰开斯特家族和约克家族的支持者之间为了英格兰王位的断续内战，因双方用红白玫瑰作为家徽得名。
[40] Tudor 都铎王朝，始自 1485 年亨利七世登基终至 1603 年伊丽莎白一世驾崩
[41] Roman Catholic Church 罗马天主教会，罗马公教会
[42] Protestant 新教徒，根据宗教改革原则脱离罗马天主教的各西方基督教会教徒
[43] Martin Luther 马丁·路德，1483—1546，德国宗教改革运动的主要人物
[44] Catherine Aragon 阿拉贡的凯瑟琳，亨利八世的王后，阿拉贡国王的女儿
[45] Bloody Mary 血腥玛丽，英格兰玛丽一世的绰号
[46] Calais 加来，法国北部渡口，1347 归英国所有，1558 年被法国收回
[47] House of Hanover 汉诺威王朝（1714—1901）
[48] Authorized Version of the Bible 基督教《圣经》的钦定英译本
[49] Cavaliers 17 世纪英国的保王党，又称骑士党
[50] Roundheads 17 世纪英国的圆颅党
[51] Oliver Cromwell 奥利弗·克伦威尔，1653—1658 任共和政体护国公
[52] the Restoration 英国 1660 年查理二世的王朝复辟
[53] William of Orange 威廉三世，玛丽二世的丈夫，1689—1702 年在位
[54] Bill of Rights 英国 1689 年《权利法案》
[55] Cabinet（英国、加拿大及其他英联邦国家的）内阁
[56] Robert Walpole 罗伯特·沃尔波尔爵士
[57] Napoleon 拿破仑一世，1804 年称帝，在滑铁卢被击败，并流放到圣海伦娜岛

[58] Waterloo 滑铁卢，比利时城镇，1815 年拿破仑军队战败处
[59] Hyde Park 英国伦敦的海德公园，因常被用作政治性集会场所而著称
[60] Charles Dickens 查尔斯・狄更斯，1812—1870，英国小说家
[61] Westminster 威斯敏斯特，位于伦敦市内，英国议院和许多政府部门坐落于此
[62] the Central Powers 同盟国，一战期间德意志帝国、奥匈帝国、奥斯曼帝国及保加利亚的联盟
[63] Allies 第一次世界大战时的协约国，以英国、法国、俄罗斯帝国为首
[64] Cavalry 骑兵
[65] U-boat U 型潜艇，两次世界大战中的德国潜艇
[66] Edward VIII 爱德华八世，唯一一位自愿退位的英国君主
[67] the Axis Powers 轴心国，第二次世界大战期间由德、意、日等国组成
[68] National Health Service 英国国民医疗服务制度
[69] the Commonwealth of Nations 英联邦，由 53 个独立国家组成
[70] European Economic Community 欧洲经济共同体
[71] IRA (Irish Republican Army)爱尔兰共和军，成立于 1919 年，其前身是“爱尔兰义勇军”，旨在建立独立的爱尔兰共和国，2005 年 9 月完全解除武装
[72] the Troubles 北爱尔兰问题，即北爱尔兰的归属问题
[73] Northern Ireland 北爱尔兰自治区，首府贝尔法斯特。1921 年 12 月，英国同爱尔兰签订条约，允许爱尔兰南部 26 郡享有自治权，北部 6 郡即北爱尔兰归英国
[74] Mrs Margaret Thatcher 玛格丽特・撒切尔夫人，英国保守党领袖，1979—1990 任首相
[75] Black Wednesday 黑色星期三，1992 年 9 月 16 日英镑陷入危机，被迫退出货币汇率机制
[76] John Major 约翰・梅杰，英国保守党政治家，1990—1997 年任首相
[77] Tony Blair 托尼・布莱尔，英国工党政治家，自 1997—2007 年任首相
[78] Gordon Brown 戈登・布朗，英国工党成员。托尼・布莱尔于 2007 年 6 月 27 日正式向英国女王递交辞呈辞去英国首相职务，由财政大臣戈登・布朗接任，入主唐宁街 10 号。他也是 20 世纪 60 年代以来第一位来自苏格兰的首相
[79] Treaty of Lisbon 《里斯本条约》，在原《欧盟宪法条约》的基础上修改而成，又被称为“简化版欧盟宪法”。2007 年 10 月 19 日，欧盟各国领导人在里斯本就新条约文本达成一致，并将之定名为《里斯本条约》，2019 年，条约获得欧盟全部 27 个成员国的批准。其第 50 条于 2009 年引入，为希望脱离欧盟的国家提供了正式的退出机制。其核心内容是，如果未得到所有欧盟成员国一致同意延期，那么启动该条款的国家将在两年后脱离欧盟。

New Words

1. **barony** /'bærəni/ *n.* the rank and estates of a baron 男爵爵位，男爵领地

2. **monarchical** /məˈnɑrkɪkl/ *adj.* connected with a ruler such as a king or a queen or with the system of government by a king or queen 君主的；君主制的
—The Declaration represented a repudiation of the pre-revolutionary monarchical regime.
这一宣言代表了对大革命前的君主政体的批判。
3. **parliament** /ˈpaːlɪmənt/ *n.* the highest legislature, consisting of the Sovereign, the House of Lords, and the House of Commons（英国）议会；议会两院
—The act was passed by the last parliament of the reign.
这项法案是上届议会通过的。
4. **controversial** /ˌkɒntrəˈvɜːʃəl/ *adj.* giving rise or likely to give rise to public disagreement（可能）引起争论的，（可能）有争议的
—The topic of argument is controversial.
这个议题是很有争议的。
5. **conspirator** /kənˈspɪrətə/ *n.* a person who takes part in a conspiracy 共谋者，阴谋家
—The conspirators took no part in the fighting which ensued.
密谋者没有参加随后发生的战斗。
6. **dictatorship** /dɪkˈteɪtəʃɪp/ *n.* government by dictator 专制，独裁
—The generals established a military dictatorship.
将军们建立了军事独裁统治。
7. **exile** /ˈeksaɪl/ *n.* the state of being barred from one's native country, typically for political reasons 流放；流亡；放逐
—He knew now that he would die in exile.
这下他明白他会在流亡中死去。
8. **agrarian** /əˈgreəriən/ *adj.* of or relating to cultivated land or the cultivation of land（与）耕地（有关）的
—People are leaving an agrarian way of life to go to the city.
人们正在放弃农业生活方式而转向城市。
9. **infant mortality** the death of children under the age of one year 婴儿夭折；婴幼儿死亡率
—The infant mortality was increasing during the war.
战争中婴儿死亡率日渐提高。
10. **coalition** /kəʊəˈlɪʃən/ *n.* a temporary alliance of political parties forming a government or of states （尤指组成政府的政党或者州的）临时结合，联合，联盟
—The several parties formed a coalition.
这几个政党组成了政治联盟。
11. **conscription** /kənˈskrɪpʃ(ə)n/ *n.* compulsory enlistment for state service, typically into the armed forces 征兵
—He's been worried that the government will introduce conscription ever since the war began.
战争开始以来，他一直担心政府会采用强制征召制度。

12. **ration** /'ræʃən/ *n.* a fixed amount of a commodity officially allowed to each person during a time of shortage, as in wartime（战争等供应短缺时期政府给予的）配给量，定量
—1947 saw the bread ration reduced on two occasions.
1947 年面包配给量曾两度下调。
13. **decolonization** /diːˌkələnaɪ'zeɪʃən/ *n.* (of a state) withdrawing from (a colony), leaving it independent（国家）使（殖民地）非殖民化
—They must decolonize India.
他们必须使印度非殖民化。
14. **dominion** /də'mɪnjən/ *n.* sovereignty; control 主权；控制权
—Man attempt to establish dominion over nature.
人类试图控制自然。
15. **protectorate** /prə'tektərət/ *n.* a state that is controlled and protected by another 受保护国
—He had been Governor of a British Protectorate.
他做过英国保护领地的总督。
16. **stagflation** /stæg'fleɪʃən/ *n.* persistent high inflation combined with high unemployment（经济）滞胀
—This country is suffering a stagflation.
这个国家正在经历一场经济滞胀。
17. **prolong** /prə'lɒŋ/ *v.* extend the duration of 延长，拖长
—This is an idea which prolonged the life of the engine by many years.
这是一个延长了引擎寿命多年的想法。

Exercises

1. Choose the correct answer.

1) In 1588 when the English navy defeated the Spain Armada, English is under the rule of ________.
A. Henry VIII　　B. Elizabeth I
C. Queen Victoria　　D. James II

2) Christianity was first brought to England by ________.
A. the Normans　　B. the Danes　　C. the Romans　　D. the Anglo-Saxons

3) The King who believed the "Divine Right" to govern, and who was executed during the English Civil War was ________.
A. Henry VIII　　B. Charles I　　C. James I　　D. James II

4) The *Authorized Version of the Bible* was translated during the reign of ________.
A. Mary I　　B. Elizabeth I　　C. James I　　D. James II

5) ________ gave up the throne to marry an American divorcee in 1936.
A. George V　　B. Edward VIII　　C. George VI　　D. Edward VII

2. Decide whether the following statements are True or False.

1) Anglo-Saxon took control of the whole island of Britain.

2) The Cabinet and the Prime Minister appeared during the reign of George I in the 18th century.

3) Henry II was the first English king to go into Ireland, and his attempts to partition Ireland were unsuccessful.

4) Britain sits with the US in the War on Terror and the Invasion of Iraq.

5) After the relative prosperity of the 1950s and 1960s, through the 1970s the UK began integration to the European Economic Community but experienced extreme industrial conflicts and stagflation following a global economic downturn.

3. Fill in the blanks according to the passage.

1) Ideas of invading Britain faded until ________ became Emperor in 41 AD.

2) ________ built by William later was used as a state prison and is now open to the public as a museum.

3) The uniqueness of the Norman Conquest in British history is that it introduced England the ________ and ________.

4) ________ passed in 1689 to limit the power of kings and being regarded as the second Magna Carta has become one of the most important documents in the political history of Britain.

5) In 2007 Tony Blair was replaced by ________.

4. Explain the following terms according to the passage.

1) The Gunpowder Plot

2) Hadrian's Wall

3) Bloody Mary

4) The Wars of Roses

5) The Glorious Revolution

5. Answer the following questions according to the passage.

1) Why do we say that the English nation is a mixture of different nationalities and cultures of Europe?

2) Why did Henry VIII start the Reformation of the Church?

3) How did the United Kingdom first come into being?

6. Discussion.

1) Why did the Civil War take place? What are the consequences of the Civil War? Why was it regarded as the beginning of modern world history?

2) "There will always be an England" was often repeated during World War II to increase morale. But what is meant by "England" or the United Kingdom? It seems to be a collection of contradictions.

Stay Positive

1. In order to win, you must expect to win.
2. Death is a challenge. It tells us not to waste time... It tells us to tell each other right now that we love each other.

Chapter 3

Politics of the United Kingdom

If you lead a country like Britain, a strong country, a country which has taken a lead in world affairs in good times and in bad, a country that is always reliable, then you have to have a touch of iron about you.

—Mrs Margaret Thatcher

1. Introduction

The politics of the United Kingdom of Great Britain and Northern Ireland takes place in the framework of a constitutional monarchy[1], in which the Monarch is head of state and the Prime Minister is the head of government. Executive power is exercised by the UK government, the regional governments of Scotland and Wales, and the Executive of Northern Ireland. Legislative power belongs to both the government and the two houses of Parliament, the House of Commons and the House of Lords, as well as in the Scottish parliament and Welsh parliament and Northern Ireland parliament. The judiciary is independent of the executive and the legislature, though several senior judges are still members of the House of Lords.

The UK is a multi-party system and since the 1920s, the two largest political parties have been the Conservative Party and the Labour Party. Though coalition and minority governments have been an occasional feature of parliamentary politics, the first-past-the-post electoral system used for general elections tends to maintain the power of these two parties, though each has in the past century relied upon a third party to deliver a working majority in Parliament.

This system of government, known as the Westminster system[2], has been adopted by other countries as well, such as Canada, India, Australia, New Zealand, Singapore, Malaysia and Jamaica, countries that made up part of the British Empire.

2. The Monarchy

The Monarchy of the United Kingdom (commonly referred to as the British monarchy) is the constitutional monarchy of the United Kingdom and its overseas territories. The present monarch, Elizabeth II[3], has reigned since February 6, 1952. She and her immediate family undertake various official, ceremonial and representational duties. Though the executive authority over the government of the United Kingdom is still by and through the monarch's **royal prerogative**, in practice these powers are only used according to laws legislated by Parliament or within the restriction of convention and precedent.

2.1 Origin of the Monarch

The British monarchy traces its origins to the days before the Norman Conquest in 1066. Its continuity was broken only once during the Civil War (1642-1651) when England was called a commonwealth (a republic) from 1649 to 1660. After the death of Oliver Cromwell, England was in disorder and the newly-elected Parliament decided to restore the monarchy by asking Charles I's son to mount the throne in 1660. Religious controversy between James II and the Parliament led to the 1688 palace coup—the Glorious Revolution [4], which marked the formal establishment of the limited constitutional monarchy.

2.2 Constitutional Role

In the uncodified Constitution of the United Kingdom, the Monarch (otherwise referred to as The Sovereign, The Crown, or His/Her Majesty, abbreviated H.M.) is the ceremonial Head of State. Oaths of allegiance are made to the King/Queen and his/her lawful successors. God Save the Queen (or God Save the King) is the British national anthem, and the monarch appears on postage stamps, coins, and paper money.

In practice, prerogative powers are only exercised on the Prime Minister's advice. The monarch holds a weekly audience with the Prime Minister. The monarch may express his or her views, but, as a constitutional ruler, must ultimately accept the decisions of the Prime Minister and the Cabinet. The royal prerogative includes the powers to appoint and dismiss ministers, regulate the civil service, issue passports, declare war, make peace, direct the actions of the military, and negotiate and ratify treaties, alliances, and international agreements. The monarch is commander in chief of the armed forces (the Royal Navy, the British Army, and the Royal Air Force [5]), accredits British High Commissioners and ambassadors, and receives diplomats from foreign states. It is the prerogative of the monarch to summon, **prorogue** and dissolve Parliament. Before a bill passed by the legislative Houses and become law, the monarch's approval is required. He/she confers noble titles and honors on those who have distinguished themselves with great achievements. He/she is the Supreme Governor of the Church of England.

The King/Queen seems very powerful, but in reality he/she is only a figure-head. His/her role in the government is a kind of formality. Monarchy is recognized as the "dignified part" rather than the "efficient part" of government.

3. The Parliament

The British Parliament is the supreme legislature of the country. It consists of three elements: the monarch, the House of Lords and the House of Commons. The primary function of the Parliament is the making of law, the control of the public revenue, and the examination

of government policy and public administration. The official head of the Parliament is the King/Queen.

3.1 The House of Lords

The House of Lords is the successor to the historical Great Council which was an advisory body to serve the king. It is now made up of two kinds of Lords: the Lords Spiritual [6] and the Lords Temporal [7] .The Lords Spiritual are the two Archbishops of Canterbury and York [8] plus 24 senior bishops of the Church of England. The Lords Temporal includes all the hereditary peers[9] (or peeresses) and life peers[10].

Unlike the House of Commons, the House of Lords does not control the term of the Prime Minister or of the Government. Only the Lower House may force the Prime Minister to resign or call elections. Thus, the House of Lords' oversight of the government is limited. Most Cabinet ministers are from the House of Commons, rather than the House of Lords. In particular, all Prime Ministers since 1902 have been members of the Lower House. If a Prime Minister wants to have enough supporters in the Upper House, he would ask the monarch to confer noble titles on his faithful followers so as to bring them into the Upper House. A noble title bearer has no right to vote in election and he cannot be elected to the House of Commons.

The House of Lords debates legislation, and has some power to amend or reject bills. However, the power of the Lords to reject a bill passed by the House of Commons is severely restricted by the Parliament Acts[11]. Under those Acts, certain types of bills may be presented for the Royal Assent without the consent of the House of Lords. The House of Lords cannot delay a money bill (a bill that, in the view of the Speaker of the House of Commons, solely concerns national taxation or public funds) for more than one month. Other public bills cannot be delayed by the House of Lords for more than two parliamentary sessions, or one calendar year, so that the Upper House could not prevent a bill from passing into law for more than two years. What's more, a Prime Minister can get a majority in the Upper House by seeking the monarch to confer peerages on his supporters. This pending threat can often bring the Upper House to submission.

However, in the judicial function it is unique. The House of Lords is the highest court in the United Kingdom hearing civil and criminal appeals from the lower courts. But we must know the fact that when acting as the final court of appeal in Britain, the House of Lords employs only "Law Lords[12]", most of whom are elevated to the House specifically for the purpose.

The procedures of the Lords are more informal than those of the Commons, and their role in saving the Commons a great amount of time is widely recognized. The House of Lords meets on three (or four) afternoons each week during the session of Parliament. All the more than 1,100 or so peers have the right to speak, vote, propose bills or ask questions of government ministers. But usually they are not enthusiastic about debates. Few moves originate in the Upper

House. In most cases only a small minority take part in the debate and vote. The smallest recorded number of the attendants is less than ten. But when an important problem is under debate, many of the Lords would be present.

3.2 The House of Commons

The House of Commons which is also known as the Lower House is where the real power lies. It is made up of 650 Members of Parliament (MPs) who are directly elected by universal adult suffrage. The 650 seats are distributed among the four regions: 533 for England, 40 for Wales, 59 for Scotland, and 18 for Northern Ireland. The four regions are divided into 650 areas (districts) and each area (known as a constituency) elects one Member of Parliament.

Each Member of Parliament (MP) is chosen by a single constituency according to the first-past-the-post[13] electoral system. British citizens and citizens of other Commonwealth countries resident in Britain may vote provided they are aged 18 or over and they are not subject to any disqualification. Each elector may cast one vote to support one candidate, normally in person at a polling station. Candidates standing for election as MPs are normally nominated and supported by different political parties. The candidate who receives the largest number of votes in a constituency is elected. The party which wins sufficient seats at a general election to command a majority of supporters in the House of Commons is asked to form the government by the King/Queen. As a result, the party itself becomes known as the Government. The party which wins the second largest number of seats becomes known as the Opposition[14]. Leaders of the Parties sit on the front benches in the House of Commons while their supporters sit on the back benches and become known as **backbenchers**. The task of the Opposition is to supervise the government, contribute to the formulation of proper policies and oppose what is objectionable. The main function of the House of Commons is law-making and the process is characterized by heated debates between the Government and the Opposition.

4. The British Government

The British Government is the supreme administrative institution which manages state affairs. The Cabinet is the core of leadership of the British government. In Britain "Government" and "Cabinet" mean different things. "Government" is the collective name for all the ministers and junior ministers, plus four legal members and about 12 ministerial **whips**. The "Cabinet" is, on the other hand, made up of the Prime Minister, the Lord President of the Privy Council, the heads of the most important departments and a few ministers without portfolios. Every important decision is made and carried out by the Cabinet, which directs and controls the armed forces, the police, the courts, the prisons and other organs. The British government can be divided into two parts—central government and local government. The former has great power since all local authorities obtain their existence, their powers and their function from it.

4.1 The Cabinet

The British Government, called Her Majesty's Government, refers to the various departments and their agencies under the leadership of the Prime Minister. The nucleus of the Government is known as the Cabinet.

The most important group of ministers, the Cabinet, has been transformed from its 18th century origins as a group of advisers to the monarch into the nucleus of the Government. The Cabinet was not established by law, but by constitutional convention. It is composed of Prime Minister and heads of the most important departments. When a party wins the majority of the seats in the Lower House at a general election, the monarch will automatically appoint the party leader Prime Minister and ask him or her to form the government. Then the Prime Minister will choose heads of departments from the MPs and ask the monarch to appoint them accordingly. A Cabinet member must be either a member of the House of Lords or a member of the House of Commons. That's why we say it is the Prime Minister who appoints the heads of departments and who has the right to remove them through face-saving resignations.

The Cabinet usually has around 20 members. The Prime Minister is limited on his choice of a cabinet. The minister of Defense, the Foreign Secretary, and the Chancellor of the Exchequer are always included. These ministers are called cabinet ministers and they make up the most powerful policy-making group in Britain. The Cabinet proposes the most important bills to be laid before Parliament and outlines government's program in the "Queen's Opening Speech". In all matters the Cabinet acts as a unit. It is the so-called Collective Responsibility of Cabinet government. If a cabinet minister has disagreement with others, he has to give up his own idea or resign his position. A Prime Minister once said to his Cabinet, "Now, is it lower the price of corn, or isn't it? It does not matter much what we say, but mind, we must all say the same thing." Since the Government commands the majority of the seats in the House of Commons, the Cabinet's measures are likely to be endorsed by Parliament. Whenever it so happens that the Government's important policy fails to pass the House of Commons, the Cabinet has to resign in a body and the Opposition Party will form a new government. The Prime Minister may also ask the monarch to dissolve the existing Parliament and order a new election. This is the so-called "**Go to the Country**"—to ask the people to make the decision. The future and destiny of the Cabinet will depend on the result of the new election. Sometimes the Prime Minister chooses the opportune time for his party and asks the Queen to dissolve Parliament and hold the general election before the ending of the five-year term.

The Cabinet usually meets once a week, but sometimes more often, especially in times of emergency. It works in great secrecy. No outsider is allowed to see any Cabinet papers until they have become only of historical significance and no member of the Cabinet may say anything about the discussions that have taken place in the Cabinet. The rule is in general well observed. Only Cabinet ministers have detailed knowledge of the inner secrets of policy, so the Cabinet is a kind of "inner government" within the British government. But the Cabinet is always answerable to Parliament. Technically the Cabinet is an informal committee of Privy Councilors as well. Whenever a person is appointed as a Cabinet minister, he is sure to be a member of the Privy Council as well and continues to be a member for the rest of his life.

4.2 The Privy Council

Historically, the Privy Council was the name given to the group of ministers who acted as chief advisers to the King or Queen. As the power of the monarch declined, the cabinet replaced the Privy Council as the UK's senior decision-making body.

Today the Privy Council's duties are largely formal, meeting to approve decisions that have been taken elsewhere and making appointments to offices of the crown. But it can exercise executive, legal and legislative powers in certain circumstances.

It has about 550 members, including all cabinet members past and present, the leaders of all the main parties, the Speaker, Archbishops, senior judges and some other important public figures. Members are entitled to use the prefix "Right Honorable"[15].

The Privy Council meets in the presence of the Queen, or one of her Counselors in State if she cannot attend, and the Lord President of the Council, a senior government minister. Usually, just a handful of Privy Councilors are called to Buckingham Palace for each meeting. But on rare ceremonial occasions such as the proclamation of a new monarch, larger meetings are convened.

Until recently, a Privy Councilor would have taken precedence over other backbench MPs when the Speaker chooses who should be allowed to contribute to a debate—but this rule has now been abandoned. The Privy Council retains the power to alter the statute book, but only in certain circumstances. It does this by issuing orders in council, which can be used, for example, to transfer powers between government departments. Technically, the Queen issues such orders "by and with the advice of Her Privy Council".

In reality, most important changes are originated by government ministers using powers given to them by acts of Parliament—this is a type of delegated legislation. But the Privy Council can exercise the right to enshrine in law executive policies independently of the parliamentary process, like the government's decision to continue to block the Chagos islanders from returning home in 2004.

The Privy Council also has a judicial arm, acting as the highest court of appeal in cases originating in the Channel Isles, the Isle of Man, some Commonwealth countries and all British overseas territories—as well as hearing appeals from some UK professional disciplinary bodies. It also oversees the administration of all organizations that have been incorporated under a royal charter.

4.3 The Prime Minister

The Prime Minister of the United Kingdom of Great Britain and Northern Ireland is the political leader of the United Kingdom and the Head of Her Majesty's Government. The Prime Minister and Cabinet are collectively accountable for their policies and actions to the Sovereign, to Parliament, to their political party, and ultimately to the electorate.

As the "Head of Her Majesty's Government", the modern Prime Minister is the highest political authority in the United Kingdom: he/she leads a major political party, commands a majority in the House of Commons (the Legislature), and is the leader of the Cabinet (the Executive). In the general election of 2010, the Conservatives won 306 seats. After five days of negotiation, David Cameron formed a coalition with the Liberal Democrats. David Cameron led the first coalition government of the United Kingdom since the World War II. The 43-year-old Cameron became the youngest British Prime Minister. The 2016 Conservative Party leadership election occurred as a result of David Cameron's resignation as leader following the European Union membership **referendum**[16], in which the United Kingdom voted to leave the European Union (EU). Cameron, who supported Britain's continued membership of the EU, made his announcement on June 24, saying that he would step down by October. Theresa May[17] won the contest on July 11, 2016. After the withdrawal of Andrea Leadsom[18], she was left as the sole candidate, succeeding Cameron as leader of the Conservative Party. Theresa May became Britain's second female prime minister.

5. The General Election

There are five types of elections in the United Kingdom: United Kingdom general elections, elections to devolved parliaments and assemblies, elections to the European Parliament, local elections and mayoral elections. Elections are held on Election Day, which is conventionally a Thursday.

United Kingdom general elections are the elections held when the MPs forming the House of Commons are elected. Following the Parliament Act 1911, parliamentary sessions last a maximum of five years, and are ended with the dissolution of Parliament. Therefore elections are not fixed, and the time is chosen by the governing party to maximize political advantage. The 2017 general election took place on June 8, 2017.

Candidates aim to win particular geographic constituencies in the UK. Each constituency elects one MP by the first-past-the-post system of election. At the 2017 general election, there were 650 constituencies, thus 650 MPs were elected to Parliament. The party with the most seats, i.e. the most MPs, usually forms the government, and the second largest party forms Her Majesty's Opposition[19]. Almost all candidates are members of a political party and the majority of voters in the UK choose who to vote for based on the candidates' parties, rather than the personalities or opinions of the individual candidates.

5.1 Eligibility

Anyone who is a citizen of the UK, the Republic of Ireland, or of a Commonwealth country, who is legally residing in the UK, and who is 18 or over on the date of the election is eligible to vote, provided that he/she is on the electoral register, unless he/she is currently a member of the House of Lords, or imprisoned for a criminal offence, or mentally incapable of making a reasoned judgment, or is an undischarged bankrupt, or has been convicted of corrupt or illegal practices in connection with an election within the previous five years. In addition, while UK, Irish and Commonwealth citizens may register to vote in all elections, European Union nationals resident in the UK may register to vote in local, European, Scottish and Welsh elections.

5.2 Timing

Since the maximum term of a parliament is five years, every five years a general election is held in Britain. A general election must take place before each parliamentary term begins. The whole of the United Kingdom is divided into 650 electoral districts, called constituencies. Each constituency has approximately an equal size of population, usually about 60, 000 voters and elects one member to the House of Commons. Because the population of some areas changes, the task of fixing the boundaries between constituencies is entrusted to impartial experts, who try to make the electoral boundaries as fair as they can. In order to win the election, each party has a local association, whose first task is to choose the candidate and help him or her to conduct his or her local campaign. A general election is full of excitement, with posters and portraits, speeches and arguments, and party political broadcasts on radio and television.

5.3 Post-election

Polls close at 10 p.m. and the votes are, in most constituencies, counted immediately. The earliest results are declared by about 11 p.m., with most having been declared by 3 or 4 a.m.; some constituencies do not declare their results until the following day. In Northern Ireland the count itself does not begin until the next morning, with results being announced from early afternoon onwards.

When all of the results are known, or when one party achieves an absolute majority of the seats in the House of Commons, the first response comes from the current (and possibly outgoing) Prime Minister. If a majority in the new Parliament has been achieved by their party, they remain in office without the need for reconfirmation or reappointment. If a majority has not been achieved, and it is obvious that another party has the numbers to form a government, the Prime Minister submits a resignation to the Monarch. The Monarch then commissions the leader of the new majority party to form a new government. The Prime Minister has the option of attempting to remain in power even if seats have been lost. The subsequent Queen's Speech (i.e., outline of the proposed legislative program) offers a chance for the House of Commons to cast a vote of confidence or no confidence in the government through accepting or rejecting the Queen's Speech. The largest party not in government becomes the Official Opposition, known as "Her Majesty's Loyal Opposition." Any smaller parties not in government are collectively known as "the opposition".

6. Political Parties

6.1 Two Major Parties

Prior to the mid-19th century politics in the United Kingdom was dominated by the Whigs[20] and the Tories[21]. These were not political parties in the modern sense but somewhat loose alliances of interests and individuals. The Whigs were associated with the newly emerging moneyed industrial classes, and the Tories were associated with the landed gentry, the Church of England and the Church of Scotland.

The Whigs' origin lay in constitutional monarchism and opposition to absolute rule. After the Restoration in 1660, Charles II became the King and reigned over Britain. When he was becoming old, he wanted his brother James, Duke of Yoke, to succeed him. Some people were against his arrangement because James was a Catholic[22] and these people favored Protestantism[23]. These opponents to the King's plan were derisively called "Whigs", a nickname once given to the rebelling Scottish drovers. The Whigs represented the interests of the big merchants of the towns. Many of them were opposed to the Church of England. To amass more wealth, the Whigs demanded social freedom and liberty. The Whigs were originally also known as the "Country Party" (as opposed to the Tories, the "Court Party"). By the first half of the 19th century, however, the Whig political program came to encompass not only the supremacy of Parliament over the monarch and support for free trade, but also Catholic emancipation, the abolition of slavery and, significantly, expansion of the **suffrage**. Towards the middle of the 19th century, they began to use another name, the Liberal Party. After the First World War, the Liberal Party began to disintegrate and soon disappeared.

The opponents to the Whig Party were derisively called the Tories—a word from the Irish term meaning robbers. The Tories represented the interests of the smaller landed gentry and tradesmen (the middle class). They were in favor of peace and a stable social order for development. They were against drastic social changes which, they feared, would cause misery. During the middle of the 19th century, the Tory Party changed its name into the Conservative Party. After the disintegration of the Liberal Party, some of its members joined the Conservative Party. Since the founding of the Conservative Party, Britain has undergone great changes. The Conservative Party has also experienced changes in its organization and doctrine. But its opposition to violent social changes still remains. The Conservatives are mainly from the middle class and they are called the "Right" because of their conservative tendency. Economically, they stand for free enterprise and less government interference.

The Conservative Party and the Liberal Party dominated the political scene until the 1920s, when the Liberal Party declined in popularity and suffered a long stream of resignations. It was replaced as the main left-wing party by the newly emerging Labour Party. The policies that the Conservatives and Liberals put into effect were sometimes different, but they were controlled by the rich. The working class became more and more unwilling to follow them. They wanted to have their own party. The Labor Party was founded in 1900 by unionists, liberals, socialists and the Fabian Society. At first it was called the Labor Representation Committee which was then changed into the Labor Party. The basic doctrine of the Labor Party is to promote communal growth. The Labor Party believes in socialism and says that socialism should promote the growth of society, not the uprising of a class. It advocates class cooperation and demands economic equality. For this purpose it supports nationalization of big enterprises. After 1922 the Labor Party gradually replaced the Liberal Party to become one of the two major parties in Great Britain.

Since then the Conservative Party and the Labor Party have dominated British politics, and have alternated in government ever since. P. S. Tregidgo says in his book *A Background to English*, "The more parties there are, the less likely it is that any one of them will be strong enough in Parliament to outvote all the others; but when there are only two, one of them is bound to have a majority of seats. This helps to ensure a strong and stable government." This may be the reason why the British have the two-party system. A general election is normally held every five years, but the Prime Minister can hold an election ahead of time during his or her office. The electoral system tends to be dominated by the two parties.

In such an old capitalist country as Britain, the Conservatives have many supporters. According to reliable estimates, a majority of the middle class vote for the Conservatives and nearly all the upper-middle classes (professional and managerial people) support them. Many of the well-to-do workers also support them. It can be said that the higher one goes up in social and economic class in Britain, the more likely he is to vote for the Conservative candidate.

Though many of the Labor leaders are from the working class, the Labor Party is not a proletarian party. It represents confusing class elements. According to estimates from general elections, about 20% of the upper-middle class, half of the middle-class, and 60% of the manual workers vote for the Labor Party. Traditionally, the Labor Party is called the Left and it represents the interests of the middle and lower-middle classes. Taking all its policies into consideration, we may say whether the Labor Party can win a general election largely depends on the economic situation in Britain. If the economic situation is rosy, the Labor Party would have less chance to win. If the economic situation is gloomy and many people want changes as a way out, the Labor Party would stand a good chance of winning the election. Certainly there are other contributing factors, such as the party's political stratagem, function of nationalism and the prestige of leaders. The big victory Mrs Thatcher won at the general election of 1983 was partly due to the influence of nationalism because England had just won the war with Argentina.

6.2 Minor Parties

The Social Democratic Party is a new party which was founded by a group of leaders from the Labor Party on March 26,1981, who defected because they thought the party was becoming too leftwing.

The Liberal Party was a term first adopted officially by the Whigs in 1868, although it had been used unofficially since the 1830s to describe reforming Whigs. At that time it was one of the main political parties in power.

The Communist Party was built up by some Marxist groups on July 21, 1920. Before the Second World War it waged a struggle against fascism and supported the Spanish people in their fight against Franco (the Spanish dictator) and opposed Chamberlain's appeasement.

7. Brexit

Brexit is a word that is used as a shorthand way of saying the UK leaving the EU —merging the words Britain and exit to get Brexit.

7.1 UK Joining the EU

The United Kingdom first joined the European Communities in January 1973, and remained a member of the European Union that it evolved into; UK citizens, and other EU citizens resident in the UK, elect 73 members to represent them in the European Parliament in Brussels and Strasbourg.

7.2 UK Leaving the EU

The UK's membership in the Union has been a major topic of debate over the years. In recent years there have been divisions in both major parties over whether the UK should form greater ties within the EU, or reduce the EU's supranational powers. Opponents of greater European integration are known as "Eurosceptics"[24], while supporters are known as "Europhiles"[25]. Division over EU is prevalent in both major parties, although the Conservative Party is seen as most divided over the issue, both whilst in Government up to 1997 and after 2010, and between those dates as the opposition. However, the Labour Party is also divided, with conflicting views over UK adoption of the euro whilst in Government (1997–2010).

British nationalists have long campaigned against European integration. The strong showing of the eurosceptic UK Independence Party (UKIP)[26] since the 2004 European Parliament elections has shifted the debate over UK relations with the EU.

In March 2008, Parliament decided to not hold a referendum on the ratification of the Treaty of Lisbon, signed in December 2007. This was despite the Labour government promising in 2004 to hold a referendum on the previously proposed Constitution for Europe.

On June 23, 2016, the United Kingdom voted to leave the European Union in a referendum. After the referendum, it was debated as to how and when the UK should leave the EU. On July 11, 2016, the Cabinet Office Minister, John Penrose failed to deliver a final answer on whether it would be at the disposal of the Prime Minister and one of the Secretaries of State, through the Royal prerogative, or of Parliament, through primary legislation.

The rules for exiting the EU are set out in Article 50 of the Treaty on European Union. This is the only lawful route for withdrawal from the EU under the Treaty. In October 2016, the Conservative Prime Minister, Theresa May, announced that Article 50 would be invoked by "the first quarter of 2017". On January 24, 2017 the Supreme Court ruled in the Miller case by a majority that the process could not be initiated without an authorising act of Parliament, but unanimously ruled against the Scottish government's claim in respect of devolution that they had a direct say in the decision to trigger Article 50. Consequently, the European Union (Notification of Withdrawal) Act 2017 empowering the Prime Minister to invoke Article 50 was passed and enacted by royal assent in March 2017.

Invocation of Article 50 by the United Kingdom government occurred on March 29, 2017, when Sir Tim Barrow[27], the Permanent Representative of the United Kingdom to the European Union, formally delivered by hand a letter signed by Prime Minister Theresa May to Donald Tusk[28], the President of the European Council in Brussels. The letter also contained the United Kingdom's intention to withdraw from the European Atomic Energy Community (EAEC or Euratom)[29]. This means that the UK will cease to be a member of the EU on March 30, 2019, unless an extension to negotiations is agreed upon by the UK and EU.

Joyful Moment

A Tough Question

If con is the opposite of pro, then isn't Congress the opposite of progress?

Notes

[1] constitutional monarchy 君主立宪制
[2] Westminster system 西敏制；威斯敏斯特体系
[3] Elizabeth II 伊丽莎白二世
[4] Glorious Revolution 光荣革命，光荣革命是英国一场和宗教有关的非暴力宫廷政变，发生在 1688 年到 1689 年
[5] the Royal Navy（英国）皇家海军, the British Army 英国陆军, and the Royal Air Force（英国）皇家空军
[6] the Lords Spiritual 上议院的神职议员
[7] the Lords Temporal 上议院世俗议员
[8] Archbishops of Canterbury and York 英国国教的两大主教：坎特伯雷大主教（The Archbishop of Canterbury）和约克大主教（the Archbishop of York）
[9] the hereditary peers 爵位能世袭的贵族

[10] life peers（爵位不能世袭的）终身贵族
[11] Parliament Acts 议会法案
[12] Law Lords 上议院议员
[13] first-past-the-post 最高票选人当选
[14] the Opposition (Party) 反对党
[15] Right Honorable 阁下（英国对某些官员的称呼）
[16] European Union membership referendum 欧洲联盟成员公投
[17] Theresa May 特雷莎 • 梅，2016 年开始任英国首相至今。
[18] Andrea Leadsom 安德烈娅 • 利德索姆，2016 年 7 月 14 日进入内阁，出任环境、食品和农村事务大臣。
[19] Her Majesty's Opposition 反对党议员为了女王陛下而对执政党的执政进行监督。
[20] Whigs 辉格党
[21] Tories 托利党
[22] Catholic 天主教的
[23] Protestantism 新教是与东正教、天主教并列的三大基督教派别之一
[24] Eurosceptics 疑欧派
[25] Europhiles 亲欧派
[26] UK Independence Party (UKIP) 英国独立党
[27] Tim Barrow 蒂姆 • 巴罗，英国驻欧盟大使
[28] Donald Tusk 唐纳德 • 图斯克，欧洲理事会主席
[29] the European Atomic Energy Community (EAEC or Euratom) 欧洲原子能共同体

New Words

1. **Royal Prerogative** /ˌrɔɪəl prɪ'rɒgətɪv/ 皇家特权
2. **prorogue** /prəʊ'rəʊg/ *vt.* to discontinue the meetings of (a legislative body) 使（议会）休会
   —The Parliament was prorogued to the tenth of February.
   国会休会到 2 月 10 日。
3. **backbencher** /ˌbæk'bentʃə/ *n.* 后排议员
4. **whip** /wɪp/ *n.* a member of a legislative body, such as the U.S. Congress or the British Parliament, charged by his or her party with enforcing party discipline and ensuring attendance. 组织秘书，政党纪律委员（英国和美国的政党中负责确保本党党员出席政府重大辩论并投票的官员）
5. **go to the country** 解散议会重新选举下议院，举行大选
6. **referendum** /ˌrefə'rendəm/ *n.* a legislative act is referred for final approval to a popular vote by the electorate 全民公决；公民投票
7. **suffrage** /'sʌfrɪdʒ/ *n.* the right or privilege of voting; franchise （政治性选举的）选举权，

投票权

Exercises

1. Choose the correct answer.

1) Which of the following is not true?

A. The Queen holds meetings of the Privy Council.

B. The Queen receives reports of cabinet meetings in her weekly sessions with the Prime Minister.

C. The Queen must take sides when a dispute arises in the Cabinet.

D. The Queen is informed and consulted on every aspect of national life.

2) How often does the general election take place?

A. At least every three years. B. At least every four years.

C. At least every five years. D. At least every six years.

3) Why are so many party members elected to Parliament in each election in Britain?

A. Because party members usually enjoy better reputation.

B. Because party members have more experience in forming a government.

C. Because party members have the backing of nationwide organizations.

D. Because people trust party members to a greater degree.

4) The executive power is in the hands of ________.

A. Parliament

B. the House of Commons

C. the Cabinet headed by the Prime Minister

D. the Queen

5) The real centre of power in Parliament is ________.

A. the Queen B. the House of Commons

C. the House of Lords D. the Cabinet

2. Decide whether the following statements are True or False.

1) The Queen is not the head of the Church of England.

2) If the Cabinet loses its majority support in Parliament, it can continue its term.

3) The supreme law-making authority in Britain is the Parliament.

4) The power of House of Lords is very limited: they can not touch money bills, and they can only hold up bills for half-year.

5) The Speaker presides over the meeting in the House of Commons and he belongs to the government party.

3. Fill in the blanks.

1) The present monarch of Britain is ________, her role is mainly ________. A general election takes place at least every ________ years. In each general election, ________

members of Parliament are elected.

2) Parliament in Britain, strictly speaking, consists of three elements: ________; ________; and ________.

3) The House of Lords has a special ________ function. It serves as________.

4) Britain, unlike France and the U.S., has no ________ constitution.

5) The leader of the party with the largest number of members returned to the House of Commons becomes ________. He is invited by ________ to form a government. The party with the next largest number of supporters in the Commons becomes the official ________ to the government.

4. Explain the following terms.

1) the British Constitution

2) party system in Parliament

3) the House of Lords

4) the House of Commons

5) Privy Council

5. Answer the following questions according to the passage.

1) What is the role of the Monarchy in the British government?

2) What does the Cabinet consist of?

3) What does the collective responsibility of Cabinet government mean?

Stay Positive

1 If a man would move the world, he must first move himself.

2. Defeat is not the worst of failure. Not to have tried is the true failure.

Chapter 4

Economy of the United Kingdom

There can be no economy where there is no efficiency.

—Disraeli, British statesman

1. General Introduction

1.1 Overview

The United Kingdom is a major developed capitalist economy. According to the GDP ranking released by the World Bank in July 2018, it is the world's fifth largest economy in nominal GDP [1]. Nominal GDP is the GDP in that year's prices, thus nominal GDP does not account for inflation. The GDP of UK is $2.809 trillion in 2018, and it is the second largest economy in Europe only after Germany. However, the UK is not among the top richest countries in Europe. On April 17, 2018, the International Monetary Fund (IMF) issued the ranking of GDP per capita. The GDP per capita [2] of UK is $39,735, ranking the 14th in Europe and the 22nd in the world. The UK has one of the world's most globalised economies. It is the 8th largest country in terms of international trade in 2017.

The UK was the first country in the world to industrialize in the 18th and 19th centuries, and possessed a leading role in the global economy for much of the 19th century. However, by the late 19th century, the U.S. had begun to challenge Britain's role as the leader of the global economy. The extensive war efforts of both World Wars in the 20th century and the **dismantlement** of the British Empire also weakened the UK economy in global terms, and by that time Britain had been **exceeded** by the United States as the chief player in the global economy. At the start of the 21st century, however, the UK still possesses a significant role in the global economy, due to its large GDP and the financial importance that its capital, London, possesses in the world.

The United Kingdom also plays a very important role in international economic organizations. It is a member of the G8, the Organization for Economic Cooperation and Development (OECD)[3], the World Trade Organization, and the European Union. Although the UK has been a major member of EU for many years, it still launched "Brexit", which is the impending withdrawal of the UK from the European Union. Following the UK's decision to leave the European Union, the Bank of England cut interest rates to a new historic low of 0.25%

for just over a year to **bolster** confidence in the economy. It also bought government and corporate bonds in order to stabilize the financial market.

1.2 Economic Performance of UK since World War II

Following the end of World War II, there was a long interval without a major **recession** (1945-1973) and a growth in **prosperity** in the 1950s and 1960s. According to the OECD, the annual growth rate of UK between 1960 and 1973 averaged 2.9%.

However, following the severe shock of the 1973 oil crisis and the 1973-1974 stock market crash [4], the British economy went into recession in 1974, with GDP falling by 1.1%, recording weaker growth than other European nations in the 1970s overall.

A new period of economic development began with the coming of the Margaret Thatcher government in 1979. Margaret Thatcher served as Prime Minister of the United Kingdom from 1979 to 1990 and leader of the Conservative Party from 1975 to 1990. In her term of office, most state-owned enterprises in the industrial and service sectors, which since the 1940s had been nationalized, were privatized. As a result, the British Government owned very few industries or businesses. GDP fell 5.9% at first then rose to 5% at its peak in 1988, as banks and other financial institutions in the UK enjoyed the **liberalization** of the regulatory structures and greater freedom to explore new investment fields with less control and regulation.

After a mild recession in the early 1990s, there followed (according to the UK Prime Minister Gordon Brown) the longest period of stable economic growth that Britain had ever seen for more than 150 years, achieving growth in every quarter between 1992 and 2007, one of the highest economic growth rates of major developed economies during that time. This boom ended in 2008 when the UK entered a recession brought about by the global financial crisis. Beginning with the collapse of Northern Rock [5], major banks failed and were nationalized.

The UK economy had been one of the strongest EU economies in terms of inflation, interest rates and unemployment, all of which remained relatively low until the 2008-2009 recessions, when unemployment rose dramatically, and interest rates fell to 0.5%. During August 2008 the IMF warned that the UK economic outlook had worsened due to a twin shock: financial crisis as well as rising commodity prices. Both developments harm the UK more than most developed countries, as the UK obtained revenue from exporting financial services while recording deficits in finished goods and commodities, including food.

The UK entered a recession in the second quarter of 2008 and exited it in the 4th quarter of 2009, according to figures produced by the Office for National Statistics [6]. The subsequently revised ONS figures show that the UK suffered six **consecutive** quarters of negative growth, making it the longest recession since records began. By the end of 2009, revised statistics from the ONS demonstrated that the UK economy shrank by 7.2% from peak to **trough**.

1.3 Causes of Financial Crisis

The financial crisis of 2007-2009 has been called the most serious financial crisis since the Great Depression [7] by leading economists, with its global effects characterized by the failure of key businesses, declines in consumer wealth estimated in the trillions of US dollars, and a significant decline in economic activity. Many causes have been proposed, with varying weight assigned by experts. What caused such serious financial crisis on earth?

The immediate cause or trigger of the crisis was the bursting of the United States housing bubble which started in 2006, and the decline accelerated in 2007 and 2008. Housing prices stopped increasing in 2006, started to decrease in 2007. The decline in prices meant that homeowners could no longer refinance when their mortgage rates were reset, which caused delinquencies and defaults of mortgages to increase sharply, especially among subprime borrowers. From the first quarter of 2006 to the third quarter of 2008, the percentage of mortgages in **foreclosure** tripled, from 1% to 3%, and the percentage of mortgages in foreclosure or at least 30 days delinquent more than doubled, from 4.5% to 10%. These foreclosure and delinquency rates are the highest since the Great Depression. The American dream of owning your own home turned into an American nightmare for millions of families.

1.4 Impact of the Financial Crisis upon the UK

The IMF said the UK had been hit hard by the global financial crisis. Economic activity weakened sharply, the unemployment rate increased, property prices dropped dramatically, and inflation had fallen despite a significant depreciation of sterling. The IMF projected a **contraction** of 4.2% in 2009, with a modest recovery starting in 2010.

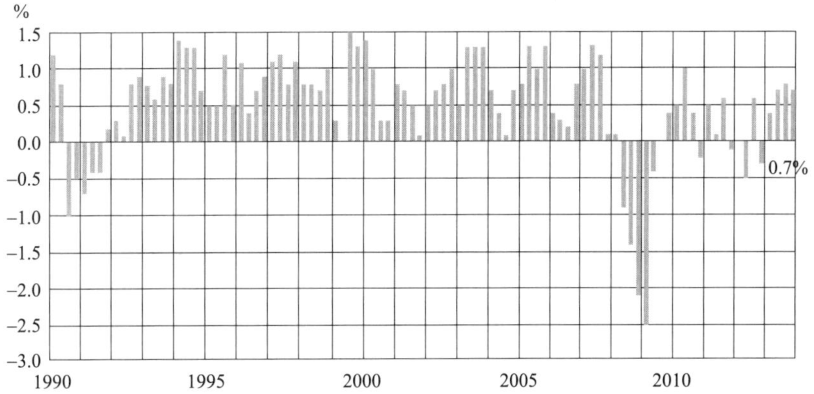

Figure 4.1 UK GDP Growth, quarter on previous quarter

As a typical capitalist economy, UK is unavoidably covered by the crisis shadow. UK GDP shrank by 1.6% in the fourth quarter of 2008. GDP in the fourth quarter of 2008 was 2.0% lower than the fourth quarter of 2007. For the year 2008 as a whole, GDP rose by 0.7%. It is the biggest quarterly fall in GDP since 1980 and the biggest annual fall in GDP since the last recession in 1991.

1.5 General Measures to Deal with Recession

At such times governments attempt to stimulate the economy. Standard macroeconomic policy includes:

- increase borrowing;
- reduce interest rates;
- reduce taxes;
- spend on public works such as infrastructure.

Borrowing at a time of recession seems risky, but the idea is that this should be complimented with paying back during times of growth.

Likewise, reducing interest rates sounds like there would be less incentive for people to save money when banks need to build up their capital reserves. However, as the real economy starts to feel the pain, reducing interest rate is an attempt to encourage people to take part in the economy.

Tax reduction is something that most people favor, and yet during times of economic downturn it would seem that a reduction in tax would result in reduced government revenues just when they need it and then spending on health, education etc., would be at risk. However, because higher taxes during downturns mean more hardship for more people, increased borrowing is supposed to offset the reduction in taxes, hopefully affording people a better chance to weather the economic storm.

Finally it is at this time that public infrastructure work, which can potentially employ many, many people, is acceptable. Often, under free market ideals, government involvement in such activities is supposed to be minimal. Even the other form of "interference" is usually not welcomed. However, most states realize that markets are not always able to function on their own; practical and sensible adoption of market systems means governments can guide development and progress as required.

Each of these measures should no doubt come under examination from opposition parties and the media to ensure they are appropriate, but some measures can be so politically sensitive that governments may be afraid to make such choices, thus making economic policies during bad times even riskier.

1.6 Recent Economic Development

In the first quarter of 2012, the UK economy was thought to have entered a **double-dip** recession by posting two consecutive negative quarters of growth. However, revised figures by the ONS showed that in fact the UK economy stagnated in quarter one with growth at 0.0%, thereby not fulfilling the technical requirement of two consecutive quarters of negative growth for a recession.

The economic growth of UK in 2013 had surprised many economists, as the budget projected annual growth of just 0.6%, but the outcome was more than expected—the annual GDP grew by 1.74%. From 2013 to 2017, the UK has achieved a stable economic development. The following figure shows the annual GDP growth rate of UK in recent years.

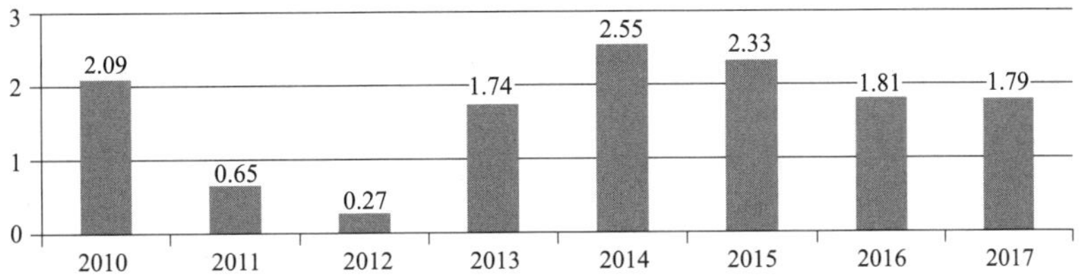

Figure 4.2 GDP Growth Rate of UK from 2010-2017

2. Economic Sectors of UK

2.1 Agriculture

The United Kingdom is an industrialized country, but its agriculture remains important. Britain's land surface is small compared to that of the United States, but British agriculture is very intensive and highly productive. Generally speaking, Britain has favorable conditions for agricultural development. Its climate is mild and there is plenty of rainfall. Britain's soil quality varies greatly. In northern areas the soils are thin, lying right above rock formations, while the south possesses areas of rich clay soil. When handled carefully, the soils of eastern and south central England are very productive. Nearly 80% of Britain's land area, or about 50 million acres, can be used for agricultural purpose, but only 26% of this land is used to grow crops.

Agriculture is a significant employer, with 1.7% of the total UK workforce involved in primary agricultural production. If the whole food chain is considered, including activities beyond the farm gate, the proportion of the workforce amounts to 14%.

The combined agricultural food sector accounts for 6.5% of the UK's total economy and generates some £80 billion in Gross Value Added, a measure of the value of goods. The UK food and drink industry contributes approximately 5% of the total UK exports.

The UK farming industry is becoming a significant supplier of renewable energy and has been at the forefront of **biofuel**, **biogas** and technological development. In the past the farming industry had been criticized for being profit driven at the expense of the environment. The past decade has seen a continuing trend towards less intensive management and the **restoration** of wildlife habitats such as hedges. The areas of farmland in England that have entered into conservation agreements now exceed six million **hectares**—almost two-thirds of the agricultural landscape. The proposed reforms to the Common Agricultural Policy will mean that environmental protection remains a priority for farmers, regardless of the pressures to intensify food production.

Agriculture therefore has an increasingly important role to play in promoting a sustainable economy, balancing the conflicting needs of people, planet and profit. The challenge for the future is to produce more food more efficiently, with fewer resources and with less waste and emissions.

2.2 Manufacturing

Britain has traditionally been a manufacturing nation and was once known as the "workshop of the world". The history of manufacturing in Britain is unique because Britain is the birthplace of the Industrial Revolution. In the 16th and 17th centuries, major manufacturing industries in Britain included silk weaving, garment making, and the manufacturing of hats, pottery, and cutlery. During the Industrial Revolution people invented new methods of manufacturing products and many products were made by machine. Production moved from small craft shops to factories. This caused population to shift to urban areas where these factories were located. With the invention of steam-powered machines, textiles, shipbuilding, iron, and steel emerged as important industries. Coal became the most important industrial fuel.

Britain's iron and steel industry remains important and Britain is still one of the world's major steel-producing nations. Britain exports a large proportion of its steel, either directly (25% of the total) or in the form of finished products every year. But Britain is not self-sufficient in iron ore and more than half of the ore it consumes comes from abroad.

Engineering and allied industries is the single largest sector. Within this sector, transport equipment was the largest contributor, with eight global car manufacturers being present in the UK—BMW, Tata (Jaguar-Land Rover), General Motors (Vauxhall Motors), Honda, Nissan, Toyota and Volkswagen with a number of smaller, specialist manufacturers and commercial vehicle manufacturers also being present. The British motor industry also comprises numerous components for the sector, such as Ford's **diesel** engine plant in Dagenham, which produces half of Ford's diesel engines globally.

Another important component of engineering and allied industries is electronics, audio and **optical** equipment, with the UK having a broad base of domestic firms, alongside a number of foreign firms manufacturing a wide range of TV, radio and communication products, scientific and optical instruments, electrical machinery and office machinery and computers.

Other important sectors of the manufacturing industry include food, drink, tobacco, paper, printing, publishing and textiles.

2.3 Service Industries

The service sector of UK accounts for more than 75% of GDP, which is no doubt the dominant sector of the UK economy, a feature normally associated with the economy of a developed country. This means that the Tertiary sector jobs outnumber the Secondary and Primary sector jobs.

2.3.1 Finance

The UK is one of the world's leading financial centers, with many major financial institutions having their headquarters located in London. The Bank of England, chartered in 1694, is the country's central bank. There are more than a dozen major commercial banks in the UK, including Lloyds TSB [8], Barclays [9], the Royal Bank of Scotland, and HSBC [10]. They provide their customers with current and savings accounts, loans and financial advice. The London Stock Exchange [11] is one of the largest exchanges in the world, where listed stocks and shares are bought and sold in public and overseas companies.

The pound sterling is the basic unit of currency in Britain. It is the oldest currency in use and the fourth most traded currency in the world, after the US dollar, the Euro and the Yen. As a member of the EU, the UK has the option of adopting the Euro as its currency. However, the subject has been politically controversial, because the British public is unwilling to see the pound to be replaced because of the former's identity as a symbol of British nationalism. Thus, the UK is continuously using its traditional currency of the pound, while other EU nations have adopted the Euro as their single currency from January 1, 2002. The British pound will be more important after the UK exits the EU.

The UK's financial exports contribute significantly towards the balance of payments. Balance of payments is an accounting record of all transactions made by a country over a certain time period, comparing the amount of foreign currency taken into the amount of domestic currency paid out. The UK has an expanding export business in financial service, which has been influenced by a mixture of unique institutions, light regulation, and a highly skilled workforce.

2.3.2 Real Estate

Real estate is a significant feature of the UK. The real estate market in the UK is the largest or second-largest in Europe (after Germany) depending on the method of measurement. The commercial real estate market in the UK has a market size of around 250 billion euros. Domestic real estate represented the largest non-financial asset in the UK. Foreign investment plays a substantial role in the UK's real estate market, particularly in London.

Average house prices in the UK have increased by 3.0% in the year to May 2018 (down from 3.5% in April 2018). This is its lowest annual rate since August 2013 when it was also 3.0%. The annual growth rate has slowed since mid-2016 and has remained under 5%, with the exception of October 2017, throughout 2017 and into 2018.

This drop of UK house price growth is driven mainly by a slowdown in the south and east of England. The lowest annual growth was in London, where prices decreased by 0.4% over the year. This is the fourth consecutive month that London house prices have fallen over the year.

The average UK house price was £226,000 in May 2018. This is £6,000 higher than in May 2017 and unchanged from last month. On a seasonally adjusted basis (series available in data downloads), average house prices in the UK decreased by 0.2% between April 2018 and May 2018, compared with an increase of 0.4% in average prices during the same period a year earlier (April 2017 and May 2017).

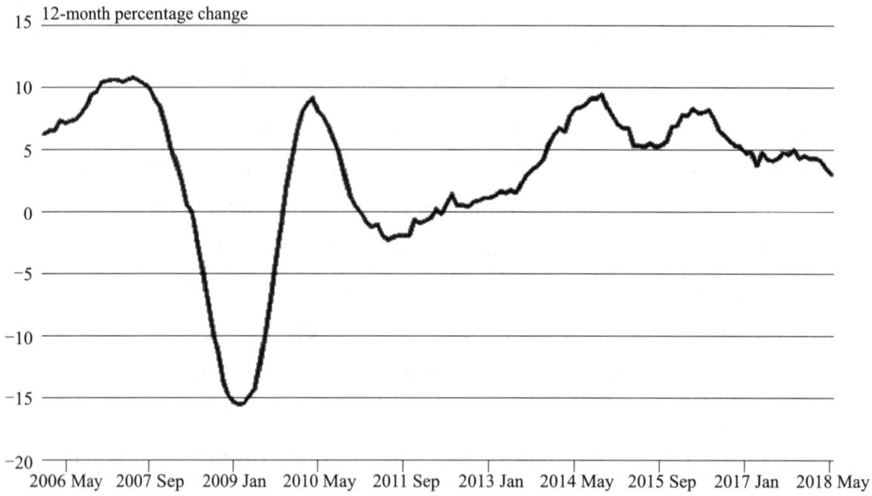

Figure 4.3 Annual House Price Rates of Change, UK all Dwellings from 2006 to 2018

Source: HM Land Registry, Registers of Scotland, Land and Property Services Northern Ireland and Office for National Statistics

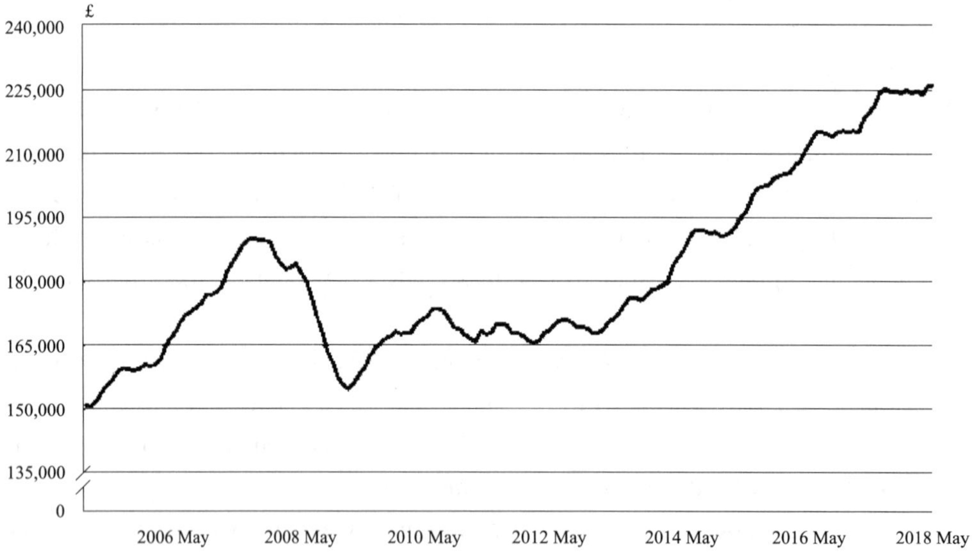

Figure 4.4 Average UK House Price, January 2006 to May 2018

Source: HM Land Registry, Registers of Scotland, Land and Property Services Northern Ireland and Office for National Statistics

3. Major Cities and Industries

3.1 London

The largest and most important city in Britain is London, which situated on the Thames River, it is the capital of both England and the United Kingdom. London is a major centre for international business and commerce, and it is one of the two global financial centers in the world (with New York City).

London's success as a service industry and business centre can be attributed to factors such as English being the native and dominant language of business, close relationship with the U.S. and various countries in Asia. Other factors include English law being the most important and most used contract law in international business and the multi-cultural infrastructure. Government policies such as low taxes, particularly for foreigners, a business friendly environment, good transport infrastructure and a deregulated economy with little intervention by the government have all contributed to London's economy becoming more service based. Over 85% (3.2 million) of the employed population of Greater London work in service industries. Another half a million employees resident in Greater London work in manufacturing and construction, almost equally divided between both.

London's largest industry remains finance, and its financial exports make it a large contributor to the UK's balance of payments. London has over 480 overseas banks, more than any other city in the world. London is home to banks, brokers, insurers and legal and accounting firms. A second, smaller financial district is developing at Canary Wharf [12] to the east of the city which includes the global headquarters of HSBC, Reuters [13], Barclays and the Magic Circle [14], which includes Clifford Chance [15], the largest law firm in the world.

Along with professional services, media companies are concentrated in London, and the media distribution industry is London's second most competitive sector. The BBC is a key employer, while other broadcasters also have headquarters around the city. Many national newspapers are edited in London, having traditionally been associated with Fleet Street [16], named after the River Fleet. They are now primarily based around Canary Wharf. Canary Wharf is a large business and shopping district in East London, located in the London Borough of Tower Hamlets, centered on the old West India Docks in the London Docklands.

Tourism is one of London's prime industries. Euromonitor International is a leading independent provider of strategic market research. It creates data and analysis on thousands of products and services around the world. In November 2017, Euromonitor ranked London at the 3rd place out of the top 100 most popular cities in the world, attracting 19 million international tourists in 2017.

3.2 Liverpool

In common with much of the rest of the UK today, Liverpool's economy is dominated by service sector industries, both public and private.

The banking, finance and insurance sectors are of the fastest growing areas of Liverpool's economy. Major private service industry concerns have also invested in Liverpool especially the financial services sector and the professional advice sector, with Barclays, JP Morgan, and the Bank of Ireland either opening or expanding their sites, a number of major call centers have opened in recent years too.

Tourism is a major factor in Liverpool's economy. In 2017 the city welcomed 839,000 foreign visitors, up from 671,000 the year before. The increase in tourism has led to a great increase in the provision of high quality services such as hotels, restaurants and clubs.

Liverpool is also well known for its strong sporting identity. The city is home of two Premier League football clubs, Liverpool F.C. [17] and Everton F.C. [18]. Matches between the two clubs are known as the Merseyside derby [19]. The world-famous Grand National also takes places annually at Aintree Racecourse [20] on the outskirts of the city.

3.2 Birmingham

The city is famous as a powerhouse of the Industrial Revolution in England, a fact which led to Birmingham being known as "the workshop of the world" or the "city of a thousand trades".

Two of Britain's "big four" banks were founded in Birmingham—Lloyds Bank (now Lloyds Banking Group) in 1765 and the Midland Bank (now HSBC Bank plc) in 1836—and today the city employs 108,000 in banking, finance and insurance.

Tourism is also an increasingly important part of the local economy. With major facilities such as the International Convention Centre and National Exhibition Center, the Birmingham area accounts for 42% of the UK conference and exhibition trade. The city's sporting and cultural venues attract large numbers of visitors.

Joyful Moment

Big Day

Teacher: What great event happened in 1809?
Little Willy: Abraham Lincoln was born.
Teacher: Correct. And what great event happened in 1812?
Little Willy: Abraham Lincoln had his third birthday.

Notes

[1] nominal GDP 名义国内生产总值，以当年价格计算的最终产品或服务的价值。

[2] GDP per capita 人均国内生产总值，将一个国家核算期内（通常是一年）实现的国内生产总值与这个国家的常住人口相比进行计算，得到人均国内生产总值。

[3] OECD 经济合作与发展组织，全称 Organization for Economic Cooperation and Development，简称经合组织，是由 36 个市场经济体组成的政府间国际经济组织，旨在共同应对全球化带来的经济、社会和政府治理等方面的挑战，并把握全球化带来的机遇。

[4] 1973-1974 stock market crash 1973—1974 年的股灾，股市暴跌从 1973 年 1 月持续至

1974 年 12 月

[5] Northern Rock 英国北岩银行

[6] Office for National Statistics 英国国家统计署（缩写为 ONS），为英国统计局的执行机构，隶属于英国国会。

[7] the Great Depression 大萧条，是指 1929 年至 1933 年之间全球性的经济大衰退。

[8] Lloyds TSB 英国劳埃德银行集团

[9] Barclays 英国巴克莱银行

[10] HSBC 汇丰银行

[11] London Stock Exchange 伦敦证券交易所（缩写为 LSE，简称“伦敦证交所”），是世界四大证券交易所之一。

[12] Canary Wharf 金丝雀码头，是英国首都伦敦一个重要的金融区和购物区，坐落于伦敦道格斯岛的陶尔哈姆莱茨区（Tower Hamlets）。

[13] Reuters 路透社，是世界上最早创办的通讯社之一，也是目前英国最大的通讯社。

[14] the Magic Circle 总部位于伦敦的五家最负盛名的国际律师事务所的非正式代称。

[15] Clifford Chance 高伟绅律师事务所，是一家总部位于英国伦敦的顶级国际律师事务所。

[16] Fleet Street 佛里特街又译舰队街，英国伦敦的一条河滨马路。18 世纪以来，它成为英国新闻和出版事业的中心，《泰晤士报》《每日邮报》的总办事处均设于此。

[17] Liverpool F.C. 利物浦足球俱乐部，位于英格兰西北部默西赛德郡利物浦市，成立于 1892 年 3 月 15 日，主场在安菲尔德球场，目前所属参赛级别为英格兰超级联赛。

[18] Everton F.C. 埃弗顿足球俱乐部，1878 年成立，位于英格兰的利物浦市。俱乐部历史悠久，是英格兰联赛创立者之一。

[19] Merseyside derby 默西赛德郡德比，或称为利物浦市德比，是指英格兰默西赛德郡利物浦市两支最成功的球队——利物浦和埃弗顿之间的同城德比战。德比，英语为 Derby Game，是体育术语，在欧洲多指足球队之间的比赛。

[20] Aintree Racecourse 安特里赛马场，位于英格兰默西赛德郡安特里，开放于 1829 年 7 月 7 日。此赛马场以每年在这里举行的英国国家大赛，即越野障碍赛马比赛而著名，这是世界上著名的赛马比赛之一。

New Words

1. **dismantlement** /ˌdɪs'mæntlment/ *n.* the act of taking something apart (as a piece of machinery) 拆除；解散

—The dismantlement appraisal date shall be the date of issuance of license for house dismantlement.

拆迁估价时点应为房屋拆迁许可证颁发之日。

2. **exceed** /ɪk'siːd/ *v.* go beyond 超过，胜过

— Exports yearly exceed imports.

出口每年超过进口。

3. **bolster** /'bəʊlstə/ *v.* to support or improve something or make it stronger 支撑；加固；提高

— More money is needed to bolster the industry. 需要更多的钱来扶持该产业。

4. **recession** /rɪ'seʃn/ *n.* a difficult time for the economy of a country, when there is less trade and industrial activity than usual and more people are unemployed 经济衰退；经济萎缩

—In the recession, our firm went through a bad time.

我们公司在经济衰退时期历尽艰辛。

5. **prosperity** /prɒ'sperəti/ *n.* the state of being successful, especially financially 兴旺；繁荣；成功；昌盛

—The new government ushered in a period of prosperity.

新政府的成立带来了一个繁荣的时期。

6. **liberalization** /ˌlɪbrəlaɪ'zeɪʃn/ *n.* the act of making less strict 自由化，放宽限制

—How would a new round of trade liberalization help poor countries?

新一轮的贸易自由化将如何帮助贫困国家呢？

7. **consecutive** /kən'sekjutɪv/ *adj.* following one after another in a series, without interruption 连续不断的；连贯的

—The poll was conducted for 26 consecutive year.

这项调查已经连续进行了 26 年。

8. **trough** /trɒf/ *n.* a low point in a process that has regular high and low points 低谷

—These cycles often take a generation to play out from peak to trough and to peak again.

这些周期经常要让一代人经历从高峰到低谷、再从低谷到高峰的漫长过程。

9. **foreclosure** /fɔː'kləʊʒə(r)/ *n.* the act of foreclosing on money that has been borrowed （抵押品）赎回权的取消

— If homeowners can't keep up the payments, they face foreclosure.

如果房主不能继续还贷，他们就面临房产抵押赎回权被取消的危险。

10. **contraction** /kən'trækʃn/ *n.* the act of decreasing (something) in size or volume or quantity or scope 收缩，紧缩

—A reading below 50 indicates economic contraction.

指数低于 50 表明经济出现收缩。

11. **double-dip** /'dʌbl'dɪp/ *adj.* In economics, a double-dip is a period when an economy goes into recession, then briefly recovers, then goes into another recession. 再度衰退，二次的

—Dismal economic findings have analysts fearing a double-dip.

对经济低潮期调查的结果使分析家们担忧经济会出现再度衰退。

12. **biofuel** /'baɪəʊfjuəl/ *n.* A biofuel is a gas, liquid, or solid from natural sources such as plants

that is used as a fuel. 生物燃料

—Biofuel production has helped some farmers and workers boost their incomes and develop their businesses.

生物燃料生产帮助了一些农民和工人增加收入和扩大生意。

13. **biogas** /'baɪəʊgæs/ *n.* a gas that is produced by the action of bacteria on organic waste matter and used as a fuel 生物气，沼气

—Both natural gas and biogas create emissions when burned, but far less than coal and oil do.

天然气和沼气燃烧时，都会产生二氧化碳，但是要比煤和石油少得多。

14. **restoration** /ˌrestə'reɪʃn/ *n.* being restored to its former good condition 恢复，复原

—There ensued a partial restoration of productive activity.

生产活动得到了部分恢复。

15. **hectare** /'hekteə/ *n.* a unit of measurement of an area of land (10,000 m^2) 公顷

—They also own about 40 hectares of coffee plantation.

同时，他们也拥有约 40 公顷的咖啡种植园。

16. **diesel** /'diːzl/ engine *n.* A diesel engine is an internal combustion engine in which oil is burned by very hot air. 柴油发动机

— Large trucks normally use diesel engines because of their strong horsepower.

大型卡车通常使用柴油发动机，因为它们的马力强劲。

17. **optical** /'ɒptɪkl/ *adj.* connected with the sense of sight or the relationship between light and sight 视力的；视觉的；光学的

—I thought I saw a ghost but it was just an optical illusion.

我以为我看见鬼了，其实只是一种幻觉。

Exercises

1. Choose the correct answer.

1) UK is the world's ________ largest by nominal GDP in 2017.

A. second

B. fourth

C. fifth

D. sixth

2) Which bank was nationalized first in 2008?

A. HSBC.

B. Northern Rock.

C. Citibank.

D. Barclays.

3) What is the dominant sector of the UK economy?

A. Agriculture.

B. Manufacturing.

C. Service industry.

D. Motor industry.

4) Which one is UK's central bank?

A. Bank of England.

B. Royal Bank of Scotland.

C. HSBC.

D. Britain Bank.

5) Which of the following is NOT the standard macroeconomic policy to stimulate the economy?

A. Increasing borrowing.

B. Reducing interest rates.

C. Increasing taxes.

D. Spending on public works.

2. Decide whether the following statements are True or False.

1) The two global "financial centers" are New York City and London.

2) Agriculture is a risky business because it has to rely on climatic conditions.

3) Since Britain was "the workshop of the world", it is self-sufficient in iron ore.

4) The pound sterling is the oldest currency in use.

5) Despite the economy is unstable, price of goods remains stable in 2007-2009 crisis.

3. Fill in the blanks according to the passage.

1) ______________ is famous as a powerhouse of the Industrial Revolution in England.

2) ______________ is the capital of Scotland.

3) ______________ in London is one of the largest exchanges in the world.

4) A new period of economics began with the coming of the ________ government in 1979.

5) In November 2017, Euromonitor ranked London at the ________ place out of the top 100 most popular cities in the world.

4. Explain the following terms according to the passage.

1) nominal GDP

2) balance of payments

3) Canary Wharf

4) Fleet Street

5) Margaret Thatcher

5. Answer the following questions according to the passage.

1) What are the factors that attribute London's success as a service industry and business center?

2) Why has the UK had an expanding export business in financial service?

3) What caused such serious financial crisis during 2007-2009?

6. Discussion.

1) The United Kingdom is an industrialized country, but its agriculture remains important. Britain's land surface is small compared to the United States, but British agriculture is very intensive and highly productive. What are the reasons?

2) Why does the UK want to exit the EU? How would "Brexit" affect the UK economy?

Stay Positive

1. Natural abilities are like natural plants that need pruning by study.
2. Opportunities are like sunrises—if you wait too long, you miss them.

Chapter 5

Military of the United Kingdom

I have nothing to offer but blood, toil, tears and sweat.

—Winston Churchill, British politician

1. Overview

The armed forces of the United Kingdom, known as His /Her Majesty's Armed Forces or sometimes the British Armed Forces, are the military services responsible for the defence of the United Kingdom, its overseas territories and the Crown dependencies. They also promote Britain's wider security interests, support international peace keeping and provide **humanitarian** aid. Today, the British Armed Forces consist of the British Army, the Royal Navy, the Royal Marines, the UK's principal land warfare branch, and the Royal Air Force.

The Commander-in-Chief of the British Armed Forces is the British monarch, Queen Elizabeth II, to whom members of the forces swear loyalty. Under British constitutional law, the armed forces are subordinate to the crown, but can only be maintained in peace time by **parliament**'s continuing consent. The UK Parliament approves the continued existence of the British Army by passing an Armed Forces Act at least once every five years, as required by the Bill of Rights 1689. The Royal Navy, Royal Air Force and Royal Marines and all other forces do not require this act. The armed forces are managed by the Defence Council of the Ministry of Defence [1], headed by the Secretary of State for Defence.

The United Kingdom is one of five recognized nuclear powers, a permanent member on the United Nations Security Council, and a founding and leading member of the NATO military alliance. In 2017, the British Armed Forces have the sixth highest declared military expenditure in the world, after United States, China, Saudi Arabia, Russia, and India.

2. History

2.1 Origin

The military history of the United Kingdom has been greatly influential in world history, beginning in 1707 with the merging of the armed forces of England and Scotland to become the armed forces of the Kingdom of Great Britain. Important conflicts in which the British took part later on in history include the Seven Years' War and the Napoleonic Wars of the 18th century/early 19th century, the Crimean War of the mid-19th Century, and the First and Second World Wars of the 20th century. The British Empire, which reached its peak in the 1920s, was the largest empire in history, almost a third of the World's population were subjects of the British Crown and it controlled a quarter of the World's total land area.

2.2 Seven Years' War

The Seven Years' War, which took part from 1756 to 1763, has sometimes been described as the first true world war, that conflict involved almost every continent and was on almost all the oceans. Although there were early setbacks, British troops eventually were victorious in every theater.

Britain's main enemy was France, as was usual. The war can be said to have started in North America, where it was known as the French and Indian War [2]. The early years saw several British defeats. The British units first dispatched to the Continent were untrained in the bush warfare they met. Partly through the naval **superiority** gained by the Royal Navy, however, Britain was eventually able to **deploy** superior strength in North America, winning a decisive battle at Quebec [3].

2.3 Napoleonic Wars

The British Army during the Napoleonic Wars experienced a time of rapid change. At the beginning of the French Revolutionary Wars in 1793, the army was small. By the end of the period, however, the numbers had vastly increased. The British infantry was "the only military force not to suffer a major reverse at the hands of Napoleonic France".

Following the conclusion of the wars, the army was reduced. Over the following decades, various regiments were added, removed or reformed to respond to military or colonial needs, but it never grew particularly large again, and the Empire became more reliant on local forces to maintain defense and order.

2.4 World War I (1914—1918)

The British Army during World War I could trace its origins to the increasing demands of imperial expansion together with inefficiencies highlighted during the Crimean War, which led to the Cardwell and Childers Reforms of the late 19th century. These gave the British Army its modern shape, and defined its **regimental** system. The Esher Report in 1904, recommended radical reform of the British Army, such as the creation of an Army Council, a General Staff and the **abolition** of the office of Commander-in-Chief of the Forces and the creation of a Chief of the General Staff. The Haldane Reforms in 1907, created an expeditionary force of seven divisions, it also reorganized the volunteers into a new Territorial Force of fourteen **cavalry brigades** and fourteen infantry divisions, and changed the old militia into the special reserve to reinforce the expeditionary force.

During the war there were three distinct British Armies. The "first" army was the small volunteer force of 400,000 soldiers, over half of which were posted overseas to garrison the British Empire. This total included the Regular Army and reservists in the Territorial Force.

Together they formed the BEF (British Expeditionary Force), for service in France and became known as the "Old Contemptibles". The "second" army was Kitchener's Army, formed from the volunteers in 1914–1915 destined to go into action at the Battle of the Somme. The "third" was formed after the introduction of conscription in January 1916 and by the end of 1918 the army had reached its peak of strength of four million men and could field over seventy divisions.

The war also saw the introduction of new weapons and equipment. The Maxim machine gun was replaced by the improved and lighter Vickers and Lewis machine guns, the Brodie helmet was supplied for better personnel protection against shrapnel and the Mark I tank was invented to try and end the stalemate of trench warfare.

The vast majority of the army fought in France and Belgium on the Western Front but some units were engaged in the Mediterranean, the Middle East, Africa and Mesopotamia, mainly against the Ottoman Empire. One battalion also fought in China during the Siege of Tsingtao.

2.5 World War II (1939-1945)

The British Army during World War II was in 1939, a volunteer army, that introduced conscription shortly after the declaration of war with Germany. During the early years of the war, the army suffered defeat in almost every theater it deployed. With mass conscription the expansion of the army was reflected in the creation of more army corps armies and army groups. From 1943, the army's fortunes turned and it hardly suffered a strategic defeat.

The army would fight around the world, with campaigns in Belgium and France in 1940 and after the collapse of both countries the army fought on in Africa, the Mediterranean and the Far East. After a series of setbacks, retreats and **evacuations**, the British Army eventually with its Allies gained the upper hand. Then in the last years of the war, the army returned to France driving the German Army back into Germany and in the Far East forced the Japanese back from the Indian border into Burma. Both the Germans and Japanese were defeated by 1945, and surrendered within months of each other.

With the expansion of the British Army, to fight a World War, new armies had to be formed, and eventually army groups were created to control even larger formations. In command of these new armies, eight Generals would be promoted to Field Marshall rank. The army commanders had to manage not only the new armies, but also a new type of soldier in formations that had been created for special service, which included the Special Air Service, Army Commandos and the Parachute Regiment.

2.6 End of the Empire and Cold War (1945-1990)

The United Nations (UN) was formed on October 24, 1945, with Britain being one of five permanent members of the UN Security Council. Britain was still considered as a global power, despite having been **eclipsed** by the two superpowers—the US and the Soviet Union—and the efforts by many colonies of the Empire to gain independence. Another global organization, known as the North Atlantic Treaty Organization (NATO), was established on April 4, 1949 with Britain being one of its founding members. The creation of NATO signified the beginning of the "Cold War" between the ideologically divided "Western Allies" and the Eastern Communist powers, controlled by the Soviet Union; they created their own NATO equivalent in 1955, known as the Warsaw Pact.

The Army was beginning to draw down its forces, beginning to demobilize shortly after the end of the war. More reforms of the armed forces took place with the 1957 Defence White Paper, which saw further reductions implemented; the Government realized after the debacle of the Suez War that Britain was no longer a global superpower and decided to withdraw from most of its commitments in the world, limiting the armed forces to concentrating on NATO, with an increased reliance upon nuclear weapons.

2.7 British De-colonialization and the British Army

The latter part of the 1940s saw the British state begin to withdraw from the Empire, the Army playing a prominent role in its **dismantlement**. The first colony the British withdrew from was India, the largest British possession as measured by population, though not the largest by geographical area.

The British Army has also played an increasingly prominent role in peacekeeping operation, gaining much respect for its comparative expertise in the area. British forces contributed as part of UNPROFOR (United Nations Protection Force) [4]. In 2000, British forces, as part of Operation Palliser, intervened in a civil war ravaged Sierra Leone, with the intention of evacuating British, Commonwealth and EU citizens. The British force remained and provided the **catalyst** for the stabilization of the country.

The early 21st century saw the world descend into a new war after the 9.11 terrorist attacks on the World Trade Center in New York City: the War on Terrorism. A US-led invasion of Taliban-ruled Afghanistan followed, with the British contribution. The British later took part in the invasion of Iraq in 2003, Britain's contribution being known as Operation Telic. The Army played a more significant role in Iraq than Afghanistan. But today, it is not unusual that soldiers were killed in Afghanistan. According to *Guardian* in Dec. 2013, a serviceman from Royal Engineers shot by enemy fire near Kabul is the 447th solider to have been killed since 2001.

3. Structure

3.1 Command Organization

As head of state, the British monarch, Queen Elizabeth II, is nominally the Commander-in-Chief of the Armed Forces. Long-standing constitutional convention, however, has vested executive authority in the office of Prime Minister and the Cabinet. The Queen, however, remains the ultimate authority of the military, with officers and personnel swearing allegiance to the monarch. It has been claimed that this includes the power to prevent unconstitutional use of the armed forces, including its nuclear weapons.

The Ministry of Defence is the Government department and highest level of military headquarters charged with formulating and executing defense policy for the Armed Forces. It employed 56,860 civilian staff as of October 1, 2015. The department is controlled by the Secretary of State for Defence and contains three deputy appointments: Minister of State for the Armed Forces [5], Minister for Defence Procurement [6], and Minister for Veterans' Affairs [7].

The Chief of the Defence Staff (CDS) is the professional head of the Armed Forces and is an appointment that can be held by an **Admiral**, Air Chief Marshal [8], or General. Before the practice was discontinued in the 1990s, those who were appointed to the position of CDS had been promoted to the most senior rank in their respective service (a 5-star rank). The CDS, along with the Permanent under Secretary, are the principal advisers to the departmental minister. The three services have their own respective professional chiefs: the First Sea Lord [9], the Chief of the General Staff [10] and the Chief of the Air Staff [11].

3.2 Naval Service

The Naval Service consists of the Royal Navy (including the Submarine Service and Fleet Air Arm) and the Royal Marines. The professional head of the Naval Service is the First Sea Lord who is an admiral and member of the Defence Council of the United Kingdom. The Defence Council delegates management of the Naval Service to the Admiralty Board, chaired by the Secretary of State for Defence.

3.2.1 Royal Navy

The Royal Navy is the UK's naval warfare force. Although warships were used by the English kings from the early medieval period, the first major maritime engagements were fought in the Hundred Years War against the Kingdom of France. The modern Royal Navy traces its origins to the early 16th century—the oldest of the UK's armed services, it is known as the "Senior Service".

As of November 2018, there are 74 commissioned ships (including submarines) in the Royal Navy, plus 12 ships of the Royal Fleet Auxiliary (RFA) [12]. There are also five Merchant Navy ships available to the RFA under a private finance initiative.

The Navy has been structured around a single fleet since the abolition of the Eastern and Western fleets in 1971. Command of deployable assets is exercised by the Commander-in-Chief Fleet, who also has authority over the Royal Marines, and the civilian Royal Fleet Auxiliary. Personnel matters are the responsibility of the Second Sea Lord/Commander-in-Chief Naval Home Command, an appointment usually held by a vice-admiral.

A submarine service has existed within the Royal Navy for over 100 years. The Royal Navy Submarine Service is the submarine element of the Royal Navy. It is sometimes known as the Silent Service, as the submarines are generally required to operate undetected. The service operates seven fleet submarines, and four ballistic missile [13] submarines. All of these

Badge

submarines are nuclear powered.

3.2.2 Royal Marines

The infantry component of the Naval Service is the Corps of Royal Marines, which are the Royal Navy's amphibious troops. Consisting of a single **maneuver** brigade and various independent units, the Royal Marines specialize in amphibious, arctic, and mountain warfare.

As a highly specialized and adaptable light infantry force, the Royal Marines are trained for rapid deployment worldwide and capable of dealing with a wide range of threats.

3.3 British Army

The British Army is the principal land warfare force of the United Kingdom, a part of British Armed Forces. The British Army is made up of the Regular Army and the Army Reserve. As of 2018, the British Army comprises just over 81,500 trained regular (full-time) personnel and just over 27,000 trained reserve (part-time) personnel. The army has a single command structure based at Andover and known as "Army Headquarters". Deployable combat formations consist of two divisions and eight brigades. Within the United Kingdom, operational and non-deployable units are administered by two divisions, Force Troops Command and London District.

3.4 Royal Air Force

The Royal Air Force is the United Kingdom's aerial warfare force. Formed towards the end of the First World War on April 1, 1918, it is the oldest independent air force in the world. Following victory over the Central Powers in 1918 the RAF emerged as, at the time, the largest air force in the world. Since its formation, the RAF has taken a significant role in British military history.

The RAF's mission is to support the objectives of the British Ministry of Defence. The RAF describes its mission statement as "... to provide an agile, adaptable and capable Air Force that is second to none, and that makes a decisive air power contribution in support of the UK Defence Mission". The mission statement is supported by the RAF's definition of air power, which guides its strategy.

The Eurofighter Typhoon is the second most expensive fighter aircraft in the world after the F-22. Consisting of both fixed-wing and rotary aircraft, the Royal Air Force has a large operational fleet that fulfills various roles.

Frontline aircraft are controlled by Air Command, which is organized into five groups defined by function: 1 Group (Air Combat) and 2 Group (Air Support), 11 Group (Air and Space Operations) and 22 Group (training aircraft and ground facilities) and 38 Group (Royal Air Force's Engineering, Logistics, Communications and Medical Operations units). Deployable formations consist of Expeditionary Air Wings and squadrons—the basic unit of the Air Force. Independent flights are deployed to facilities in Afghanistan, the Falkland Islands, Iraq, and the United States.

4. Uniforms

The British Army uniform developed along roughly the same lines as uniforms in other European armies. Its signature color had become standardized as red for both infantry and cavalry units by the end of the 17th century, except for the Royal Horse Guards and Royal Artillery who wore dark blue; then khaki (for everyday wear) and blue (for parade) in the 1930s.

British army uniforms currently exist in several grades, which are worn depending on the requirements of a unit or individual, ranging from ceremonial uniforms to combat dress. While there are officially 15 different grades (or "numbers"), many of these are rarely worn or phased out altogether. Note that uniform distinctions can vary greatly from one regiment or corps to another, and the following descriptions are generalization.

The British army numbers its uniforms for ease of instruction. Fourteen "orders" of dress are authorized and prescribed to be worn on various occasions; a "full dress" is also prescribed for the most important ceremonies.

Full Dress

As with the other regiments of the Foot Guards, a tall Bearskin is worn. Full dress is the most elaborate order worn by the British Army. It was withdrawn from general issue in 1914; the Household Division resumed wearing their scarlet full dress in 1920, but for the remainder of the Army, red coats were only authorized for wear by regimental bands and in mess dress or on certain limited social or ceremonial occasions. The reason for not generally reintroducing the distinctive full dress was primarily financial, as the scarlet cloth required expensive red cochineal dye.

Full dress is now rarely worn except by the Foot Guards and the Household Cavalry. It is issued at public expense to these units other units may obtain and wear full dress for use in historical displays, when acting as ushers or lining parties at weddings, and when acting as sword guards to the Royal Horse Artillery. However, these uniforms must be purchased and maintained from non-public funds.

No.1 Temperate Ceremonial Uniform

No.2 Service Dress (temperate parade uniform)
No.3 Warm Weather Ceremonial Uniform
No.4 Warm Weather Service Dress (officers only)
No.5 Desert Combat Dress
No.6 Warm Weather Parade Uniform (bush jacket)
No.7 Warm Weather **Barrack** Dress
No.8 Temperate Combat Dress
No.9 Tropical Combat Dress
No.10 Temperate Mess Dress
No.11 Warm Weather Mess Dress
No.12 Protective Clothing
No.13 Temperate Barrack Dress
No.14 Shirt Sleeve Order
No.15 Blue Patrols

5. Recruitment

The British Army came into being with unification of the Kingdoms of England and Scotland into the United Kingdom of Great Britain in 1707. The new British Army incorporated regiments that had already existed in England and Scotland. The British Army has traditionally relied upon volunteer recruits, the only exceptions were during the latter part of the First World War, the Second World War and only once during peace time, when conscription was enacted.

5.1 The First World War

At the start of 1914 the British Army had a reported strength of 710,000 men including reserves, of which 247,432 were regular troops, also including 80,000 regular troops formed as the British Expeditionary Force.

It was abundantly clear that the army which the Kaiser had referred to as a "contemptible little army" would need thousands more recruits. Young Britons answered the call, for King and Country, and voluntarily joined the British Army. The Kitchener recruitment campaign had proved to be very successful, as on September 1, 1914, over 30,000 men enlisted. With each day passing, thousands more were **clamoring** to be taken. By the end of World War I almost 1 in 4 of the total male population of the United Kingdom of Great Britain and Ireland had joined, over five million men.

5.2 The Second World War

The pre-war army was an all-volunteer army and recruits were arranged to the corps of their wishes. This led to men being allocated to the wrong or unsuitable corps. In early 1939, Neville Chamberlain [14] was allowed to introduce conscription to meet the threat of Germany, with the Military Training Act of 27 April 1939. The Act required all men aged 20 and 21 to take six months military training. This Act was extended on the declaration of the war, to include all fit men between the ages of 18 and 41. Conscription was gradually brought in, starting in October 1939 and applying to all fit men between 20 and 23, and the age group was increased as the war continued.

The Local Defense Volunteers was formed early in 1940. Very large numbers of civilians too old or too young for the Army, or barred from serving if they were in reserved occupations, volunteered for the new force. The organization was eventually renamed the "Home Guard" and was to be part of the defense of Britain in the advent of a German invasion of Britain.

5.3 Present Day

The Army mainly recruits within the United Kingdom, and normally has a recruitment target of around 25,000 soldiers per year. Low unemployment in Britain has resulted in the Army having difficulty in meeting its target, and in the early years of the 21st century there has been a marked increase in the number of recruits from mostly Commonwealth countries.

The minimum recruitment age is 16, although soldiers may not serve on operations below 18; the maximum recruitment age was raised in January 2007 from 26 to 33. The normal term of engagement is 22 years, and once enlisted soldiers are not normally permitted to leave until they have served at least 4 years. After 22 years of service a soldier may be offered a two-year extension. After the two years, the soldier or officer may take a further two years service and thereafter until they reach 55 years of age.

All three services of the British Armed Forces recruit primarily from within the United Kingdom, although citizens from the Commonwealth of Nations and the Republic of Ireland are equally eligible to join. In 2008 Commonwealth origin volunteers comprised approximately 6.7% of the Army's total strength. In total 6,600 foreign soldiers from 42 countries were represented in the Army, not including Gurkhas [15]. In 2014, the yearly intake into the armed forces is 11,880. Excluding the Brigade of Gurkhas and the Royal Irish Regiment, as of April 1, 2014 there are approximately 11,200 black and minority ethnic persons serving as regulars across the three service branches; of those, 6,610 were recruited from outside the United Kingdom. In total, black and minority ethnic persons represent 7.1% of all service personnel.

Joyful Moment

A retired four-star general ran into his former orderly, also retired, in a Manhattan bar and spent the rest of the evening persuading him to come to work for him as his valet. "Your duties will be exactly the same as they were in the army," the general said. "Nothing to it—you'll catch on again fast."

Next morning promptly at eight o'clock, the ex-orderly entered the ex-general's bedroom, pulled open the drapes, gave the general a gentle shake, strode around the other side of the bed, spanked his employer's wife on her bottom and said, "OK, sweetheart, it's time back to the village for you."

Notes

[1] Defence Council of the Ministry of Defence 国防部国防委员会
[2] French and Indian War 法国—印第安人战争
[3] Quebec 魁北克城，加拿大东部重要城市和港口，位于圣劳伦斯河与圣查尔斯河汇合处
[4] UNPROFOR (United Nations Protection Force) 联合国保护部队（联保部）
[5] Minister of State for the Armed Forces 武装部队国务部长
[6] Minister for Defense Procurement 国防采购部长
[7] Minister for Veterans' Affairs 退伍军人事务部长
[8] Air Chief Marshal 空军上将
[9] First Sea Lord 第一海务大臣
[10] Chief of the General Staff 总参谋长
[11] Chief of the Air Staff 空军参谋长
[12] Royal Fleet Auxiliary 皇家海军辅助舰队
[13] ballistic missile 弹道导弹
[14] Neville Chamberlain 亚瑟·内维尔·张伯伦（1869—1940），英国政治家，1937 年到 1940 年任英国首相，由于在二次世界大战中对纳粹德国实行绥靖政策而倍受谴责。
[15] Gurkhas 廓尔喀人，来自尼泊尔的士兵。英军的廓尔喀雇佣兵部队因骁勇善战而享誉盛名。

New Words

1. **humanitarian** /hjuˌmænɪ'teərɪən/ *adj*. If a person or society has humanitarian ideas or behaviors, they try to avoid making people suffer or help people who are suffering. 人道主义的

   —WHO is providing humanitarian aids to the region which suffered an earthquake last week.
   世界卫生组织正在对上个星期发生地震的地区提供人道主义援助。

2. **parliament** /'pɑːləmənt/ *n*. a group of people who are elected to make and change the laws of a country 议会；国会

   —Which party does your Member of Parliament belong to?
   你那区的国会议员属于哪一个政党？

3. **superiority** /suːpɪəri'ɒrəti/ *n*. the state or quality of being better than others 优越（性）

   —The goal was power superiority at all costs.
   目标是不惜任何代价的力量优势。

4. **deploy** /dɪ'plɔɪ/ *v*. to deploy troops or military resources means to organize or position them so that they are ready to be used; to use something effectively 调动部署，展开；有效地利用

—He warned them not to hold on to this new capital, but to deploy it.
他警告他们不要手持这一新资金，而是使用这一资金。

5. **regimental** /ˌredʒɪ'mentl/ *adj.* connected with a particular regiment of soldiers 团的；团队的
—A rider came pounding up with an order from the regimental commander.
一个骑马的人带着团长的命令飞驰而来。

6. **abolition** /ˌæbə'lɪʃn/ *n.* the ending of a law, a system or an institution （法律、制度等的）废除，废止
—Abolition of property in land and application of all rents of land to public purposes.
废除土地形式的财产，将土地的所有租赁收入用于公共目的。

7. **cavalry** /'kævlri/ *n.* (in the past) the part of the army that fought on horses; the part of a modern army that uses tanks（旧时的）骑兵；装甲兵
—The cavalry is much superior in mobility than the infantry.
骑兵在机动性方面比步兵优越得多。

8. **brigade** /brɪ'geɪd/ *n.* a military unit that is typically composed of two to five regiments or battalions 旅（军事单位）
—The last of these brigades came home this month, he said.
他说，这些部队的最后几个旅于本月回国。

9. **evacuation** /ɪˌvækjʊ'eɪʃn/ *n.* to send them to a place of safety 撤退
—A mass evacuation of New Orleans is on, with officials telling residents to leave.
政府官员告知市民离开，新奥尔良大规模疏散工作已经开始了。

10. **eclipse** /ɪ'klɪps/ *v.* a loss of importance, power, etc.（重要性、权势等的）丧失
—During the seventies, her acting career was eclipsed.
在七十年代，她的表演生涯黯然失色。

11. **catalyst** /'kætəlɪst/ *n.* a person or thing that causes a change 促使变化的人，引发变化的因素
—Competition is the catalyst for social development and an impetus to mankind civilization.
竞争是社会发展的催化剂，是促进人类文明的动力。

12. **admiral** /'ædmərəl/ *n.* an officer of very high rank in the navy 海军上将，舰队司令
—The admiral felt very annoy about his son in drug habit.
那位海军上将因儿子染上毒瘾而十分苦恼。

13. **maneuver** /mə'nuːvə/ *n.* [plural, 复数] military activities, such as pretending to fight a battle, which are done as practice or training 军事演习
—Large-scale military maneuvers are being carried out near the border.
边境附近正在进行大规模军事演习。

14. **barracks** /'bærəks/ *n.* a group of buildings where soldiers live 兵营
—The battalion formed up by company on the barracks square.
全营以连为单位在军营广场上列队。

15. **clamor** /'klæmə/ *v.* (a group of people) shout loudly and insistently 大声疾呼
—The public are clamoring for a change of government.
公众大声疾呼要求撤换政府。

Exercises

1. Choose the correct answer.

1) The British Armed Forces however have the ________ highest declared expenditure of any military in the world in 2017.
A. third B. fourth C. fifth D. sixth

2) The ________ War, which took part from 1755 to 1763, has sometimes been described as the first true world war.
A. Seven Years' B. Napoleonic
C. French and Indian D. Queen Victoria

3) World War I happened in________.
A. 1913-1918 B. 1914-1918 C. 1916-1919 D. 1914-1916

4) Britain is one of five permanent members of the ________ Security Council.
A. US B. UN C. EU D. OPEC

5) The creation of NATO signified the beginning of the "__________" between the ideologically divided "Western Allies" and the Eastern Communist powers
A. Cold War B. Seven Years' War
C. Napoleonic War D. Independence War

2. Decide whether the following statements are True or False.

1) The first colony the British withdrew from was India.
2) The Ministry of Defence is the Government department and highest level of military headquarters.
3) Royal army is the oldest service within the British Armed Forces.
4) No. 2 service dress is the most elaborate order worn by the British Army.
5) The British Army has traditionally relied upon volunteer recruits.

3. Fill in the blanks.

1) The minimum recruitment age is ________.
2) The United Kingdom is deemed to have the _________ highest power projection capability behind the United States.
3) During Seven Years' War, Britain winning a decisive battle at ________.
4) During the long reign of_________, British society underwent great changes such as industrialization and the enactment of liberal reforms.
5) At the beginning of World War II, British Army was a volunteer army, but it introduced _________ shortly after the declaration of war with Germany.

4. Explain the following terms.

1) The Ministry of Defence
2) The Chief of the Defence Staff
3) NATO
4) Corps of Royal Marines
5) No.3 dress

5. Answer the following questions.

1) What is the mission of the British Armed Forces?
2) What is the influence of the Industrial Revolution to the British Army?
3) What are the three distinct British Armies during World War I?

6. Discussion

1) Great Britain's struggle with France during the Napoleonic wars required the British Army to expand rapidly. What were the main methods used for recruiting?
2) The British Army during World War II was in 1939, a volunteer army, that introduced conscription shortly after the declaration of war with Germany. What happened to the Army during this period of time?

Stay Positive

1. Goals determine what you are going to be.
2. Life is not a matter of counting the days. It's making the days count.

Chapter 6

Culture and Education of the United Kingdom

The roots of education are bitter, but the fruit is sweet.

—Aristotle, Ancient Greek philosopher

1. Introduction

As we mentioned in previous chapters, the Untied Kingdom is composed of four regions—England, Northern Ireland, Scotland and Wales—each of which has distinct customs, cultures, **symbolism** and education system.

2. Culture

The culture of the United Kingdom refers to the patterns of human activity and symbolism associated with the United Kingdom and its people since its formation in 1707. It is influenced by the UK's history, major power, and Christian religious life. **Humanism**, Protestantism[1], and representative democracy[2] are borrowed from broader Western culture. The social structure of Britain has played a central cultural role throughout the history of British society. As a result of the history of the formation of the United Kingdom, the cultures of England, Scotland, Wales and Northern Ireland are diverse and have varying degrees of overlap and distinctiveness.

2.1 Social Class

British society is considered to be divided into three main groups of classes—the Upper Class, the Middle Class, and the Lower or Working Class. This is known as the Class System and it is important to know something about it if you want to understand the British people and society. Most British people grow up with a deep knowledge and understanding of the class system even if they are not very conscious of it. Most people know which class they belong to by the way they speak, their clothes, their interests or even the type of food they eat.

Social class is not only about behavior and attitudes. For example, although many upper class people are rich and may own a lot of land, having a lot of money does not make a person upper class. It is also important to come from a particular kind of family, have friends who are considered suitable, have been to a certain type of private school and speak with the right kind of accent. Many people do not like the class system but it is impossible to pretend that these differences do not exist.

2.2 Family Structure

Historically most people in the United Kingdom lived either in extended families or nuclear families. This reflected an economic landscape where the general people tended to have less spending power, meaning that it was more practical to stick together rather than go their individual ways. This pattern also reflected gender roles. Men were expected to go out to work and women were expected to stay at home and look after families.

In the 20th century the **emancipation** of women, the greater freedoms enjoyed by both men and women in the years following the Second World War, greater affluence and easier divorce have changed gender roles and living arrangements significantly. The general trend is a rise in single people living alone and the extinction of extended family.

From the 1990s, the high cost of living, combined with rising cost of accommodation, further education and higher education, means that many young people cannot afford to live independent lives from their families. Young people are tending to continue to live in the parental home for much longer than their predecessors in the 21st century.

2.3 Cuisine

2.3.1 Traditional Cuisine

British food has traditionally been based on beef, lamb, pork, chicken and fish and generally served with potatoes and one other vegetable. The most common and typical foods eaten in Britain include the sandwich, fish and chips, pies like the Cornish pasty[3], trifle and roasted dinners.

Sunday roast

Each region within the United Kingdom has its own specialties. Traditional examples of English cuisine include the Sunday roast, featuring a roasted joint, usually beef, lamb or chicken, served with assorted boiled vegetables, Yorkshire pudding and gravy. Other prominent meals include fish and chips and the full English breakfast—consisting of bacon, grilled tomatoes, fried bread, black pudding, baked beans, fried mushrooms, sausages and eggs.

Fish and chips

A full breakfast consists of bacon, sausages and eggs, often served with a variety of side dishes and a beverage such as coffee or tea. It is especially popular in the UK and Ireland and in UK-influenced cultures, including the United States, Australia, New Zealand, Canada and South Africa. It is sometimes referred to as an English breakfast or a "full English breakfast". Sometimes it may be shortened to "full English" or "fry-up". The phrase "full breakfast" differentiates it from the European Continental breakfast, traditionally consisting of tea, milk or coffee and fruit juices with bread, croissants or pastries.

Full breakfast

2.3.2 Traditional Drinks

Britain is a tea drinking nation. Around 200, 000 tons of tea are consumed every year. Most Britons like their tea strong and dark, but with a lot of milk. In Britain, if someone asks you if you "would like a cuppa", they are asking if you would like a cup of tea. If someone says "let me be mother" or "shall I be mother", they are offering to pour out the tea from the teapot.

Recently, coffee is as popular as tea in Britain. People either drink it with milk or have it black, either have freshly-made coffee or instant coffee. Britain is also famous for its ale which tends to be dark in appearance. It is also called 'bitter'. Britain's wine industry is growing rapidly and now has over 300 wine products. The most famous vineyard is Kent.

2.4 Holidays

Several holidays are celebrated during the year in the United Kingdom.

Christmas is the biggest and the most popular British holiday celebrated on December 25th each year to **commemorate** the birth of Jesus Christ. People usually decorate homes with evergreen plants, Christmas trees and ornaments. They also exchange gifts and Christmas cards. Stores stock Christmas items earlier and earlier and everyone is urged to buy presents for their families and friends. At Christmas everyone gives and receives gifts, especially the children. Presents are placed under the Christmas tree or beside the children's beds where they can be easily seen when the children awake. The children are told that Father Christmas (Santa Clause) brings the presents. Children also hang up stockings, which are mystically filled with small toys, nuts and fruit before Christmas morning. Three typical British traditions on Christmas are: the Christmas Pantomime[4], the Queen's speech over the TV and radio, and the Boxing Day. The Boxing Day is a typical British tradition celebrated on the day after Christmas. People used to give Christmas gifts or money to their staff or servants on this day. And now they mostly do shopping, pay visits, enjoy eating and just relax.

Easter, a religious holiday, occurs in the spring. It is the most important Christian festival for many church-goers. Easter weekend begins on Good Friday, commemorating the crucifixion[5] of Jesus Christ, and ends on Easter Sunday, celebrating Christ's **resurrection** from the dead. Easter Monday is also a holiday in England. Families usually gather for an Easter meal and the children are given baskets filled

Easter eggs and rabbit

with chocolate eggs and chickens. The Easter egg, originally a Christian symbol of new life, is the main symbol of Easter for most people. Rabbits and chicks are also animals traditionally associated with Easter.

The official birthday of Queen Elizabeth II is marked every year by a military parade and march-past, known as Trooping the Color (carrying of the flag). It has an official name as "the Queen's Birthday Parade". Each June, the Queen and other members of the Royal Family attend the Trooping the Color ceremony on Horse Guards Parade, Whitehall in London. The Queen attends the ceremony to take the salute from thousands of guardsmen who parade the Color (their regiment's flag). A regiment's colors embody its spirit and service, as well as its fallen soldiers. The loss of a color, or the capture of an enemy color, was respectively considered the greatest shame, or the greatest glory on a battlefield. Consequently, regimental colors are respected by officers and soldiers of all ranks.

The name Bank Holiday comes from the time when Banks were shut and so no trading could take place. Now, even though Banks are still closed on these days many shops remain open. Traditionally on a Bank Holiday many businesses are closed to enable the workers to have a holiday. This time is often spent with the family on mini breaks and outings. Anyone who works on Bank Holidays usually gets paid extra "time and a half" or even "double time," negotiated for them by the Trade Unions.

Table 1 The Bank and Public Holidays in the UK

Date	Name	England and Wales (8)	Scotland (9)	Northern Ireland (10)
January 1	New Year's Day	√	√	√
January 2	2 January		√	
March 17	St. Patrick's Day			√
The Friday before Easter Sunday	Good Friday	√	√	√
The day after Easter Sunday	Easter Monday	√		√
First Monday in May	May Day Bank Holiday	√	√	√
Last Monday in May	Spring Bank Holiday	√		√
First Monday In June	June Bank Holiday		√	
July 12	Battle of the Boyne – Orangeme's Day			√
First Monday in August	Summer Bank Holiday		√	
Last Monday in August	Summer Bank Holiday	√		√

continued

Date	Name	England and Wales (8)	Scotland (9)	Northern Ireland (10)
Last Monday in October	October Bank Holiday			
November 30	St. Andrew's Day		√	
December 25	Christmas Day	√	√	√
December 26	Boxing Day, St. Stephen's Day	√	√	√

2.5 Media

Media of the UK consist of several different types of communications media: television, radio, newspapers, magazines, and web sites.

2.5.1 Newspapers

UK newspapers can be split into more serious-minded newspapers (usually referred to as the broadsheets due to their large sizes), sometimes known collectively as "the quality press", and less serious newspapers, generally known as **tabloids**, and collectively as "the popular press", which have tended to focus more on celebrity coverage and human interest stories rather than political reporting or overseas news.

theguardian
Labour's chief union backer attacks Miliband
PM throws backing behind new royal yacht
We are terrified: the families putting their trust in the Lords

The major national papers are as follows:

◆ *The Times* (former broadsheet, compact since November 2004). It often reflects the view held by the Government and politically it is more sympathetic with the Conservative Party. It has a reputation for its cautiousness in its attitudes.

◆ *The Guardian* (Berliner[6] since September 12, 2005). It was called Manchester Guardian until 1959. Now it has moved its base to London and has become a national paper. Politically, it is closer to the Labor Party than to the Conservatives.

◆ *Daily Express* (compact). It is a popular paper and owes much of its success to its skills of popular journalism.

◆ *Daily Mirror* (tabloid). It is called a "tabloid" because it carries a lot of pictures, strip cartoons and interesting stories for popular appeal. Since its special appeal is to young people of about 16, its political reporting is rather scant.

• *The Sun* (tabloid). *The Sun* is a tabloid newspaper published in the United Kingdom and the Republic of Ireland. It is published by the News Group Newspapers division of News UK. Since *The Sun on Sunday* was launched in February 2012, the paper has been a seven-day

operation. *The Sun* previously had the largest circulation of any daily newspaper in the United Kingdom, but was overtaken by rival *Metro* in March 2018.

Britain's daily papers have no Sunday editions, but there are Sunday papers which are closely related to the national daily papers. Most of the Sunday papers are less serious and often carry reports about scandals and crimes, such as *Sunday Mirror*, *Sunday Express*, *Sunday Times*, *The Observer*.

2.5.2 Periodicals

A large range of magazines are sold in the United Kingdom covering most interests and potential topics. British magazines and journals that have achieved worldwide circulation include *The Economist*, *Nature*, and *New Scientist*, *Private Eye*, *Hello!*, *The Spectator*, *Radio Times* and *NME (New Musical Express)*.

2.5.3 Television

Television in the United Kingdom is made up of two chartered public broadcasting companies (the BBC and Channel Four) and two franchised commercial television companies (ITV and Five). There are five major free-to-air analogue channels: BBC One, BBC Two, ITV (Independent Television), Channel Four and Five.

2.5.4 Radio

Radio in the UK is dominated by the BBC, which operates radio stations both in the United Kingdom and abroad. The BBC World Service radio network broadcasts in more than 40 languages globally. The English-language service broadcasts 24 hours a day. Rather than operating as independent entities, many commercial local radio stations are owned by large radio groups which broadcast a similar format to many areas. There are also regional stations broadcasting in some main parts of the UK.

2.6 Sports

Sports play an important part in people's life in Britain and are a popular leisure activity. The United Kingdom has given birth to a range of major international sports including: association football, baseball, rugby (union and league), cricket, golf, tennis, table tennis, badminton, etc. The national sport is cricket although football is the most popular. Some of England's football teams are world famous, the most famous being Manchester United, Arsenal and Liverpool. Hundreds of thousands of people play football in parks and playgrounds. The highlight is the FA (Football Association) Cup Final each May.

The world's most famous tennis tournament is Wimbledon. It begins on the nearest Monday to June 22, at a time when England has the finest weather. Millions of people watch the Wimbledon Championships on TV live.

Scotland is traditionally regarded as the home of golf. There are over 400 golf courses in

Scotland alone. Horse racing and greyhound racing are popular spectator sports. People can place bets on the races at legal off-track betting shops.

Table tennis was invented in England in 1880. It began with Cambridge University students using cigar boxes and champagne corks. Although the game originated in England, British players don't have much luck in international championships. Angling is one of the most popular sports in the UK, with an estimated 3.3 million people participating in the sport on a regular basis. Fishermen can be seen sitting beside rivers and lakes.

3. Education

The current British education system is highly complex and it consists of many types of schools and schooling, such as preschools, public schools and grammar schools. Each region of the UK has separate systems. Broadly speaking, the systems in England, Wales and Northern Ireland are fairly similar, with the Scottish system being completely separate. The two systems have different emphases. Traditionally the English, Welsh and Northern Irish system has emphasized depth of education whereas the Scottish system has emphasized breadth.

3.1 Different Types of Schools

There are two main categories of school—state schools and independent schools. In the UK 93% of the children go to state schools. State schools are free to children from the age of 5 to 16, funded from taxes and most are organized by local authorities. As for independent schools, parents pay for their children's education.

Eton Public School

A public school is an independent secondary school. Public schools in England are not run by the government. The entrance exams used by most public schools are known as Common Entrance Exams (CEE) and are taken at the age of 11 (girls) or 13 (boys). The most famous public schools are Eton, Harrow and Winchester.

3.2 Stages of Education

In each country there are five stages of education: early years, primary, secondary, further education and higher education. Education is compulsory for all children between the ages of 5 (4 in Northern Ireland) and 16; before this children can be educated at nursery. Further education is non-compulsory, and covers non-advanced education which can be taken at further education colleges and higher education institutions. The fifth stage, higher education, is study beyond GCE [7] A levels (and their equivalent) which, for most full-time students, takes place in universities and other HEIs (higher education institutions) and colleges.

3.2.1 Preschool Education

In the UK, preschool education in nursery classes or schools is fully funded by local government for children aged over three. Preschool education can be provided by childcare centers, playgroups, nursery schools and nursery classes within primary schools. Private voluntary or independent nursery education is also available throughout the UK and varies between structured preschool education and a service offering child-minding facilities. Nursery in England is also called FS1 (Foundation Stage 1), which is the first year of foundation before they go into primary. The curriculum goals of a nursery school are more specific than a childcare center, but less **strenuous** than a primary school.

3.2.2 Primary Education

Primary or elementary education is the first years of formal, structured education that occurs during childhood. In most Western countries, it is compulsory for children to receive primary education. Typically, primary education is provided in schools. Children are usually placed in classes with one teacher who will be primarily responsible for their education and welfare for that year. The major goals of primary education are achieving basic literacy and **numeracy** among all their students, as well as establishing foundations in science, geography, history and other social sciences.

3.2.3 Secondary Education

Secondary education is a period of education which follows directly after primary education. The purpose of a secondary education can be preparing for either higher education or vocational training. The exact boundary between primary and secondary education varies from region to region and even within them, but is generally around the seventh to the tenth year of education. Primary and secondary education together are sometimes referred to as "K-12" education (K is for kindergarten, 12 is for twelfth grade). In secondary education, nearly 88% of pupils go to comprehensive schools, which provide a wide range of secondary education. Comparatively, grammar schools are selective, they offer academically oriented general education. Entrance is based on a test of ability, namely "11+ exam" or "11 plus exam". After leaving a grammar school, as with any other secondary school, a student may go into further education at a college or university.

3.2.4 Further Education

Further education (often abbreviated to FE) in the United Kingdom and Ireland, refers to post-compulsory education, which is distinct from the higher education offered in universities. It may be at any level above compulsory secondary education, from basic skills training to higher vocational qualifications such as PGCE[8], NVQ [9], HNC [10], and so on.

A distinction is usually made between FE and higher education (HE), an education at a higher level than secondary school, usually provided in distinct institutions such as universities. FE in the United Kingdom is usually a means to attain an intermediate or follow up qualification necessary to attend university, or begin a specific career path, e.g. quantity surveyor, town planner or veterinary surgeon, for anyone over 16 years old, primarily available at Colleges of Further Education, work-based learning, or adult and community learning institutions.

3.2.5 Higher Education

Higher education is education provided by universities and other institutions that award academic degrees, such as university colleges, and liberal arts colleges. Higher education includes both the teaching and the research activities of universities, and it includes both the undergraduate level and the graduate (or postgraduate) level. Higher education differs from other forms of post-secondary education such as vocational education. However, most professional education is included within higher education, and many postgraduate qualifications are strongly vocationally or professionally oriented, for example in disciplines such as law and medicine.

There is a three-level hierarchy of degrees (Bachelor, Master, Doctor) currently used in the United Kingdom. A graduate student is an individual who has completed a bachelor's degree (B.A., B.S., etc.) and is pursuing further higher education, with the goal of achieving a master's degree (M.A., M.S., etc.) or doctorate (Ph.D.)

3.3 Education in England

Education in England is overseen by the Department for Education and the Department for Business, Innovation and Skills. Local authorities take responsibility for implementing policy for public education and state schools at a local level.

The education system is divided into early years (ages 3-4), primary education (ages 4-11), secondary education (ages 11-18) and tertiary education[11] (ages 18+). Full-time education is compulsory for all children aged between 5 and 18. Students may then continue their secondary studies for a further two years (sixth form), leading most typically to A-level qualifications. State-provided schooling and sixth form education is paid for by taxes. England also has a tradition of independent schooling, and parents may choose to educate their children by any suitable means.

Table 2 Common Patterns for Schooling in the State Sector in England

<table>
<tr><th>Age on Sep. 1st</th><th>Year</th><th>Curriculum stage</th><th colspan="3">Schools</th></tr>
<tr><td>3</td><td>Nursery</td><td rowspan="2">Foundation stage</td><td colspan="3">Nursery school</td></tr>
<tr><td>4</td><td>Reception</td><td rowspan="3">Infant school</td><td rowspan="7">Primary school</td><td rowspan="5">First school</td></tr>
<tr><td>5</td><td>Year 1</td><td rowspan="2">Key stage 1</td></tr>
<tr><td>6</td><td>Year 2</td></tr>
<tr><td>7</td><td>Year 3</td><td rowspan="4">Key stage 2</td><td rowspan="4">Junior school</td></tr>
<tr><td>8</td><td>Year 4</td></tr>
<tr><td>9</td><td>Year 5</td><td rowspan="2">Middle school</td></tr>
<tr><td>10</td><td>Year 6</td></tr>
</table>

continued

<table>
<tr><th>Age on 1st Sep.</th><th>Year</th><th>Curriculum stage</th><th colspan="3">Schools</th></tr>
<tr><td>11</td><td>Year 7</td><td rowspan="3">Key stage 3</td><td rowspan="5">Secondary school</td><td rowspan="7">Secondary school with sixth form</td><td rowspan="2">Middle school</td></tr>
<tr><td>12</td><td>Year 8</td></tr>
<tr><td>13</td><td>Year 9</td><td rowspan="5">Upper school</td></tr>
<tr><td>14</td><td>Year 10</td><td rowspan="2">Key stage 4/
GCSE</td></tr>
<tr><td>15</td><td>Year 11</td></tr>
<tr><td>16</td><td>Year 12</td><td rowspan="2">Sixth form/
A-level</td><td rowspan="2">Sixth form college</td></tr>
<tr><td>17</td><td>Year 13</td></tr>
</table>

Children are allowed to be educated at home. The legislation places no requirement for parents who choose not to send their children to school to follow the National Curriculum, or to give formal lessons, or to follow school hours and terms, and parents do not need to be qualified teachers. A small but increasing numbers of parents do choose to educate their children outside the conventional school systems, officially referred to as “Elective Home Education”. The state provides no financial support to parents who choose to educate their children outside of school.

Higher education often begins with a three-year bachelor’s degree. Postgraduate degrees include the master degree, either taught or by research, and the doctorate degree, a research degree that usually takes at least three years. Universities require a Royal Charter in order to issue degrees.

3.4 Education in Wales

Education in Wales differs in certain respects from the systems used elsewhere in the United Kingdom. A significant number of students all over Wales are educated either wholly or largely through the medium of Welsh; lessons in the language are compulsory for all until the age of 16. Welsh medium education is available to all age groups through nurseries, schools, colleges and universities and in adult education. There are also plans to increase the number of Welsh medium schools.

Currently, demand has passed supply for education through the medium of Welsh especially in Cardiff and the surrounding South Wales Valleys. Some schools in South Wales now have to turn Welsh students away as there are no spaces in the schools compared with the English schools where in some cases pupil levels are only reaching 50% capacity.

3.5 Education in Scotland

Scotland has a long history of universal provision of public education, and the Scottish education system is distinctly different from other parts of the United Kingdom. Traditionally, the Scottish system has emphasized breadth across a range of subjects, while the English, Welsh and Northern Irish systems have emphasized greater depth of education over a smaller range of subjects at secondary school level. Following this, Scottish universities generally have courses a year longer (typically 4 years) than their counterparts elsewhere in the UK, though it is often possible for students to take more advanced specialized exams and join the courses at the second year. One unique aspect is that the ancient universities of Scotland issue a Master of Arts as the first degree in humanities.

State schools are owned and operated by the local authorities which act as Education Authorities, and the compulsory phase is divided into primary school and secondary school (often called high school). Inspections and audits of educational standards are conducted by three bodies: Care Commission inspects care standards in preschool provision; Her Majesty's Inspectorate of Education for preschool, primary, education, further and community education; the Scottish office of the Quality Assurance Agency for Higher Education (QAA Scotland [12]) responsible for higher education.

3.6 Education in Northern Ireland

Education in Northern Ireland differs slightly from systems used elsewhere in the United Kingdom, though it is more similar to that used in England and Wales than it is to Scotland. A child's age on July 1st determines the point of entry into the relevant stage of education unlike England and Wales where it is September 1st. Northern Ireland's results at GCSE[13] and A-Level are consistently top in the UK.

3.7 Famous Universities

3.7.1 University of Cambridge

The University of Cambridge (informally Cambridge University, or simply Cambridge), located in the City of Cambridge, Cambridgeshire, United Kingdom, is the second oldest university in the English-speaking world. The name is sometimes abbreviated to Cantab.

The university grew out of an association of scholars in the city of Cambridge that was formed, early records suggest, in 1209 by scholars leaving Oxford after a dispute with townsfolk there. The universities of Oxford and Cambridge are often jointly referred to as "Oxbridge". In addition to cultural and practical associations as a historic part of British society, the two universities also have a long history of rivalry with each other.

Academically, Cambridge is consistently ranked in the world's top five universities and as the best university in Europe. About 104 affiliates of the University of Cambridge have been awarded the Nobel Prize since 1904.

3.7.2 University of Oxford

The University of Oxford (informally Oxford University, or simply Oxford), located in the City of Oxford, Oxfordshire, United Kingdom, is the oldest university in the English-speaking world. It is also regarded as the second best university in the UK according to many of the most recent league tables of British universities. The name is sometimes abbreviated to Oxon. in post-nominals (from the Latin Oxoniensis), although Oxford is sometimes used in official publications. The university has 38 independent colleges and six permanent private halls.

Although the exact date of foundation remains unclear, there is evidence of teaching there as far back as the 11th century. After a dispute between students and townsfolk broke out in 1209, some of the academics at Oxford fled north-east to the town of Cambridge, where the University of Cambridge was founded. Academically, Oxford is ranked in the world's top 10 universities.

3.7.3 University of London

The University of London is a federal university and one of the oldest, largest and most diverse universities in the UK. Established by Royal Charter in 1836, the university is recognized globally as a world leader in Higher Education.

It consists of 19 self-governing colleges of outstanding reputation, together with the prestigious institutes of the School of Advanced Study and a number of other central academic activities.

The university has a very diverse student population of over 161,270 students, with a further 52,000 students studying by distance learning on the University's External System. The colleges of the university differ in size, age and tradition as well as in the courses of study they offer. Some are multi-faculty institutions with large student populations, while others are specialist and smaller in size. Through its member institutions, the University of London offers almost every subject covered in any university curriculum, delivering huge flexibility and choice to its students.

Joyful Moment

Nest and Hair

My sister, a primary school teacher, was informed by one of her pupils that a bird had built its nest in the tree outside the classroom.

"What kind of bird?" my sister asked.

"I didn't see the bird, ma'am, only the nest," replied the child.

"Then, can you give us a description of the nest?" my sister encouraged her.

"Well, ma'am, it just resembles your hair."

Notes

[1] Protestantism 新教教义，基督教新教，是由16世纪宗教改革运动中脱离罗马天主教会的教会和基督徒形成的一系列新宗派的统称。

[2] representative democracy 代议制民主，公民选举代表掌握国家决策权力的民主形式。代议制民主下，公民的民主权利主要体现在选举代表的权利上。

[3] Cornish pasty 康瓦尔郡菜肉烘饼。传统的肉饼里面有牛肉丁、马铃薯和洋葱，而现在制作时则多在膨胀的面团里添加胡萝卜和绿豌豆，既可以是午饭便当的首选，也可以是配上新鲜蔬菜沙拉的主菜。

[4] Christmas Pantomime 圣诞哑剧

[5] crucifixion 十字架苦刑，the Crucifixion 耶稣受难

[6] Berliner 柏林版式，是欧洲大陆流行的三种主要报纸版式之一。采用这种版式的报纸通常的尺寸为470 mm×315 mm（18 inch×12.4 inch）。柏林版式比起小报或紧凑版式略高略宽，而比大报略短略窄。

[7] GCE (General Certificate of Education) 普通教育证书

[8] PGCE (Postgraduate Certificate of Education) 研究生教育证书

[9] NVQ (National Vocational Qualification) 国家职业资格认证

[10] HNC（Higher National Certificate）(英国技术职业教育的)国家高级合格证书

[11] tertiary education 高等教育

[12] QAA Scotland (Quality Assurance Agency for Higher Education) 苏格兰高等教育质量管理署

[13] GCSE (General Certificate of Secondary Education) 普通中等教育证书

New Words

1. **symbolism** /'sɪmbəlɪzəm/ *n.* a system of symbols and symbolic representations 象征；象征意义

   —The symbolism of every gesture will be of vital importance during the short state visit.

   这次短暂的国事访问中的一举一动都有极其重要的象征意义。

2. **humanism** /'hjuːmənɪzəm/ *n.* the doctrine that people's duty is to promote human welfare; the doctrine emphasizing a person's capacity for self-realization through reason 人道主义；人本主义

   —Enterprise should cultivate and carry out humanism idea in practice.

   企业应该培植并在实践中全面贯彻人本理念。

3. **emancipation** /ɪˌmænsɪ'peɪʃən/ *n.* freeing someone from the control of another 解放

   —The emancipation of women depends on themselves.

   妇女的解放依靠她们自己。

4. **commemorate** /kə'meməreɪt/ *v.* mark by some ceremony or observation; call to

remembrance 纪念；庆祝

—In order to commemorate the day, they nicknamed it Singles Day.

为了纪念这一天，他们给它命名为“光棍节”。

5. **resurrection** /ˌrezəˈrekʃən/ *n.* the rising of Christ on the third day after the Crucifixion; a revival from inactivity and disuse 复活；复苏

—His resurrection frightened us.

他的复活吓坏了我们。

6. **tabloid** /ˈtæblɔɪd/ *n.* sensationalist journalism 通俗小报

—As the tabloid has hit on hard times, the check of checkbook journalism have shrink.

随着小报纸的不景气，买断独家采访权的金额也跟着缩减了。

7. **strenuous** /ˈstrenjuəs/ *adj.* characterized by or performed with much energy or force 费力的

—Greece, Spain and Italy all made strenuous efforts to qualify for the euro.

希腊、西班牙和意大利为加入欧元区都做出了艰苦的努力。

8. **numeracy** /ˈnjuːmərəsi/ *n.* skill with numbers and mathematics 计算能力，识数

—Six months later John had developed literacy and numeracy skills, plus confidence.

六个月后，约翰已经能够识字和算数了，也有了自信。

Exercises

1. Choose the correct answer.

1) In Britain, the great majority of parents send their children to________.

A. private schools B. state schools

C. independent schools D. public schools

2) Which is the national sport of the UK?

A. Cricket. B. Football.

C. Tennis. D. Table tennis.

3) In terms of press, ________are directed at readers who want full information on a wide range of serious public matters.

A. quality newspapers B. tabloids

C. popular newspapers D. mid-market newspapers

4) Many of Britain's public schools have gained a reputation for ________.

A. low academic standards and snobbery

B. exclusiveness and short history

C. average academic standards, exclusiveness, and short history

D. high academic standards, exclusiveness, and snobbery

5) The Universities of Oxford and Cambridge date from________.

A. the 10th and 11th century B. the 12th century

C. the 12th and 13th century D. the 13th century

2. Decide whether the following statements are True or False.

1) Young people are tending to continue to live in the parental home for much longer than their predecessors in the 21st century.

2) Grammar schools select children at 11, through an exam called "the 11-plus".

3) Easter commemorates the crucifixion and resurrection of Jesus Christ, while Christmas commemorates the birth of Jesus Christ.

4) In Britain, if someone asks you if you "would like a cuppa", they are asking if you would like a cup of coffee.

5) Schooling is compulsory between the ages of 7 and 16 in the UK.

3. Fill in the blanks according to the passage.

1) The culture of the United Kingdom refers to the patterns of human activity and ________ associated with the United Kingdom and its people since its formation in 1707.

2) British society is considered to be divided into three main groups of classes—________, the Middle Class, and the Lower or Working Class.

3) ________ is a typical British tradition celebrated on the day after Christmas.

4) There is a three-level hierarchy of degrees (________, ________, ________) currently used in the United Kingdom.

5) Traditionally, the Scottish system has emphasized ________ across a range of subjects, while the English, Welsh and Northern Irish systems have emphasized greater ________ of education over a smaller range of subjects at secondary school level.

4. Explain the following terms according to the passage.

1) Christmas

2) Bank Holidays

3) public schools

4) Oxbridge

5) BBC

5. Answer the following questions according to the passage.

1) Does the class system exist in British society? If yes, could you describe it?

2) Please explain stages of education in the UK.

3) What's the difference between FE (further education) and HE (higher education)?

6. Discussion.

1) Illustrate traditional English cuisine. Which one is your favorite?

2) Direction: Read the following passage and answer the question below.

The Wedding

The wedding tradition of "something old, something new, something borrowed, something blue" has been around for hundreds of years. Many brides have been asked on their respective wedding days if they have gathered something old, new, borrowed, and blue to carry with them as they walk down the aisle. The tradition of carrying or wearing one of each item is said to bring luck and fortune to the newly married couple.

Have you ever stopped to think what the saying really means? What is its origin and what does each item represent?

The original saying dates back to the Victoria times and states, "Something old, something new, something borrowed, something blue and a silver sixpence in your shoe."

Something old...

A bride may wear or carry something old to represent her continued ties to her family and her old life. Many brides wear a piece of family jewelry as their old item. Some brides wear the wedding dress worn by their mother or grandmother. In many cases, something old may also be something borrowed.

Something new...

Wearing something new is supposed to represent success and hope in the bride's new life and in her marriage. If the bride purchased her wedding dress new, it may represent her new item, but any item that is new may be used. Something "new" is usually the easiest category to fill.

Something borrowed...

The borrowed item should be something borrowed from a friend that is happily married. It is suggested that their happiness will rub off on you and bring lasting happiness to your marriage. Some brides borrow an item of clothing, a piece of jewelry, a handkerchief or perhaps a beaded purse.

Something blue...

Wearing something blue dates back to biblical times when a blue wedding dress was worn to represent purity, fidelity and love. Over time this has changed from wearing a blue dress to wearing just a blue and around the bottom of the bride's wedding dress to modern times where it is commonplace for the bride to wear a blue garter.

Silver sixpence...

Placing a silver sixpence in the bride's left shoe is said to be a symbol of wealth. This not only refers to financial wealth, but also a wealth of happiness and joy throughout her married life. Since most brides probably don't even know what a sixpence is, this part of the tradition is not used very often in modern times. However, if a bride would like to include it in her wedding, she can purchase a silver sixpence from many companies that sell bridal supplies such as garters and invitations.

Some brides are more traditional than other and may take a great deal of care in selecting one item for each category. Others brides are not bound by tradition but still may choose to carry out the custom at someone else's request. If they don't want to carry numerous items, they may simply carry two handkerchiefs in a small beaded bag—she may choose to buy a new, white handkerchief and borrow a blue one from a family member. That would provide them with something new—the white handkerchief, as well as something that is old, borrowed and blue—the blue handkerchief. The handkerchief just may come in handy during the wedding for drying their joyful tears.

Question:

How does the traditional Britain wedding compare with the traditional Chinese wedding?

Stay Positive

1. If you want to be an extraordinary person, not an ordinary one, you must do something extra each day.
2. The road to success is lined with many tempting parking spaces.

Chapter 7

Religion of the United Kingdom

For me the different religions are beautiful flowers from the same garden, or they are branches of the same majestic tree. Therefore they are equally true, though being received and interpreted through human instruments equally imperfect.

—Mohandas Karamchand Gandhi, Indian statesman

1. General Introduction

The United Kingdom has one of the most religiously diverse populations in the European Union. Religious practice cuts across ethnic groups and ethnic groups are multi-religious. Christians may be Britons, Asians, Indians or other Europeans. Indians for example may be Sikhs[1], Hindus[2], Muslims[3], Christians or other faith.

People in the UK are free to choose and follow their own religious beliefs. The United Kingdom guarantees freedom of religion to its citizens and residents through three different regulations. One of these laws is the European Convention on Human Rights, which guarantees the right to free religious choice. Although freedom of religion is well established and practiced, some religious preference is given by the government. In the case of the monarchy for example, only Protestants may become king or queen (although they are now free to marry Catholics without losing their **succession** to the throne).

In a YouGov[4] poll 2011, 35% of the total respondents were either very or fairly religious vs. 63% who were not very religious or not religious at all, with the remaining 2% unsure. Christianity is the majority religion, followed by Islam, Hinduism, Sikhism, Judaism[5] and Buddhism[6] in terms of number of adherents. Among Christians, Anglicans[7] are the most common denomination, followed by the Catholics[8], Presbyterians[9], Methodists[10] and Baptists[11].

UK Religion Poll, 2011

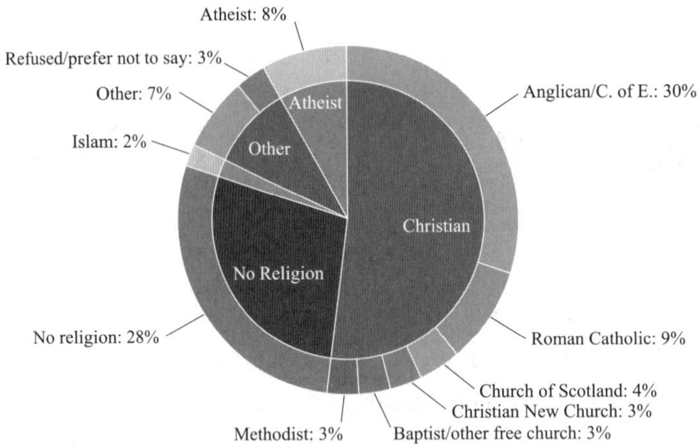

2. Role in History and Modern Society

Religion plays an important role in the UK and has a huge and far-reaching influence on British people in various aspects and different ways.

2.1 Role in History

In history, religion had great effects on social life and behavior, for example, during the last part of the 19th century and the early part of the 20th century. The Protestants were very active in the fight against the obvious forms of sin and hated all **self-indulgence**. According to old Puritan tradition, drinking and gambling were restricted, many activities were forbidden and the pursuit of pleasure was bitterly criticized. It insisted on hard work and self-sacrifice.

Apart from the effects on behavior and ideas, religion took part in social activities. Since the early 19th century religion has inspired a lot of work for good causes. Innumerable organizations, which have religion origins, have been built up to help people in need.

On the other hand, religion also caused blood and disturbance in the history of Britain. Britain was Roman Catholic until the Reformation in the 16th century[12]. Then King Henry VIII refused to accept the doctrine of the Catholic Church or the authority of the Pope and set up the Church of England. Henry's daughter Mary Tudor tried to make England Catholic again by force. She had many Anglicans buried alive, including Henry's **Archbishop** of Canterbury, Tomas Crammer. Mary's plan failed completely. Elizabeth I strongly supported the Church of England her father founded. She executed Catholics, treating them as **traitor**s working for England's great enemy, Philip II of Spain and the Pope.

2.2 Role in Modern Society

In modern society, religion does not play an important role as it did in the 19th century in national life.

In 2018, according to a study conducted by London's St Mary's University's Benedict XVI

Centre for Religion and Society and the Institut Catholique de Paris, and based on data from the European Social Survey 2014-2016 collected on a sample of 560, among 16 to 29 years-old British people 21% were Christians (10% Catholic, 7% Anglican, 2% other Protestant and 2% other Christian), 6% were Muslims, 3% were of other religions, and 70% were not religious.

The British public, both adults and children, are almost wholly ignorant of the basic facts surrounding Christians and other world religions. They may tell you frankly that they cannot see that religion is of any use. Some never really think about it. Others who do not go to church still believe in God and Heaven in a confused way. They like to get married in church and perhaps have their children christened in church, and they would certainly like to have a Christian funeral when they die, however, they seldom go to church or pray otherwise.

3. Christianity

3.1 Christianity at a Glance

Christianity is the world's biggest religion, with about 2.1 billion followers worldwide. It is based on the teachings of Jesus Christ who lived in the Holy Land 2,000 years ago.

3.1.1 Christian Beliefs

Christians believe that God made the world. The term "Christian" is form Jesus Christ who was God's son. Jesus was born or came to Earth because people were forgetting God—Jesus came to tell us all about God and remind us how to behave and to save humanity from the consequences of its sins. Jesus was born to Mary about 2000 years ago. He is known by several names: Son of God, Light of the World, Lamb of God and The Good Shepherd. Jesus was fully human, and experienced this world in the same way as other human beings of his time.

One of the most important concepts in Christianity is that of Jesus giving his life on the Cross and rising from the dead after the third day.

Christians believe that there is only one God, but that there are three elements to this one God: God the Father, God the Son, The Holy Spirit[13].

Christians worship in churches. Their spiritual leaders are called priests or ministers.

The Christian holy book is the Bible, and consists of the Old and New Testaments. The Old Testament tells the stories of Jewish history while the New Testament tells the story of Jesus life and teaching. Parts of the writing contained in the Old Testament are also sacred to Jewish and Muslim people.

3.1.2 Christianity in Britain

Although Britain has been predominantly Christian since Saxon times, following the Reformation in the sixteenth century many different Christian denominations have existed. The three main churches found in Britain today are the Anglican or Church of England, the Roman Catholic Church and several Protestant denominations Though they share the same origins and have many common beliefs, historically they developed different forms of **ritual**s and doctrines which have led to some major differences among the churches. These are often expressed in the different forms of worship the churches have adopted.

3.2 History of Christianity in Britain

Christianity was first brought to Britain during the days of the Roman Empire. With the departure of the **legion**s and the Anglo-Saxon invasions of the fifth century Christianity was reduced to pockets of support in Wales, Scotland and Ireland. This situation changed with the arrival of **missionaries** sent by the Pope led by Augustine[14]in 597. The next few centuries saw Christianity established throughout Britain. Augustine, meanwhile, became the first Archbishop of Canterbury.

Bishops were also established in a number of other centers, and by the end of the eleventh century a system of **diocese**s and **parish**es had been established across much of England. This system remains the basis of the structure of the Church of England.

In the 16th century, the Great Britain underwent the English Reformation. The English Reformation was the series of events in 16th century England by which the Church of England first broke away from the authority of the Pope and the Roman Catholic Church.

Based on Henry VIII's desire for a divorce, the English Reformation was at the beginning more of a political than a religious issue. Before the break with Rome, it was the Pope that decided everything. The split from Rome made the English monarch the Supreme Governor of the English church, thereby making the Church of England the established church of the nation. In Scotland, the medieval Church was replaced by the established Presbyterian Church[9]of Scotland. Roman Catholicism survived in strength only in Ireland.

The Reformation was followed by further divisions. Conflicts over beliefs, led to a series of separation from the Church of England in the course of the sixteenth and seventeenth centuries. These Free Churches, as they are now called, were joined in the eighteenth and nineteenth centuries by the Methodists[10]. This and the revival of Roman Catholicism throughout Britain in the course of the nineteenth century, largely as a result of immigration, particularly from Ireland, produced an increasingly diverse religious scene.

3.3 The Church of England

3.3.1 Hierarchy

There are two established or state churches in Britain: the Church of England, or Anglican Church[15]as it is also called, and the Church of Scotland, or "Kirk"[16].

The Church of England is divided into two provinces—Canterbury in the South of England and York in the North. Each province has a head or archbishop—the Archbishop of Canterbury who is "Primate of All England", and the Archbishop of York, who is "Primate of England". Both provinces are divided into dioceses, each with a bishop in charge and a **cathedral** as the central church. Canterbury is the larger province, containing 30 dioceses, while York contains only 14. A diocese is divided into smaller districts called parishes. Each parish is in the care of a priest, who is called either a vicar or a rector.

The Archbishop of Canterbury is head of the Anglican Communion, which is a worldwide family of churches in more than 160 different countries. Once in every ten years the Archbishop of Canterbury invites all the bishops of the Anglican Communion to a conference at Lambeth[17] in London to exchange views and debate issues of concern.

The Church is governed by its bishops. In that sense it is a hierarchical organization. Nevertheless its regulating and legislative body is the General Synod[18], made up of three "Houses", the House of Bishops, the House of Clergy and the House of Laity. The General Synod is the supreme authority of the Church of England.

3.3.2 The Church of England as a Broad Church

The Church of England is frequently considered to be a "broad" church because it includes a wide variety of beliefs and practices. It is, in the words of one journalist, "a Church where there has traditionally been seat for **heretic**s and unbelievers, doubters and skeptics". It avoids making clear statements where it can, to keep its broad body of believers together. Most of its members are happy with the arrangement. In that sense the Church of England is profoundly typical of the English character. It prefers the illogical but practical atmosphere of "live and let live" within a broader church climate. Consequently there is always a concern to ensure that all wings of the Church are represented among the bishops.

Some Anglican priests have broken away from tradition to the extent that in some services they introduce new religious songs, composed by young people who accompany them on guitars in the church. They also use the church as a place where people can discuss the problems of everyday life.

3.3.3 Legislative Role

The Church of England also has a law-making role in Britain. Twenty-six bishops (including the two Archbishops) sit in the House of Lords and are known as the Lords Spiritual[15]. They are thought to bring a religious idea to the secular process of law.

3.3.4 Civic Duties

The Church of England fulfills a civic responsibility too. Its bishops and priests are responsible for performing state weddings and funerals, acts of remembrance, memorial services as well as grand occasions like the coronation. After events like the Gulf War or major disasters, the country comes together to mourn under the spiritual guidance of the Church of England.

3.4 Current Issues

As the main religion in Britain, Christianity and the changes and current issues about it frequently attract media attention. These are just a few of the key issues facing it at the beginning of the 21st century.

3.4.1 The decline of Christianity

Freedom from religion in Britain is becoming as important as freedom of religion, according to a United Nations investigation.

A 23-page report by Asma Jahangir, the UN special reporter on freedom of religion or belief, claims that two thirds of British people do not admit to any religious affiliation. The UK is following the religious trends of the rest of Europe: Christianity is in free-fall.

In the past when life had fewer **distractions** people measured Church attendance on a weekly basis, but today regular churchgoing is often measured as those that go at least once a month.

Some say that declining church attendance and the rise in multiculturalism meant that Christian Britain is dead. The fall in church marriages and baptisms revealed that Britain was no longer a Christian nation.

3.4.2 The Ordination of Women in the Church of England

After a long debate, the Church finally accepted the ordination of women in 1992. The first group of about 1000 women was ordained in 1994. About 470 male clergy left the church in protest soon after, 58 subsequently returned.

Some female priests complained that they are heavily discriminated against. Some claimed that they have been accused of being witches. Anyway, by the year 2000, only three out of the 44 dioceses in the Church of England still refused to ordain female priests. In mid-2008, about one quarter of the Church of England clergy are women. It was not until summer 2014 that it was finally agreed to open up all orders of the ministry to both genders.

4. Other Religions

Today nearly all of the world's other religions are also practiced in Britain. Apart from Christianity, there are at least five other religions with a substantial number of adherents in Britain. The most influential two are Judaism and Islam.

4.1 Judaism

The oldest is the Jewish community, which is in rapid decline in Britain today. Even so, it is the second largest Jewish community in Western Europe.

Jews returned to England in the seventeenth century, after they were forced to leave in the thirteenth century. The Jews are divided into different religious groups. The largest group, approximately 120,000, are Orthodox[20] and belong to the United Synagogues. They look to the Chief Rabbi[21]of Great Britain for spiritual leadership. Unlike leaders in many other faiths, a rabbi is not a priest and has no special religious status. The two progressive groups, the Reform and Liberal Jews have no acknowledged single leader, but they do have a number of rabbis who command a following among those who admire their wisdom.

4.2 Islam

Muslim believes in Islam which is the second most popular religion in the world with over a thousand million followers. The Arabic word "Islam" means obedience, and derives from a word meaning "peace". It is more often thought of as a complete way of life rather than a religion.

4.2.1 Basic belief and Six Main Beliefs

The basic belief of Islam is that there is only one God, whose name is Allah[22].

The six articles of faith are the main doctrines of Islam. All Muslims share beliefs in the following.

◆ **God**

Islam believes that there is only one Supreme and Eternal entity, Allah (God). He alone is the creator of all the universe. Quran[23] declares "That is God, your Lord. There is no god but Him, the Creator of everything. So worship Him. He is responsible for everything."

◆ **Angels**

Muslims believe in angels. They are comprised of light, and each has different purposes.

◆ **Scriptures**

It refers to believing in all the four books: the Torah (Moses), the Psalms (David), the Gospel (Jesus) and the Quran (Mohammad)[24]. Muslim beliefs and practices are rooted in the Quran and Muslims believe it is "the word of God".

◆ **Prophets**

It is obligatory on every Muslim to believe in all the messengers from Adam to Mohammad without any discrimination. Quran treats all the prophets equally.

◆ **Resurrection**[25]

Muslims have faith that after the end of the world, every human will be resurrected from the grave. They will be held according to whatever they have done in their lives. The day is known as the Day of Judgment. The innocent ones will stay in Heaven, whereas, the corrupted ones will go to hell.

◆ **Divine Creed**[26]

It is one of the main aspects of Islam. Believing in divine creed refers to **predestination**. Everything that has happened, is happening, or will happen is evident to God.

4.2.2 Worship in Mosques

The Muslim building for communal worship is called mosque.

Very often Mosques have a domed roof and a tall tower called a minaret[27]. Muslims are called to prayer from the minaret. In Britain, calling Muslims to pray this way is not allowed, so some Islamic communities broadcast the call to prayer on a radio frequency which Muslims can pick up in their homes and places of work using a small receiver.

There are no pictures or statues in a mosque. They are decorated with patterns and words from the Quran. There is also very little furniture inside because Muslims use prayer mats[28]for prayers.

When people go into the mosque they take off their shoes. This is to keep it clean for prayers.

There is often a fountain or pool, or at least an area with water where people can wash. Muslims wash their hands, mouth, throat, nose, ears, arms up to the elbow and feet. This is a sacred wash that symbolizes spiritual cleansing and purity in readiness for coming before God.

There is always a qibla wall[29] in a mosque which is beautifully decorated. This wall is facing Mecca[30]. It is important that Muslims always know the direction of Mecca.

Women do not pray in the same place as men, there is usually a screened-off area for them.

Services are held every day at the mosque. The most important service is held at the mosque on Friday at noon.

4.2.3 Muslims in Britain

Islam is the second largest religion in the United Kingdom of Great Britain and Northern Ireland. The vast majority of Muslims in the United Kingdom live in England.

Within the British Muslim community as a whole, which like Jewish and Christian communities, is divided into different sects and traditions. During the past quarter century, since large numbers of Muslims arrived in Britain, there has been a tension between those Muslims who sought an accommodation between Islam and Western secular society, one might call them modernists, and those who have wanted to uphold traditional Islamic values even when these directly conflicted with secular social values. Until 1989 it might be said that those Muslims who were relatively successful economically and socially were the prevailing example of how Muslims could live successfully in the West.

Mosque attendance increased and religious observance became an outward symbol of Muslim assertion. In 1985 only about 20% of Muslims were actually religiously observant. By 1995 that figure had risen to about 50%. Yet the Islam of young British Muslims is different from that of their parents. Young Muslims come from several different ethnic origins but they all share their religion and their British culture and education. This is leading to a Britain-specific form of Islam.

According to analysis based on the 2011 census, Muslims in the United Kingdom face poor standards of housing, poorer levels of education and are more vulnerable to long-term illness, and that Muslims in the UK have the highest rate of unemployment, the poorest health, the most disability and fewest educational qualifications among religious groups. The figures were, to some extent, explained by the fact that Muslims were the least well-established group, having the youngest age profile.

5. Religious Views about Social Issues

5.1 On Euthanasia

Euthanasia, sometimes known as "mercy-killing", is illegal in most of the world. It has been a controversial issue in Britain for many years. It formed the basis of one of the 2013 Westminster Faith Debates on religion and personal morality.

Since religion concerns itself with issues of life, death, meaning and morality, it is not surprising that, for many people, religious beliefs are the main basis for their views of euthanasia.

5.1.1 Christians' Views

Christians are mostly against euthanasia. In June, 2009, three of Britain's most senior religious leaders, the Archbishop of Canterbury, the Archbishop of Westminster and the Chief

Rabbi, have come together for the first time to reject proposals that would allow families to help loved ones to die. The arguments about euthanasia are usually based on the beliefs that life is given by God, and that human beings are made in God's image. Below are some of the main ideas from the anti-euthanasia Christians:

- Life is a gift from God.
- Human beings are valuable because they are made in God's image.
- The process of dying is spiritually important, and should not be disrupted.
- All human lives are equally valuable.

Some features of Christianity suggest that there are some obligations that go against the general view that euthanasia is a bad thing:

- Christianity requires us to respect every human being.
- If we respect a person we should respect their decisions about the end of their life.
- We should accept their rational decisions to refuse burdensome and useless treatment.

Some turn to Bible for reference. There are only two mentions of suicide in the Old Testament: King Saul and David's counselor, Ahitophel, both of which required the assistance of another person and are thus similar to euthanasia. The Bible does not comment on either of these instances, though it has been noted that none of the persons who commit suicide in the Bible are heroic or sympathetic figures.

5.1.2 Jews' Views

The message of Judaism is that one must struggle until the last breath of life. Until the last moment, one has to live and feel happy and give thanks to the Creator. In Jewish law, any form of active euthanasia is strictly prohibited and condemned as plain murder. The fact that the patient is in pain and pleads for assistance in ending his life does not change the law.

5.1.3 Muslims' Views

Muslims are of the similar opinions. They believe that human life is sacred because it is given by Allah, and that Allah chooses how long each person will live. Human beings should not interfere in this. Suicide and euthanasia are explicitly forbidden. The Prophet said: "There was a man who got a wound and growing impatient (with its pain), he took a knife and cut his hand with it and the blood did not stop till he died. Allah said, 'My Slave hurried to bring death upon himself so I have forbidden him (to enter) Paradise.' "

Despite these traditional beliefs, in May 2014, 73% of respondents to a YouGov/Dignity in Dying poll supported Lord Falconer's proposals to legalise assisted dying for the terminally ill. Only 13% were against the proposals. Majorities of religious believers support assisted dying. Separate YouGov polls in 2013 found that:

78% who attend a place of worship at least monthly support the practice;

62% of strongly religious people support assisted dying for the terminally ill.

5.2 On Abortion and Contraception

The British Social Attitudes Survey 2012 found that there is an overwhelming **consensus** in the UK that abortion is justified in cases of:

a health risk to the parent, with 95% in favour

the diagnosis of a defect, with 85% in favour

the parents not wishing to have a child, with 76% in favour

Only 6% of Catholics questioned in a poll by YouGov agreed that abortion should never be allowed, and only 11% believed abortion should only be permitted as an indirect consequence of a life-saving treatment for the mother. In contrast 30% agreed that abortion should be a matter of individual choice, and 44% agreed that abortion should be permitted on grounds of "rape, incest, severe disability to the child or as an indirect consequence of life-saving treatment for the mother".

Only 4% of Catholic adults questioned believed artificial contraception is wrong and should not be used. 71% agreed it should be used more often, 23% believed it was a matter entirely for couples.

A 2013 YouGov poll found that the percentage of the population wanting an outright ban on abortion had declined from 12% in 2005, to 7% in 2013. Whilst 44% of those polled agreed that life begins at conception, most of this group did not support a ban on abortion.

Joyful Moment

A Case of Mistakenly Identity

A middle-aged woman had a heart attack and was taken to the hospital. While on the operating table she had a near-death experience. During that experience she saw God and asked if this is it. God said no and explained that she has another 30-40 years to live.

Upon her recovery she decided to just stay in the hospital and have a face lift (整容), liposuction(吸脂), breast augmentation(丰胸), and a tummy tuck(腹部拉皮). She even had someone come in and change her hair color. She figured that since she's got another 30 or 40 years she might as well make the most of it.

She walked out the hospital after the last operation and was killed by an ambulance speeding up to the hospital.

She arrived in front of God again and asked, "I thought you said I had another 30-40 years?"

God replied, "Sorry, I didn't recognize you."

Notes

[1] Sikhs 锡克教徒，显著特征为裹头巾、留长发、蓄胡须

[2] Hindus 印度教徒

[3] Muslims 穆斯林，信奉伊斯兰教的人统称为"穆斯林"

[4] YouGov 舆观调查，英国民意调查委员会（British Polling Council）的成员之一

[5] Judaism 犹太教
[6] Buddhism 佛教
[7] Anglicans 英国圣公会教徒
[8] Catholics 天主教徒
[9] Presbyterian 长老会成员
[10] Methodist 卫理公会教徒
[11] Baptist 浸礼会教徒
[12] Reformation in the 16th century 16 世纪宗教改革
[13] God the Father, God the Son, The Holy Spirit 圣父、圣子、圣灵三位一体，基督教信仰的基础
[14] St. Augustine 圣奥古斯丁，其 597 年的传教使不列颠几近被摧毁的基督教得以恢复
[15] Anglican Church 英国国教，英国在宗教改革中建立的民族教会
[16] Kirk 苏格兰教会
[17] Lambeth 伦敦朗伯斯区，伦敦坎特伯雷大主教官邸所在地
[18] General Synod 英国圣公会总议会，英国国教的管理组织
[19] Lords Spiritual（英国的）上议院神职议员
[20] Orthodox 东正教徒，东正教与天主教、新教并称基督教三大教派
[21] Chief Rabbi 首席拉比
[22] Allah 阿拉，伊斯兰教信奉的唯一真主
[23] Quran 古兰经，伊斯兰教的经典
[24] Torah, the Psalms, the Gospel and the Quran 伊斯兰教的正典，分别为《摩西五经》《诗篇》《福音书》和《古兰经》
[25] resurrection 死后复活
[26] Divine Creed 信前定，认为世间的一切都是由阿拉预先安排好的
[27] Minaret 伊斯兰教清真寺的尖塔，高而细，上有突出的阳台
[28] prayer mats（穆斯林祈祷时用的）跪垫，跪毯
[29] qibla wall 朝拜墙
[30] Mecca 麦加，是穆罕默德诞生地，伊斯兰教第一圣地

New Words

1. **succession** /sək'seʃən/ *n.* the act of taking over an official job or position, or the right to be the next to take it 继任，继承，接任；继承权

   —His divorce will not prevent the Prince of Wales' succession to the throne.

   离婚不会影响威尔士亲王继承王位。

2. **denomination** /dɪˌnɒmɪ'neɪʃən/ *n.* a branch of the Christian Church（基督教）教派

   —What religious denomination does he belong to?

他属于哪个教派？

3. **self-indulgence** /ˌselfɪn'dʌldʒəns/ *n.* the act of allowing oneself to have or do the things that one enjoys very much 放纵，任性

—She allowed herself only a few moments' self-indulgence.

她只许自己任性了几分钟。

4. **archbishop** /ˌɑːtʃ'bɪʃəp/ *n.* a bishop of the highest rank, responsible for all the churches in a large area 大主教

—We saw the archbishop crown the queen.

我们看见大主教为女王加冕。

5. **traitor** /'treɪtər/ *n.* a person who betrays his friends, his country, etc. 叛徒，卖国贼

—They branded him a traitor.

他们给他加上叛逆者的污名。

6. **ritual** /'rɪtʃuəl/ *n.* a series of actions that are always carried out in the same way, especially as part of a religious ceremony 程序，仪规，礼节，（尤指）宗教仪式

—Some religions employ ritual more than others.

有的宗教举行仪式时特别注重仪规。

7. **legion** /'liːdʒən/ *n.* a large group of soldiers who form a part of an army 军团，兵团

—Caesar's Legions marched through France and crossed into Britain.

恺撒的兵团穿过法国，进入英国。

8. **missionary** /'mɪʃənrɪ/ *n.* a person who is sent to a foreign country to teach people about Christianity 传教士

9. **diocese** /'daɪəsɪs/ *n.* a district for which a bishop is responsible 主教辖区

—There has been various rumours the moment he arrived in the diocese.

他一进入主教辖区就有各种各样的谣言传出。

10. **parish** /'pærɪʃ/ *n.* an area that has its own church and that a priest is responsible for 堂区，教区

—Her family came upon the parish.

她一家人穷得靠教区布施。

11. **cathedral** /kə'θiːdrəl/ *n.* the main church of a district, under the care of a bishop 主教堂，教区总教堂

—St. Pauls Cathedral is the most famous cathedral in England.

圣保罗大教堂是英国最著名的教堂。

12. **heretic** / 'herətɪk/ *n.* someone whose beliefs or actions are considered wrong by most people 异教徒，异端者

—He was regarded as heretic by the common people.

他被大众视为异教徒。

13. **distraction** /dɪ'strækʃən/ *n.* an activity that amuses or entertains people 娱乐，消遣

—Fishing is his major distraction.
钓鱼是他主要的娱乐。

14. **ordination** /ˌɔːdɪ'neɪʃən/ *n.* the act or ceremony of making somebody a priest or minister of a church（圣职的）授予
—It is the central issue in the debate over the ordination of women.
这是授圣职给女性之争的核心问题。

15. **synagogue** /'sɪnəgɒg/ *n.* a building where Jews meet for religious worship and teaching 犹太会堂，犹太教堂
—Many Jews come to this synagogue on saturday.
星期六的时候，许多犹太人到这所犹太教会堂来。

16. **scripture** /'skrɪptʃə/ *n.* refers to writings that are regarded as holy in a particular religion, for example the Bible in Christianity.（某宗教的）圣典，经文，经典
—The devil can cite Scripture for his purpose.
为了达到目的，魔鬼也会援引圣经。

17. **prophet** /'prɒfɪt/ *n.* (in the Christian, Jewish and Muslim religions) a person sent by God to teach the people and give them messages from God （基督教、犹太教和伊斯兰教的）先知
—Mohammed is the prophet of the Muslims.
穆罕默德是穆斯林的先知。

18. **predestination** /ˌpriːdestɪ'neɪʃən/ *n.* the theory or the belief that everything that happens has been decided or planned in advance by God or by fate and that humans cannot change it 宿命论，命定说
—Would you accept the concept of predestination?
你可以接受宿命的概念吗？

19. **mosque** /mɒsk/ *n.* a Muslim house of worship 清真寺
—Here is the remains of a mosque.
这里是一所清真寺的废墟。

20. **euthanasia** /ˌjuːθə'neɪziə/ *n.* the practice (illegal in most countries) of killing without pain a person who is suffering from a disease that cannot be cured 安乐死
—People are divided on the issue of euthanasia.
人们在安乐死这一问题有截然不同的观点。

21. **consensus** /kən'sensəs/ *n.* a generally accepted opinion or decision among a group of people 一致的意见，共识
—The general consensus in the office is that he can't do his job.
办公室成员一致认为他无法胜任工作。

Exercises

1. Choose the correct answer.

1) The Christian holy book is the________.

A. Gospel　　B. New Testaments

C. The Ten Commandments　　D. Bible

2) ________are God's Revelation found in the Bible's Old Testament and they are central to the Christian faith.

A. The Ten Commandments　　B. Gospel

C. Torah　　D. The New Testament

3) The Jewish spiritual leaders are called________.

A. Chief Rabbi　　B. Priest　　C. Abraham　　D. Jesus

4) There are two established or state churches in Britain: the ________and the Church of Scotland.

A. Kirk　　B. Methodist Church

C. Church of England　　D. Canterbury Cathedral

5) The Arabic word "Islam" means obedience, and derives from a word meaning "________".

A. love　　B. democracy　　C. mercy　　D. peace

2. Decide whether the following statements are True or False.

1) Canterbury is the larger province, containing 30 dioceses, while York contains only 14.

2) King Henry VIII was a devout Roman Catholic.

3) 42 million Britons see themselves as nominally Christian, and almost all of them are actively practicing.

4) The Mormons were forced out of several established communities because they abstain from all alcohol, tobacco, coffee and tea.

5) All the writings contained in the Old Testament are also sacred to Jewish and Muslim people.

3. Fill in the blanks according to the passage.

1) Britain was ________ until the Reformation in the 16th century.

2) Christianity is based on the teachings of________ who lived in the Holy Land 2,000 years ago.

3) The Archbishop of________ is head of the Anglican Communion, which is a worldwide family of churches in more than 160 different countries.

4) After a long debate, the Church finally accepted the ordination of________ in 1992.

5) Islam believes that there is only one Supreme, Eternal,________ and Unparalleled entity.

4. Explain the following terms according to the passage.

1) English Reformation

2) Christian Beliefs
3) Lords Spiritual
4) Resurrection
5) qibla wall

5. Answer the following questions according to the passage.

1) What do Christians believe?
2) Why is the Church of England regarded as a broad church?
3) What do Muslims believe in?

6. Discussion.

Below is a married couple's prayer. Read it and think about how religion functions in building intimacy in their marriage.

Dear Heavenly Father,

Thank you for this life, for the gift of love, and the blessing of our marriage. We give you praise for the joy you've poured into our hearts through this love, for the contentment of family, and the happiness of our home. May we always treasure the experience of loving each other in this holy union. Help us to remain forever committed to our vows, those we made to each other, and to you, Lord.

We will need your strength daily Lord, as we live together with the goal of following and serving you. Develop within us the character of your Son, Jesus, that we might love each other with the love he demonstrated—with patience, respect, understanding, honesty, forgiveness and kindness.

Let us always be a support to one another—a friend to listen and encourage, a refugee from the storm, and most importantly, a warrior in prayer.

Holy Spirit, guide us through the difficult moments of life and comfort us in our grief. May our lives together bring glory to you, our Savior, and testify of your love.

In Jesus' Name,
Amen

Stay Positive

1. Meet success like a gentleman and disaster like a man.
2. It always seems impossible until it's done.

Chapter 8

Literature and Arts of the United Kingdom

To use books rightly, is to go to them for help; to appeal to them when our own knowledge and power fail; to be led by them into wider sight and purer conception than our own, and to receive from them the united sentence of the judges and councils of all time, against our solitary and unstable opinions.

—John Ruskin (1819-1900), English art critic

1. Literature

English literature has a long history and a secure position in world literature. It has a rich literary tradition with authors such as Chaucer, Shakespeare, Wordsworth, Dickens, Eliot, George Orwell and H. G. Wells. Famous English poets, playwrights and novelists are well known, quoted and loved all over the world.

1.1 The Old English Period and Middle English Period (450-1500)

The earliest form of English literature developed after the settlement of the Saxons and other Germanic tribes in England and is known as Old English. The bloody Anglo-Saxon epic poem *Beowulf*[1] is the most famous work in Old English. Beowulf, a Swedish warrior in the 6th century, comes to help King of Danes who is attacked by Grendel, a defeated sea monster. Later, *Beowulf*, King of his own land, dies killing a fire dragon that was threatening his people. *Beowulf* is a Christian epic on the grounds that its hero-king stands for Christian virtues. He lives his life and goes to his death in devoted service to other people.

With the Norman Conquest in 1066, Britain entered the Middle Ages (1066-1485). The most significant English author in the Middle Ages was the poet Geoffrey Chaucer[2](1340? - 1400). His life experience gave him a wide range of knowledge about people from different walks of life.

Chaucer's masterpiece is *The Canterbury Tales*[3], a collection of stories set within a framing story of a **pilgrimage** to Canterbury Cathedral[4]. The poet joins a band of pilgrims who assemble at the Tabard Inn outside London for the journey to Canterbury. Ranging in status from a Knight to a humble Plowman, they are a microcosm of 14th century English society.

Since the travel is arduous and wearing, the Host proposes a storytelling contest to kill the time on the road. In the tales, Chaucer treated such universal subjects as love, sex and death.

1.2 The Renaissance (1500-1660)

During the 15th and 16th century an intellectual movement called the Renaissance[5]swept Western Europe. The word means "rebirth" and refers especially to the revival of ancient Greek learning. The sonnet[6] and other Italian literary influence began to appear in English literature.

1.2.1 Drama

More than any other form of literature, drama flourished in this age. A large number of comedies, tragedies, and examples of intermediate types were produced for London theaters.

Christopher Marlowe (1564-1593) is the great pioneer of English drama, whose style is thought to have been a great influence on Shakespeare. His masterpiece is *The Tragical History of Doctor Faustus*, in which Faustus, a young and brilliant scholar, sells his soul to the devil in return for power and knowledge. Marlowe also began the tradition of the chronicle play[7], about the fatal deeds of kings and potentates, a few years later with the tragedies *Tamburlaine the Great, Part I*, and *Edward II*.

William Shakespeare (1564-1616) is recognized in much of the world as the greatest of all dramatists. A complete account of Shakespeare's life does not exist, but it is generally accepted that he came from a middle-class family in Stratford-upon-Avon[8] and became a successful playwright and director in London. Shakespeare is the most widely quoted author in history, and his plays have probably been performed more times than those of any other dramatist.

Shakespeare had a remarkable knowledge of human behavior, which he was able to communicate through his portrayal of a wide variety of characters. He was able to enter fully into the point of view of each of his characters and to create vivid dramatic situations in which to explore human motivations and behavior. His mastery of poetic language and of the techniques of drama enabled him to combine these multiple viewpoints, human motives, and actions to produce a unique theatrical experience.

Shakespeare's 37 plays fall into three categories: comedy, tragedy and historical play. His comedies include *A Midsummer Night's Dream*, *The Merchant of Venice*, *As You Like It* and *Twelfth Night*[9]. The last two depict the endearing as well as the ridiculous sides of human nature. His major historical plays are *Richard III*, *Henry IV* and *Antony and Cleopatra*. His great tragedies include *Hamlet*, *Othello*, *King Lear*, and *Macbeth*[10], looking deeply into the springs of action in the human soul. Shakespeare's last plays are the so-called dramatic romances, including *The Tempest*.

Hamlet is regarded as a milestone in Shakespeare's dramatic development. It tells the story of the prince's effort to revenge the murder of his father, who has been poisoned by Hamlet's uncle, Claudius, the man who then becomes Hamlet's stepfather and the king. The play ends in a spectacular scene of death. Hamlet is certainly Shakespeare's most intellectually engaging and **elusive** play, to which literary critics and actors turn again and again. *The Night Banquet*, a 2006

Chinese *wuxia*(swordman)-drama film directed by Feng Xiaogang, is widely regarded as a loose adaption of Hamlet.

1.2.2 Poetry

In English Renaissance period, poetry is the other major literary form.

Spenser's uncompleted *The Faerie Queene* (Books I-III, 1590; Books IV-VI, 1596) is the most famous work of the period. *The Faerie Queene* is not only famous for the extensive imagination, rich vocabulary, but also for the Spenserian Stanza[11], a nine-line verse stanza that the first eight lines are iambic pentameter, and the ninth, iambic hexameter.

Although Shakespeare is well known for his talents in drama, his poems certainly bring him a prominent status in literary history. Actually, his sonnets represent the finest poetic craftsmanship of Elizabethan poetry. He wrote 154 sonnets which are profound in their moral depth and more complex in their expressed feelings.

1.3 The Neo-Classical Period (1660-1785)

Neo-classical period[12] in English literature refers to the years between the return of the Stuarts[13] to the English throne in 1660 and the full development of Romanticism. In this period, there was a revival of interest in the old classical works. This tendency is known as neo-classicism.

John Milton (1608-1674) is the last great poet of the English Renaissance. His masterpiece is the epic *Paradise Lost*[14], in which Milton narrated the tricks of Satan leading to the fall of Adam and Eve from the state of innocence to express the central Christian truths of freedom, sin, and **redemption** as he conceived them.

John Dryden (1631-1700), a poet laureate[15], is "the father of English criticism". His talents were diversified and his works abundant. The bulk of Dryden's work was in drama and his best tragedy was *All for Love*.

In the age of Alexander Pope (1688-1744), the classical spirit in English literature reached its highest point. Pope's brilliant satiric masterpiece, T*he Rape of the Lock*[16], makes an epic theme of a trifling drawing-room episode: the contention arising from a young lord's having stealthily snipped a lock of hair from a young lady's head.

Jonathan Swift (1667-1745) wrote a number of satirical prose narratives. His best-known work, *Gulliver's Travels*[17], claims to be a ship doctor's account of his voyages into strange places, but in reality it is a criticism on the human race. The accounts of Gulliver's first two voyages are often read as a children's book.

A quite different kind of journalism is represented by the work of the middle-class adventurer, hack writer, and political agent Daniel Defoe (1660-1731). He produced a series of seemingly true but actually fictitious stories. The first of these, and the greatest, is *Robinson Crusoe*[18], which reports the life and adventures of a shipwrecked sailor. He was viewed as one of the **progenitor**s of the novel in the English language.

The age of Samuel Johnson (1709-1784), from 1744 to about 1784, was a time of changing literary ideals. His curiously lovable and upright personality, along with his intellectual excellence, has been preserved in the most famous of English biographies, *The Life of Samuel Johnson*, by James Boswell, a Scottish writer with an appetite for literary celebrities. Johnson worked his way up from poverty by honest literary labors, among which was his *Dictionary of the English Language*, which he worked hard on for 7 years.

1.4 The Romantic Period (1785-1830)

Extending from about 1785 until 1830, the romantic age[19] stressed emotion over reason. The romantic age in English literature was characterized by the subordination of reason to intuition and passion, the primacy of the individual will over social norms of behavior, and the interest in what is distant in time and place.

1.4.1 Poetry

The first important expression of romanticism was in the *Lyrical Ballads*[20] of William Wordsworth and Samuel Taylor Coleridge. In its preface, Wordsworth stated his belief that poetry results from the spontaneous overflow of powerful feeling; it is viewed as romantic poetry's "Declaration of Independence". Coleridge's main contribution, *The Rime of the Ancient Mariner*, masterfully creates an illusion of reality in relating strange, exotic, or obviously unreal events.

For William Wordsworth (1770-1850) the great theme remained the world of simple, natural things, in the countryside or among people. Wordsworth's great works include his long poem *The Prelude* and short poem *I Wandered Lonely as a Cloud.*

A second generation of romantic poets scorned social convention and often used poetry as a political voice. They brought the Romantic Movement to its height.

George Gordon Byron (1788-1824), known as Lord Byron, is one of the exemplars of a personality in tragic revolt against society. His masterpiece is *Don Juan*[21]. Byronic hero, who is a proud, mysterious rebel figure of noble origin, is Byron's chief contribution to the world literature. Byron's satirical spirit and strong sense of social realism kept him apart from other English romantics.

The other great poet-revolutionary of the time, Percy Bysshe Shelley (1792-1822), seems much closer to the serious spirit of the other romantics. His most thoughtful poetry expresses his two main ideas, that the external cruelty of rulers, customs, or superstitions is the main enemy, and that inherent human goodness will, sooner or later, remove evil from the world. It is, perhaps, in his masterpiece *Prometheus Unbound*[22] that these ideas are most completely expressed.

1.4.2 Prose

The works of the majority prose writers in this period were characterized by a "more personal and intimate tone", which is called familiar essay. They were no longer afraid of talking about their personal life and opinions.

Charles Lamb (1775-1834), an English writer whose retellings of the classic works of literature especially that of Shakespeare's tales, is still popular today. Lamb remained single and devoted his whole life caring for his sister, Mary Ann Lamb, who had suffered from insanity. Lamb is best known for his occasional essays, *the Essays of Elia* [23].

1.5 The Victorian Era (1837-1901)

The Victorian era[24], from the coronation of Queen Victoria in 1837 until her death in 1901, was an era of several unsettling social developments that forced writers to take positions on the immediate issues inspiring the rest of society.

1.5.1 Novel

The Victorian era was the great age of the English novel—realistic, thickly plotted, crowded with characters, and long. The dominant feature of Victorian novels might be their close representation to the real social life of the age—Realism.

Charles Dickens (1812-1870) was the greatest English realist and wrote numerous novels including his most autobiographical *David Copperfield.* He is considered as the spokesman for the poor, for he brought much attention to the oppressed and the have-nots. His first novel *The Pickwick Papers* made him famous at the age of twenty-four. Next after *The Pickwick Papers* came *Oliver Twist*, the story of an orphan child drawn into crime in the London **underworld** only later to discover the error of his ways through the love and understanding of an older mentor. Of the others, *Bleak House*, and *A Tale of Two Cities* are among the best.

For the first time in English history, female authors assumed a central role.

Jane Austen (1775-1817) first gave novel its modern character through the treatment of everyday life. The most urgent task of her bright, young heroines is **courtship** and finally marriage. Austen herself never married. Her best-known books include *Sense and Sensibility, Pride and Prejudice* and *Emma*[25].

The story of the three Bronte sisters—Charlotte (1816-1855), Emily (1818-1848) and Anne (1820-1849)[26], all talented and all dead young, is one of the saddest pages in the history of English literature. The Brontes tried writing fiction to pour out their pent-up emotions. A novel by each sister appeared in 1847: *Jane Eyre* by Charlotte, aged 31; *Wuthering Heights* by Emily, aged 29; and *Agnes Grey* by Anne, aged 27.

George Eliot is the pen name of Mary Ann Evans (1819-1880), a gifted woman writer who adopted a masculine name in order to survive in a male-dominated world. Her novels are about lives of ordinary people and their day-to-day problems of survival. Her masterpiece *Middlemarch* is noted for its realism.

Thomas Hardy (1840-1928)[27], is one of the representatives of English critical realism at the turn of the 19th century. He has preferred to deal chiefly with persons in the middle and poorer classes of society. He believes in fatalism—that man has no control over his fate. In Hardy's works, the pessimistic interpretation of modern science is expressed frankly and fully. *Far from the Madding Crowd* and *The Return of the Native* are among his best novels, though the sensational frankness of *Tess of the D'Urbervilles* has given it greater reputation.

1.5.2 Drama

The spirit of social criticism inspired the plays of the Irish-born George Bernard Shaw (1856-1950)[28]. A powerful public speaker with great wit, Shaw was awarded the Nobel Prize for Literature in 1925. He exposed in his plays the sickness and stupidity of individuals and societies in England. His masterpiece is *Saint Joan* but he is best-known for *Pygmalion*, and musical *My Fair Lady*.

1.5.3 Neo-Romanticism and Aestheticism

Other literary trends prevailed at the end of the 19th century, such as neo-romanticism[29] and aestheticism[30]. Dissatisfied with the ugly social reality, and yet trying to avoid the positive solution of the acute social contradictions, some writers led the novel back toward storytelling and romance. This new trend is known as neo-romanticism. Robert Louis Stevenson (1850-1894) is one of its representatives. His *Treasure Island* thrilled readers young and old.

Aestheticism is the belief that artists have no obligation other than to strive for beauty—"art for art's sake", which means that art is to be enjoyed for its own sake, rather than any moral message it might seem to contain. The works of these aesthetes are characterized by profuse use of symbols. The most important artist associated with aestheticism in England is Oscar Wilde (1854-1900). *The Picture of Dorian Gray*, a novel full of descriptions of the depraved life and divided personality of a young man is the only published novel by Oscar Wilde.

1.6 20th Century Literature (1914-1999)

The 20th century English literature can be roughly divided into two periods: modernism and postmodernism.

Modernism in literature began before the Second World War. Modernist writers express the difficulty they see in understanding and communicating how the world works. Modernist writing seems disorganized and hard to understand.

Postmodernism generally refers to literature after the Second World War. It's characterized by a high degree of experimentation. George Orwell's *1984* marks the beginning postmodernism in English literature. The horrors of the Second World War weakened ideas of human progress, and of meaning in life. One of the characteristics of postmodernism is to give up the search for meaning in life. So while modernists were scientists of human existence, looking for buried meaning below confusing surfaces, postmodernists can be thought of as abandoning that search.

1.6.1 Post-World War I Fiction

Joseph Conrad (1857-1924) is one of the most famous English modernist writers. Polish-born, Conrad was brought up in Poland and was in his twenties before he knew any English. After becoming a British subject, he wrote brilliant novels in his adopted tongue. His most well-known novel is *The Heart of Darkness*.

Virginia Woolf (1882-1941)[31] is regarded as a modernist writer and one of the most famous writers of the century. In her writing, she uses the technique called the stream of consciousness which tells the story through a continuous flow of ideas, thoughts, and feelings, as they are experienced by the main character. It is usually regarded as a special form of interior monologue and is characterized by associative leaps in sentence structure and punctuation that can make the prose difficult to follow, tracing a character's disconnected thoughts and sensory feelings. One of her best novels is *Mrs. Dalloway*.

James Joyce (1882-1941), an Irish novelist, poet and short-story writer, is famous for *Ulysses*. In *Ulysses*, he focused on the events of a single day and related them to one another in thematic patterns based on Greek mythology.

D.H. Lawrence (1885-1930) was one of the most famous modernist writers in English literature. His novels were critical of the modern world, especially of the modern industrial society. One of the features of his writings is that his language is easy and sentences are short. His best known novels and short stories are *Sons and Lovers*, *Women in Love* and *Lady Chatterley's Lover*.

1.6.2 Fiction after World War II

George Orwell (1903-1950) wrote one of the most famous novels *1984* in the postwar period in English. It is set in an extremely unpleasant England ruled absolutely by "Big Brother". This depressing story is characteristic of the postwar years.

William Golding (1911-1993)[32] is one of the 20th century's greatest novelists. In 1983 he was awarded the Nobel Prize for literature. His allegorical *Lord of the Flies*, published when Golding was 43, gained him international success. It is a terrifying story that tells how a group of British school boys stranded on a desert island in the wake of a nuclear war.

V.S. Naipaul (1932-2018)[33] won the Nobel Prize for literature in 2001. From his long period of travels in the 1960s and early 1970s in India, South-America, Africa, Iran, Pakistan, Malaysia and the U.S., Naipaul produced *India: A Wounded Civilization*, and *A Bend in the River*, a pessimistic novel about Africa, proclaiming the corruptibility of mankind. Central themes in Naipaul's works are damaging effects of colonialism upon the people of the Third World.

1.6.3 Modern Poetry

Two of the most remarkable poets of the modern period, William Butler Yeats and T. S. Eliot combined tradition and experiment in their works.

William Butler Yeats (1865-1939)[34], an Irish poet, dramatist and prose writer, was more traditional. In his romantic poetry, written before the turn of the century, he exploited ancient Irish traditions and then gradually developed a powerfully honest, profound, and rich poetic idiom, at its maturity in *The Tower* and *The Winding Stair*. He won the Nobel Prize for Literature in 1923.

The younger poet, T. S. Eliot (1888-1965), born in America, achieved more immediate acclaim with *The Waste Land*. It is a long poem that caught the mood of despair and confusion felt by many people during the years between the two World Wars when everything seemed to be changing and uncertain. The poem remains one of the great works of 20th-century literature although it is very difficult to understand.

1.6.4 Modern Drama

Harold Pinter (1930-2008)[35], the recipient of the 2005 Nobel Prize in literature, wrote plays set in a working-class environment. His plays are noted for the use of silence to increase tension and to suggest that unknown truths are being avoided. His famous play, *The Birthday Party*, deals with an ordinary man who is threatened by strangers for an unknown reason.

Outside the literary mainstream was the Irish-born novelist-dramatist Samuel Beckett (1906-1989)[36], recipient in 1969 of the Nobel Prize for literature. His plays are concerned with human suffering and survival, and his characters are struggling with meaninglessness and the world of the Nothing. His most famous work is the play *Waiting for Godot*.

1.7 21th Century Literature (2000-)

As the 21st century got under way, history remained the outstanding concern of English literature. Although contemporary issues such as global warming and international conflict received attention, writers were still more disposed to look back.

Bennett's play *The History Boys* (filmed 2006) premiered in 2004 at the Royal National Theatre in London and it portrayed pupils in a school in the north of England during the 1980s. Although *Cloud Atlas*—a far-reaching book by David Mitchell (1969-), one of the more ambitious novelists to emerge during this period—contains chapters that describe future eras damaged by malign technology and climactic and nuclear devastation, it devotes more space to scenes set in the 19th and early 20th centuries. In doing so, it also displays another preoccupation of the 21st century's early years: the imitation of earlier literary styles and techniques. There was a marked vogue for **pastiche** and revisionary Victorian novels. McEwan's *Atonement* worked masterly variations on the 1930s fictional procedures of authors such as Elizabeth Bowen. In *Saturday*, the model of Virginia Woolf's fictional presentation of a war-shadowed day in London in *Mrs. Dalloway* stood behind McEwan's vivid depiction of that city on Feb. 15, 2003, a day of mass demonstrations against the impending war in Iraq. Heaney continued to revisit the rural world of his youth in the poetry collections *Electric Light* and *District and Circle* while also reexamining and reworking classic texts, a striking instance of which was *The Burial at Thebes*, which infused Sophocles' *Antigone* with contemporary resonances. Although they had entered into a new millennium, writers seemed to find greater imaginative stimulus in the past than in the present and the future.

2. Arts

The British people began to be engaged in the artistic activity during the Anglo-Saxon times, and with the development of the society, the British people have achieved great feasts in arts.

2.1 Architecture

British architecture has made an international impact in the field of architectural planning and designing. Widely dispersed in corners of Britain, the architectural wonders are representatives of particular periods in the history of Britain.

2.1.1 Norman Architecture

Norman architecture actually features the styles of Romanesque architecture that dominated during the 11th and 12th centuries. Numerous castles, **fortifications**, churches, abbeys and cathedrals with round arched windows and doorways fall under this architectural pattern.

2.1.2 Gothic Architecture

Gothic architectural form was mainly propounded in Britain by Thomas Rickman (1776-1841).

Buildings under this style show significant French influence. Its characteristic features include the pointed arch, the ribbed vault and the flying buttress. Wells Cathedral, Salisbury Cathedral and Bath Abbey are some examples of this architecture.

2.1.3 Anglo-Saxon Architecture

Although Anglo-Saxon Architecture is not predominant in Britain at present, some unique constructions are found dating back to 600-725 or 900-1050.

2.2 Movies

The industry of British movies is characterized by remarkably high artistic excellence. The British film industry also exhibits a high level of technology that is clearly projected on screen. Many worldwide **blockbuster**s like the Harry Potter film series[37] and the animation super grosser *Chicken Run*[38] were conceptualized, directed, made, and post-produced in Britain.

2.2.1 Beginnings

The first British film was shot by William Friese Greene in 1889. It was, however, a non-commercial piece. The first commercial film was *Incident at Clovelly Cottage* in 1895. The medium attracted investors resulting in a number of British films being produced at that time.

2.2.2 Between the Wars

The period between the two World Wars saw the British film industry slide into decline. This was largely the effect of the United States film industry marketing in British audiences. The period also announced the beginning of talkies[39], films that made with sound. Alfred Hitchcock directed *Blackmail*—the first British film with concurrent sound. The 1930s saw the emergence of British documentary films.

2.2.3 War Aftermath

The end of World War II saw British films being made primarily for the domestic audience. The films produced in Britain showcased the heroism of British soldiers during the Second World War.

The 1950s saw a large number of comedy films like the *Doctor in the House* and *Genevieve* being made in Britain. The latter years of the decade saw horror films like *Dracula* and *Frankenstein* being shot.

The 1960s were a happy period for British cinema. The film industry saw the emergence of spy films that achieved box office successes worldwide. The James Bond film franchise emerged at that time.

2.2.4 Decline

The 1970s saw a decline in British cinema. This was largely the offshoot of the economic recession. Richard Attenborough made two films—*A Bridge Too Far* and *Young Winston* in this period.

2.2.5 Re-emergence of the British Film Industry

The 1990s saw British cinema gaining a new confidence in the world stage. Films like *Lock, Stock and Two Smoking Barrels* and *The Full Monty* achieved stunning success worldwide. Many North American film companies also began to shoot their films in Britain.

The turn of the millennium saw British cinema increasingly starting to look for newer pastures in film-making. Cartoon blockbusters like *The Curse of the Were-Rabbit* were made in 2005. Independent film production companies like Working Title shot and marketed many British blockbusters like *Love Actually* and *The Last King of Scotland* around the world.

2.3 British Folk Music

Traditional British music has its roots in the rich folk traditions of England, Wales and Scotland. Each region had its own folk tradition, which has been handed down over centuries. However, it was from the 1960s onwards that Britain started to feature as one of the strongest forces in the world of music, following the rock and roll revolution.

2.3.1 English Folk Music

England has a long and diverse history of folk music dating back at least to the medieval period and including many forms of music, song and dance. Much of the tradition has been preserved and continues to be practiced. It led to the creation of a number of fusions with other forms of music that produced sub-genres such as electric folk, folk punk[40] and folk metal.

2.3.2 Northern Irish Music

Northern Ireland (along with the Republic of Ireland) has vibrant folk traditions. The popularity of traditional instruments such as fiddles has remained throughout the centuries even as those in Great Britain died out.

2.3.3 Scottish Folk Music

Scottish folk music includes many kinds of songs, including ballads and **lament**s, sung by a single singer with accompaniment by bagpipes[41], fiddles or harps[42].

2.3.4 Welsh Folk Music

Welsh music includes male voice choirs and songs accompanied by a harp. Having long been subordinate to English culture, Welsh musicians in the late 20th century had to reconstruct traditional music when a roots revival began. This revival achieved some mainstream success in the UK in the 1980s.

2.4 British Theater

British theaters are recognized worldwide for their splendid quality. The British stage has seen works for great playwrights and performances from the best actors from all over the world.

2.4.1 Early British Theater

The theaters that were performed in Britain during medieval times served the purpose of educating their audiences of the power of God. The passage of time, however, made British theater increasingly secular.

The first of the British theater buildings in the middle of the 16th century was made of timber with thatched roofs. Majority of the public theaters had a rounded internal layout for better **acoustic** effects. The lowest ticket price was fixed at 1 penny.

Earlier British theaters featured only male actors. A number of noted male actors specialized in playing female roles. Another distinct feature of the earlier British theaters was the sheer **prolificacy** and the consequent low repetition of plays.

2.4.2 Modern British Theater Venues

Modern British theaters cater to the mass audience by performing acts that are believed to be more acceptable to the modern British audience. Musical theater is very popular. Other contemporary British theater genres include Showcase Theater and Community Theater. These theaters are less commercial.

2.5 Art Galleries

Most Britain art galleries do not charge visitors a fee to view the exhibits. Both government and private art galleries exist in the country. The National Gallery in London is counted as one of the premier art display areas in the world.

The Britain art galleries are known for their extensive collection of traditional as well as contemporary art. The government-owned art galleries in Britain display art with a non-profit motive. The privately owned art galleries of Britain display art with profit as one of the primary motives. Paintings and sculptures are publicly displayed so that they may be bought by potential interested buyers. No entry charges are applicable to gain entry to both private and government art galleries.

2.6 British Crafts

The British crafts are known for their unique designs. The modern British crafts are made from relatively exotic base materials like pearls, silver and gold. High quality leather items are also lovingly made. Items painstakingly made from sycamore[43] and maple trees are also sold.

Joyful Moment

Lord Byron's Gift

Byron once gave his publisher, John Murray, a splendidly bound Bible, and the recipient was proud of it until he happened to discover that his friend donor had altered the last verse of the 18th chapter of St. John so as to read: "Now Barrabas was a publisher." (Now Barrabas was a robber)

Notes

[1] *Beowulf*《贝奥伍甫》，古英语英雄叙事长诗
[2] Geoffrey Chaucer 杰弗里·乔叟，英国中世纪著名作家
[3] *The Canterbury Tales*《坎特伯雷故事集》
[4] Canterbury Cathedral 坎特伯雷座堂，英国最古老、最著名的基督教建筑之一
[5] Renaissance 文艺复兴，被认为是中古时代和近代的分界
[6] sonnet 十四行诗，欧洲一种格律严谨的抒情诗体
[7] chronicle play 历史剧，编年史剧
[8] Stratford-upon-Avon 埃文河畔斯特拉特福，威廉·莎士比亚的故乡
[9] *A Midsummer Night's Dream*, *The Merchant of Venice*, *As You Like It* and *Twelfth Night* 莎士比亚四大喜剧：《仲夏夜之梦》《威尼斯商人》《皆大欢喜》《第十二夜》
[10] *Hamlet*, *Othello*, *King Lear* and *Macbeth* 莎士比亚四大悲剧：《哈姆雷特》《奥赛罗》《李尔王》和《麦克白》
[11] Spenserian Stanza 斯宾塞诗体，每诗节九行，诗格数不限
[12] neo-classical period 英语文学的新古典主义时期
[13] the Stuarts 斯图亚特王室
[14] *Paradise Lost*《失乐园》，弥尔顿的一部史诗
[15] poet laureate 桂冠诗人，起于英国颁给优秀诗人的称号
[16] *The Rape of the Lock*《秀发劫》（《夺发记》），亚历山大·蒲柏的代表作
[17] *Gulliver's Travels* 乔纳森·斯威夫特的经典讽刺小说《格列佛游记》
[18] *Robinson Crusoe* 丹尼尔·笛福的《鲁滨逊漂流记》
[19] romantic age 英语文学的浪漫主义时期
[20] *Lyrical Ballads*《抒情歌谣集》，收录了华兹华斯著名的《丁登寺》（*Tintern Abbey*）和柯勒律治的巨作《古舟子咏》（*The Rime of the Ancient Mariner*）
[21] *Don Juan*《唐·璜》，19 世纪英国著名的诗人拜伦的长篇诗体小说
[22] *Prometheus Unbound*《解放了的普罗米修斯》，英国浪漫主义诗人雪莱的诗剧，取材于古希腊罗马神话
[23] *Essays of Elia*《伊利亚随笔》，英国著名作家查尔斯·兰姆的随笔作品
[24] The Victorian era 维多利亚时代
[25] *Sense and Sensibility*, *Pride and Prejudice*, *Emma* 简·奥斯汀的三部小说《理智与情感》《傲慢与偏见》《爱玛》
[26] Bronte sisters 布朗特三姐妹，夏洛特·布朗特、艾米莉·布朗特、安妮·布朗特。其代表作分别为《简爱》《呼啸山庄》和《阿格尼斯·格雷》

[27] Thomas Hardy 托马斯·哈代，英国诗人、小说家，作品有《远离尘嚣》《还乡》和《德伯家的苔丝》

[28] Bernard Shaw 伯纳德·肖（萧伯纳），爱尔兰剧作家，获 1925 年诺贝尔文学奖，其喜剧作品《卖花女》（*Pygmalion*）被好莱坞改编为卖座电影《窈窕淑女》

[29] neo-romanticism 新浪漫主义

[30] Aestheticism 唯美主义，提倡“为艺术而艺术”，强调超然于生活的纯粹美

[31] Virginia Woolf 弗吉尼亚·伍尔芙，英国女作家，批判家，意识流小说的代表人物之一，代表作《达洛维夫人》

[32] William Golding 威廉·戈尔丁，英国小说家，著有长篇小说《蝇王》

[33] V.S. Naipaul 印度裔英国作家 V.S.奈保尔，著有《印度：受伤的文明》

[34] William Butler Yeats 威廉·巴特勒·叶芝，爱尔兰诗人，著有《塔楼》

[35] Harold Pinter 哈罗德·品特，英国剧作家及剧场导演

[36] Samuel Beckett 塞缪尔·贝克特，爱尔兰作家，著有《等待戈多》

[37] Harry Potter film series《哈利·波特》电影系列

[38] Chicken Run 动画片《小鸡快跑》

[39] talkies 有声电影

[40] folk punk 民谣朋克

[41] bagpipe 风笛

[42] harp 竖琴

[43] sycamore 小无花果树；大枫树

New Words

1. **pilgrimage** /'pɪlgrɪmɪdʒ/ *n.* a journey to a sacred place 朝圣
   —The Muslim delegation is shortly going on a pilgrimage to Mecca.
   这个穆斯林代表团很快就要去麦加朝圣了。
2. **elusive** /ɪ'luːsɪv/ *a.* difficult to find, describe, remember, or achieve 难懂的，难以捉摸的
   —She did not know; it was too subtle and elusive to name.
   她不知道，这太微妙难以言喻。
3. **redemption** /rɪ'dempʃən/ *n.* the act of saving or state of being saved from the power of evil; the act of redeeming 拯救；救赎
   —The boy is beyond redemption.
   这个男孩子不可救药了。
4. **progenitor** /prəʊ'dʒenɪtə/ *n.* a person who starts an idea or a development 创始人，先驱
   —Arnold Schoenberg was a progenitor of modern music.
   勋伯格是一位现代音乐的先驱。
5. **underworld** /'ʌndəwɜːld/ *n.* the people and activities involved in crime in a particular place 黑社会；黑道

—That quiet man was an underworld kingpin.
那个安静的人是个黑社会老大哥。

6. **courtship** /'kɔːtʃɪp/ *n.* the time when two people have a romantic relationship before they get married; the process of developing this relationship 求爱期；求爱，追求
—He won her heart after a brief courtship.
经过短时期的追求，他赢得了她的芳心。

7. **pastiche** /pæs'tiːʃ/ *n.* a piece of art, music, literature, etc. that intentionally copies the style of someone else's work or is intentionally in various styles, or the practice of making art in either of these ways（艺术、音乐、文学作品等的）模仿作品
—The movie is a skilful, witty pastiche of "Jaws".
该影片是对《大白鲨》巧妙而诙谐的模仿。

8. **fortification** /ˌfɔːtɪfɪ'keɪʃən/ *n.* a tower, wall, gun position, etc. built to defend a place against attack 碉堡，围墙，炮台，防御工事
—These fortifications were built during the last war.
这些防御工事是上次战争时修建的。

9. **blockbuster** /'blɒkˌbʌstə/ *n.* something very successful, especially a very successful book or film/movie 一鸣惊人的事物，（尤指）非常成功的书或电影
—That new movie is a blockbuster.
那部新片是部大片。

10. **lament** /lə'ment/ *n.* a song, poem or other expression of great sadness for sb who has died or for sth that has ended 挽歌，哀诗，悼辞
—Short pleasure, long lament.
痛快一时，痛苦一世。

11. **acoustic** /ə'kuːstɪk/ *a.* related to sound or to the sense of hearing 声音的，音响的，听觉的
—The company has come up with a new acoustic-optical device.
这家公司已制造出一种新的声光装置。

12. **prolificacy** /prə'lɪfɪkəsɪ/ *n.* great fertility; producing of a large number of literary or artistic works（文学或艺术作品的）多产
—He is famous for prolificacy.
他以多产而闻名。

Exercises

1. Choose the correct answer.

1) Of the following books, ________ is not included in Shakespeare's tragedies.
A. *Hamlet* B. *Othello*
C. *Antony and Cleopatra* D. *King Lear*

2) *Lyrical Ballads* is composed by William Wordsworth in collaboration with________.

A. Coleridge B. Southey C. Blake D. Byron

3) Of Dickens' novels, ________ is considered autobiographical.

A. *A Tale of Two Cities* B. *Bleak House*

C. *Oliver Twist* D. *David Copperfield*

4) Daniel Defoe's fictitious story ________ reports the life and adventures of a shipwrecked sailor.

A. *Robinson Crusoe* B. *Gulliver's Travels*

C. *Life on the Mississippi* D. *The Adventures of Tom Sawyer*

5) The Victorian era was the great age of the English—realistic, thickly plotted, crowded with characters, and long ________.

A. drama B. poetry C. novel D. prose

2. Decide whether the following statements are True or False.

1) *The Canterbury Tales* is a representative work of the Old English Period.

2) John Dryden is regarded as "the father of English criticism".

3) The romantic age stressed reason over emotion.

4) Charles Dickens (1812-1870) was the greatest English realist.

5) Postmodernism generally refers to literature after the World War I.

3. Fill in the blanks according to the passage.

1) The most important work of Old English literature is________.

2) In Hardy's works, the ________interpretation of modern science is expressed frankly and fully.

3) ________, who is a proud, mysterious rebel figure of noble origin, is Byron's chief contribution to the world literature.

4) The National Gallery is located in________.

5) The British crafts are known for their unique ________.

4. Explain the following terms according to the passage.

1) Stream of consciousness

2) Aestheticism

3) Modernism in literature

4) Postmodernism in literature

5) Gothic architecture

5. Answer the following questions according to the passage.

1) Describe the features of the earlier British theater.

2) How did the British film industry re-emerge?

3) Explain Shakespeare's great contribution to English literature.

6. Discussion.

1) Three years before the publication of *Oliver Twist*, the British Parliament passed a controversial amendment to the nation's "poor-laws". This amendment stipulated that the poor could receive public assistance only if they lived in official workhouses and abided by their regulations. In these workhouses, husbands were separated from wives, and living conditions were often very poor. Behind the establishment of workhouses were the assumptions that moral virtue lay in work, that work led necessarily to success, that economic failure was the result of laziness, and that, therefore, poverty was a sign of moral degeneracy. Read Chapter 2 of *Oliver Twist* which describes the conditions in the workhouse to which the orphan Oliver has just been sent and discuss Charles Dickens's opinion of the nation's "poor-laws".

2) Read the following poem and think about the questions.

Daffodils

I wandered lonely as a cloud
That floats on high o'er vales and hills,
When all at once I saw a crowd,
A host, of golden daffodils;
Beside the lake, beneath the trees,
Fluttering and dancing in the breeze.

Continuous as the stars that shine
And twinkle on the Milky Way,
They stretched in never-ending line
Along the margin of a bay;
Ten thousand saw I at a glance,
Tossing their heads in sprightly dance.

The waves beside them danced; but they
Out-did the sparkling waves in glee;
A poet could not but be gay,
In such a jocund company;
I gazed—and gazed—but little thought
What wealth the show to me had brought;

For oft, when on my couch I lie
In vacant or in pensive mood,
They flash upon that inward eye

Which is the bliss of solitude;
And then my heart with pleasure fills,
And dances with the daffodils.

Questions:

a) What did the poet see?

b) With what does the poet compare the daffodils?

c) What resemblance does he find between the stars and the daffodils?

d) How can the heart dance?

e) In the poem how does Wordsworth achieve the seemingly effortless effect of implying the unity of his consciousness with nature?

Stay Positive

1. It is awfully easy to be hard-boiled about everything in the daytime, but at night it is another thing.
2. If you spend too much time thinking about a thing, you'll never get it done.

Part Two
The United States of America

Chapter 1

Introduction to the United States of America

Progress is the activity of today and the assurance of tomorrow.

—Emerson, American thinker

1. Introduction

The United States of America (commonly referred to as the United States, the U.S., the USA, or America) is a federal constitutional republic comprising 50 states and a federal district. The country is situated mostly in central North America, where its 48 **contiguous** states and Washington D.C., the capital district, lie between the Pacific and Atlantic Oceans, bordered by Canada to the north and Mexico to the south. The state of Alaska is in the northwest of the continent, with Canada to its east and Russia to the west across the Bering Strait. The state of Hawaii is an **archipelago** in the mid-Pacific. The country also possesses several territories, or **insular** areas, in the Caribbean and the Pacific.

The United States is the third or fourth largest country by total area and the third largest by land area and population. The United States is one of the world's most **ethnically** diverse and multicultural nations, the product of large-scale immigration from many countries. The U.S. economy is the largest national economy in the world. U.S. nominal GDP was $19.5 trillion in 2017. Annualized nominal GDP reached $20.5 trillion in 2018, the first time it exceeded the $20 trillion level.

The nation was founded by thirteen colonies of Great Britain located along the Atlantic seaboard. On July 4, 1776, they issued the Declaration of Independence, proclaimed their independence from Great Britain and their formation of a cooperative union. The rebellious states defeated Great Britain in the American Revolutionary War, the first successful colonial war of independence. The Philadelphia Convention adopted the current United States Constitution on September 17, 1787; its **ratification** the following year made the states part of a single republic with a strong central government. The Bill of Rights, comprising ten constitutional amendments guaranteeing many fundamental civil rights and freedoms, was ratified in 1791.

In the 19th century, the United States acquired land from France, Spain, the United Kingdom, Mexico, and Russia, and **annexed** the Republic of Texas[1] and the Republic of Hawaii[2]. Disputes between the **agrarian** South and industrial North over states' rights and the expansion of the institution of slavery provoked the American Civil War of the 1860s. The North's victory prevented a permanent split of the country and led to the end of legal slavery in the United States. By the 1870s, the national economy was the world's largest. The Spanish-American War and World War I confirmed the country's status as a military power. In 1945, the United States emerged from World War II as the first country with nuclear weapons, a permanent member of the United Nations Security Council, and a founding member of NATO. The end of the Cold War and the **dissolution** of the Soviet Union left the United States as the sole superpower. The country accounts for approximately a third of global military spending and is a leading political and cultural and scientific force in the world.

2. Location and Area

2.1 Location

The United States is a country in the Western Hemisphere[3]. It consists of 48 contiguous states on the North American continent, Alaska, an enormous **peninsula** which forms the northwestern most part of North America, and Hawaii, an archipelago in the Pacific Ocean. It also holds several United States territories in the Pacific and Caribbean. The term "United States", when used in the geographical sense, means the continental United States, Alaska, Hawaii, Puerto Rico, Guam, and the Virgin Islands[4] of the United States. The country shares land borders with Canada and Mexico and water borders with Russia, the United Kingdom, and the Bahamas.

2.2 Area

The total area of the US is 9,629,091 square kilometers given by the United Nations Statistics Division (Great Lakes area included but not coastal waters). These sources consider only the 50 states and the Federal District, and exclude overseas territories.

Both China and the United States follow behind Canada and Russia in total area, and are followed by Brazil. By land area (exclusive of waters), the United States is the world's third largest country, following Russia and China. In total area (including inland water), Russia and Canada are larger than the United States. Ranking for third-largest status is disputed. Some sources (including Encyclopedia Britannica and all publications of the People's Republic of China), list China as larger than the U.S. Many other sources list the U.S. as larger. The dispute appears to **hinge** on the inland of Taiwan, without which China takes fourth place. But it is a plain fact that Taiwan is an inseparable part of China, an offshore province just like Hainan.

3. Climate

Due to its large size and wide range of geographic features, the United States contains examples of nearly every global climate. The climate is temperate in most areas, tropical in Hawaii and southern Florida, polar in Alaska, semiarid in the Great Plains west of the 100th meridian, Mediterranean in coastal California and arid in the Great Basin. Its comparatively generous climate contributed (in part) to the country's rise as a world power, with infrequent severe drought in the major agricultural regions, a general lack of widespread flooding, and a mainly temperate climate that receives adequate **precipitation**.

The main influence on U.S. weather is the polar jet stream, which brings in large low pressure systems from the northern Pacific Ocean. The Cascade Range, Sierra Nevada, and Rocky Mountains pick up most of the moisture from these systems as they move eastward. Greatly **diminished** by the time they reach the High Plains, much of the moisture has been **sapped** by the orographic effect as it is forced over several mountain ranges. However, once it moves over the Great Plains, uninterrupted flat land allows it to reorganize and can lead to major clashes of air masses. In addition, moisture from the Gulf of Mexico is often drawn northward. When combined with a powerful jet stream, this can lead to violent thunderstorms, especially during spring and summer. Sometimes during late winter and spring these storms can combine with another low pressure system as they move up the East Coast and into the Atlantic Ocean, where they intensify rapidly. These storms are known as Northeasters and often bring widespread, heavy snowfall to the Mid-Atlantic and New England. The uninterrupted flat grasslands of the Great Plains also leads to some of the most extreme climate swings in the world. Temperatures can rise or drop rapidly and winds can be extreme, and the flow of heat waves or Arctic air masses often advance uninterrupted through the plains.

The Great Basin and Columbia Plateau (the Intermontane Plateaus) are arid or semiarid regions that lie in the rain shadow of the Cascades and Sierra Nevada. Precipitation averages less than 15 inches (38cm). The Southwest is a hot desert, with temperatures exceeding 100℉[5] (37.8℃) for several weeks at a time in summer. The Southwest and the Great Basin are also affected by the **monsoon** from the Gulf of California[6] from July to September, which brings localized but often severe thunderstorms to the region.

Much of California consists of a Mediterranean climate[7], with sometimes excessive rainfall from October to April and nearly no rain the rest of the year. In the Pacific Northwest rain falls year-round, but is much heavier during winter and spring. The mountains of the west receive abundant precipitation and very heavy snowfall. The Cascades[8] are one of the snowiest places in the world, with some places averaging over 600 inches (1,524cm) of snow annually, but the lower **elevations** closer to the coast receive very little snow. Another significant (but localized) weather effect is lake-effect snow that falls south and east of the Great Lakes, especially in the hilly portions of the Upper Peninsula of Michigan[9] and on the Tug Hill Plateau[10] in New York. The lake effect dumped well over 5 feet (1.52m) of snow in the Buffalo[11], New York area throughout the 2006-2007 winter. The Wasatch Front[12] and Wasatch Range[13] in Utah can also receive significant lake effect accumulations off of the Great Salt

Lake.

4. Topography

Deciduous **vegetation** and grasslands prevail in the east, transitioning to **prairies**, northern forests, and the Rockies in the west, and deserts in the southwest. In the northeast, the coasts of the Great Lakes and Atlantic seaboard host much of the country's population.

The United States shares land borders with Canada (to the north) and Mexico (to the south), and a territorial water border with Russia in the northwest. The contiguous 48 states are otherwise bounded by the Pacific Ocean on the west, the Atlantic Ocean on the east, and the Gulf of Mexico to the southeast. Alaska borders the Pacific Ocean to the south, the Bering Strait to the west, and the Arctic Ocean to the north, while Hawaii lies far to the southwest of the mainland in the Pacific Ocean.

Forty-eight of the States are in the single region between Canada and Mexico; this group is referred to, with varying **precision** and **formality**, as the **continental** or contiguous United States, and as the Lower 48. Alaska, which is not included in the term contiguous United States, is at the northwestern end of North America, separated from the Lower 48 by Canada. The State of Hawaii is an archipelago in the Pacific Ocean. The capital city, Washington, District of Columbia, is a federal district located on land donated by the state of Maryland. (Virginia had also donated land, but it was returned in 1849.) The United States also has overseas territories with varying levels of independence and organization.

5. Rivers and Lakes

The longest river in the in North America is the Missouri River. The Missouri River starts in Montana and covers 2,341 miles before flowing into the Mississippi River. The Missouri-Mississippi river system is the fourth longest in the world. The longest undammed river in the contiguous USA is the Yellowstone River at 692 miles in length.

5.1 Missouri River

The Missouri River[14], rising in the Rocky Mountains of western Montana, flows east and south for 2,341 miles (3,767 km) before entering the Mississippi River north of St. Louis, Missouri. The river takes **drainage** from a sparsely populated, semi-arid watershed of more than half a million square miles (1,300,000 km^2), which includes parts of ten U.S. states and two Canadian provinces. When combined with the lower Mississippi River, it forms the world's fourth longest river system.

For over 12,000 years, people have depended on the Missouri River and its **tributaries** as a source of sustenance and transportation. More than ten major groups of Native Americans populated the watershed, most leading a nomadic lifestyle and dependent on enormous bison herds that once roamed through the Great Plains. The first Europeans encountered the river in the late 17th century, and the region passed through Spanish and French hands before finally becoming part of the United States through the Louisiana Purchase[15]. The Missouri river was long believed to be part of the Northwest Passage—a water route from the Atlantic to the Pacific-but when Lewis and Clark became the first to travel the river's entire length, they confirmed the mythical pathway to be no more than a legend.

The Missouri River was one of the main routes for the westward expansion of the United States during the 19th century. The growth of the fur trade in the early 19th century laid much of the groundwork as trappers explored the region and blazed trails. Pioneers headed west in the 1830s, first by covered wagon, then by the growing numbers of steam boats entering service on the river. Former Native American lands in the watershed were taken over by settlers, leading to some of the most longstanding and violent wars against indigenous peoples in American history.

During the 20th century, the Missouri River basin was extensively developed for irrigation, flood control and the generation of hydroelectric power. Fifteen dams impound the main stem of the river, with hundreds more on tributaries. **Meanders** have been cut and the river channelized to improve navigation, reducing its length by almost 200 miles (320 km) from pre-development times. Although the lower Missouri valley is now a populous and highly productive agricultural and industrial region, heavy development has taken its toll on wildlife and fish populations as well as water quality.

5.2 Mississippi River

The Mississippi River[16], with a length of 2,320 miles (3,730 km), flows entirely in the United States from its source in Lake Itasca[17] in Minnesota[18] to its mouth in the Gulf of Mexico[19].

Native Americans have lived along the Mississippi River and its tributaries for thousands of years. Most were hunter-gatherers, but some, such as the Mound Builders[20], formed prolific agricultural societies. The arrival of Europeans in the 16th century changed the native way of life as first explorers, then settlers, ventured into the basin in increasing numbers. The river served first as a barrier, forming borders for New Spain, New France, and the early United States, and then as a vital transportation artery and communications link.

Formed from thick layers of the river's silt deposits, the Mississippi **embayment** is one of the most fertile regions of the United States; steamboats were widely used in the 19th and early 20th centuries to ship agricultural and industrial goods. During the American Civil War[21], the Mississippi's capture by Union forces marked a turning point towards victory, due to the river's strategic importance to the Confederate war effort. Because of substantial growth of cities and the larger ships and barges that replaced steamboats, the first decades of the 20th century saw the construction of massive engineering works such as levees, locks and dams, often built in combination.

Since the 20th century, the Mississippi River has also experienced major pollution and environmental problems—most notably elevated **nutrient** and chemical levels from agricultural runoff, the primary contributor to the Gulf of Mexico dead zone.

5.3 Great Lakes

The Great Lakes[22], also called the Laurentian Great Lakes or the Great Lakes of North America, are a series of **interconnected** freshwater lakes primarily in the upper mid-east region of North America, on the Canada-United States border, which connect to the Atlantic Ocean through the Saint Lawrence River[23]. The Great Lakes consist of Lake Superior[24], Lake Michigan[25], Lake Huron[26], Lake Erie[27], and Lake Ontario[28], although **hydrologically**, there are four lakes, Lake Superior, Lake Erie, Lake Ontario, and Lake Michigan-Huron. The connected lakes form the Great Lakes Waterway[29].

The Great Lakes are the largest group of freshwater lakes on Earth by total area, and second-largest by total volume, containing 21% of the world's surface fresh water by volume. The total surface is 94,250 square miles (244,106 km^2), and the total volume (measured at the low water datum) is 5,439 cubic miles (22,671 km^3), slightly less than the volume of Lake Baikal[30] (23,615 km^3, 22-23% of the world's surface fresh water). Due to their sea-like characteristics (rolling waves, sustained winds, strong currents, great depths, and distant horizons) the Great Lakes have also long been referred to as inland seas. Lake Superior is the largest freshwater lake by surface area, and the third largest freshwater lake by volume. Lake Michigan is the only one of the five Great Lakes that is entirely within one country.

The Great Lakes began to form at the end of the last glacial period around 14,000 years ago, as retreating ice sheets exposed the basins they had carved into the land which then filled with melt water. The lakes have been a major source for transportation, migration, trade, and fishing, serving as a habitat to a large number of aquatic species in a region with much **biodiversity**.The surrounding region is called the Great Lakes region, which includes the Great Lakes Megalopolis[31].

6. Mountains and Hills

The Rocky Mountains[32], also known as the Rockies, are a major mountain range in western North America. The Rocky Mountains stretch more than 4,800 kilometers (3,000 mi) from the northernmost part of British Columbia, in western Canada, to New Mexico in the Southwestern United States. Located within the North American Cordillera[33], the Rockies are somewhat distinct from the Pacific Coast Ranges, Cascade Range[34], and the Sierra Nevada[35], which all lie farther to the west.

The Rocky Mountains formed 80 million to 55 million years ago, in which a number of plates began sliding underneath the North American plate. The angle of subduction was shallow, resulting in a broad belt of mountains running down western North America. Since then, further tectonic activity and erosion by glaciers have **sculpted** the Rockies into dramatic peaks and valleys. At the end of the last ice age, humans began inhabiting the mountain range. After Europeans, such as Sir Alexander Mackenzie[36], and Americans, such as the Lewis and Clark expedition[37], began the exploring of the range, minerals and furs, which drove the initial economic exploitation of the mountains, although the range itself never experienced dense population.

7. Population

The United States is the third most populous country in the world with an estimated population of 328,285,992 as of January 12, 2019. It is highly urbanized, with 82.3% of the population residing in cities and suburbs. Large urban clusters are spread throughout the eastern half of the United States (particularly the Great Lakes area, northeast, east, and southeast) and the western tier states; mountainous areas, principally the Rocky Mountains and Appalachian[38] chain, deserts in the southwest, the dense boreal forests in the extreme north, and the central prairie states are less densely populated; Alaska's population is concentrated along its southern coast—with particular emphasis on the city of Anchorage[39]—and Hawaii's population is centered on the island of Oahu[40]. California[41] and Texas[42] are the most populous states, as the mean center of U.S. population has consistently shifted westward and southward. New York City is the most populous city in the United States.

The United States Census Bureau[43] shows a population increase of 0.75% for the twelve-month period ending in July 2012. Though high by industrialized country standards, this is below the world average annual rate of 1.1%. The total fertility rate in the United States estimated for 2018 is 1.73 children per woman, which is below the replacement **fertility** rate of approximately 2.1.

The American population almost **quadrupled** during the 20th century—at a growth rate of about 1.3% a year—from about 76 million in 1900 to 281 million in 2000. It is estimated to have reached the 200 million mark in 1967, and the 300 million mark on October 17, 2006. Population growth is fastest among minorities as a whole, and according to the Census Bureau's estimation for 2012, 50.4% of American children under the age of 1 belonged to racial and ethnic minority groups.

White people constitute the majority of the U.S. population, with a total of about 245,532,000 or 77.7% of the population as of 2013. Non-Hispanic whites make up 62.6% of the country's population. In an official census report, it was reported that 54.4% (2,150,926 out of 3,953,593) of births in 2010 were non-Hispanic white. This represents an increase of 0.3% compared to the previous year, which was 54.1%. The non-Hispanic white population of the U.S. is expected to fall below 50% by 2045.

Hispanic and Latino Americans accounted for 48% of the national population growth of 2.9 million between July 1, 2005 and July 1, 2006. Immigrants and their U.S.-born descendants are expected to provide most of the U.S. population gains in the decades ahead. According to Pew Research Center study released in 2018, by 2040, Islam will surpass Judaism to become the second largest religion in the US due to higher immigration and birth rates.

The Census Bureau projects a U.S. population of 417 million in 2060, a 38% increase from

2007 (301.3 million), and the United Nations estimates the U.S. population will be 402 million in 2050, an increase of 32% from 2007.

8. Languages

The most commonly used language in the United States is English (specifically, American English), which is the de facto national language. Nonetheless, many other languages are also spoken, or historically have been spoken in the United States. These include indigenous languages, languages brought to the country by colonists, enslaved people and immigrants from Europe, Africa and Asia. There are also several languages, including creoles and sign languages, that developed in the United States. Approximately 430 languages are spoken or signed by the population, of which 176 are indigenous to the area. Fifty-two languages formerly spoken in the country's territory are now extinct.

The United States has never had an official language at the federal level. However, 32 states of the United States, in some cases as part of what has been called the English-only movement, have adopted legislation granting official status to English. Out of 50 states, 30 have established English as the only official language, while Hawaii recognizes both English and Hawaiian as official, and Alaska has made some 20 native languages official, along with English.

Moreover, English is one of the official languages in all of the U.S. territories. In Puerto Rico both English and Spanish are official, although Spanish has been declared the principal official language. The school system and the government operate almost entirely in Spanish.

English is the primary language used for legislation, regulations, executive orders, treaties, federal court rulings, and all other official **pronouncements**. Nonetheless, laws require documents such as ballots to be printed in multiple languages when there are large numbers of non-English speakers in an area. American schools, public as well as private, require English classes at every grade level, even in bilingual or dual-language learning situations. Semesters of English composition are compulsory in virtually all U.S. colleges and universities to satisfy requirements for associate's and bachelor's degrees.

Joyful Moment

Bedtime Prayers

Julie was saying her bedtime prayers. "Please God," she said, "Make Naples the capital of Italy. Make Naples the capital of Italy."

Her mother interrupted and said, "Julie, why do you want God to make Naples the capital of Italy?"

And Julie replied, "Because that's what I put in my geography exam!"

Notes

[1] Republic of Texas 德克萨斯共和国（1836—1845），德克萨斯共和国于 1836 年从墨西哥独立出来，国旗上只有一颗星，加入美国后被称为孤星州（lone star state）。德克萨斯到 1845 年才被接纳为美国的一个州。德克萨斯是唯一以独立国家身份加入联邦的，所以它是唯一有权利自行退出联邦的州，其他 49 个州在法律上没有这个权利。

[2] Republic of Hawaii 夏威夷共和国（1894—1898）。夏威夷王国是在 1810 年由瓦胡、毛伊、考爱、莫洛凯和夏威夷等岛屿的小型独立部落，在经过一场战争后统一而成的王国。1893 年，当地的美国人发动政变，软禁了夏威夷女王；1894 年，夏威夷共和国成立，夏威夷王国灭亡。1898 年夏威夷共和并入美国，成为美国的一个地区，1959 年成为美国的一个州。

[3] Western Hemisphere 西半球

[4] Virgin Islands of the U.S.美属维尔京群岛，位于大西洋的加勒比海，1917 年美国从丹麦购得，通用语为英语，多数人信奉基督教。

[5] ℉华氏温度计符号，是温度计量的一种。水的冰点为 32 度，沸点为 212 度，刻度方法是德国物理学家华伦海特制定的。

[6] Gulf of California 加利福尼亚湾，墨西哥西北的狭长海湾，太平洋深入北美大陆的狭长边缘海，位于墨西哥西北部和下加利福尼亚半岛之间，呈西北—东南走向，北窄南宽形似喇叭状，长约 1 200 千米，宽度 90～210 千米，面积约 16 万平方千米。

[7] mediterranean climate 地中海气候，亚热带、温带的一种气候类型，因地中海沿岸地区最典型而得名。地中海气候是由西风带与副热带高气压带交替控制形成的，在地中海地区，夏季受副热带高气压带控制，地中海水温相比陆地低，从而形成高压，加大了副热带高气压带的影响势力，冬季地中海的水温又相对较高，形成低压，吸引西风，又使西风的势力大大加强。夏季炎热干燥，高温少雨，冬季温和多雨。

[8] Cascades 喀斯喀特山脉，北美洲环太平洋海岸山脉的一部分，由南向北跨越加利福尼亚州、俄勒冈州、华盛顿州，延伸至加拿大的不列颠哥伦比亚省。

[9] Upper Peninsula of Michigan 密歇根州的上半岛。密歇根州由两大半岛组成，分隔两半岛的水面叫做麦基诺水道。南为下半岛，是该州的主体，面积较大。北部为上半岛，面积比下半岛小。

[10] Tug Hill Plateau 塔格山高原

[11] Buffalo 布法罗，又称水牛城，美国纽约州西部的城市

[12] Wasatch Front 瓦萨奇区

[13] Wasatch Range 瓦萨奇山脉，北起犹他州和爱达荷州交界处，南至犹他州中部

[14] Missouri River 密苏里河

[15] Louisiana Purchase 路易斯安那购置地，美国于 1803 年向法国购买超过 828 000 平方米的土地，总价为 1 500 万美元

[16] Mississippi River 密西西比河

[17] Lake Itasca 伊塔斯加湖

[18] Minnesota 明尼苏达州
[19] Gulf of Mexico 墨西哥湾
[20] Mound Builders 美国原始印第安人
[21] American Civil War 南北战争，又称美国内战
[22] Great Lakes 美国五大湖
[23] Saint Lawrence River 圣劳伦斯河
[24] Lake Superior 苏必利尔湖，北美五大湖中的第一大湖
[25] Lake Michigan 密歇根湖
[26] Lake Huron 休伦湖，北美五大湖中的第二大湖
[27] Lake Erie 伊利湖，北美五大湖之一
[28] Lake Ontario 安大略湖
[29] Great Lakes Waterway 北美大湖水道
[30] Lake Baikal 贝加尔湖，世界上最深的淡水湖
[31] Great Lakes Megalopolis 五大湖区城市群，是由一群位于北美洲，围绕大湖区的城市群。
[32] Rocky Mountains 落基山脉，位于北美洲的西部，北起加拿大西部的不列颠哥伦比亚，南至美国西南部的新墨西哥州，绵延超过 4800 千米
[33] North American Cordillera 是科迪勒拉山系（American Cordillera）位于北美的部分，科迪勒拉山系是世界上最长的褶皱山系
[34] Cascade Range 喀斯喀特山脉，北美洲环太平洋海岸山脉的一部分
[35] Sierra Nevada 内华达山脉，美国加利福尼亚州东部的花岗岩块状山脉
[36] Sir Alexander Mackenzie 亚历山大 • 麦肯齐爵士（1764–1820），出生于苏格兰，是第一位由东到西横跨北美的苏格兰探险家，比刘易斯与克拉克远征早 12 年
[37] Lewis and Clark expedition 刘易斯与克拉克远征（1804–1806）是美国国内首次横越大陆、西抵太平洋沿岸的考察活动。领队为美国陆军的梅里韦瑟 • 刘易斯上尉（Meriwether Lewis）和威廉 • 克拉克少尉（William Clark），该活动是由杰斐逊总统所发起。
[38] Appalachian 阿巴拉契亚山脉，指美国东部的纽约州南部、阿拉巴马州北部、密西西比州北部和佐治亚州北部一带
[39] Anchorage 安克雷奇，又译为安克拉治，是美国阿拉斯加州最大的城市，位于阿拉斯加中南部
[40] Oahu 瓦胡岛，夏威夷群岛的第三大岛，位于该岛东南角的火奴鲁鲁，是夏威夷州的首府
[41] California 加利福尼亚州，美国西部太平洋沿岸的一个州
[42] Texas 德克萨斯州，美国南方最大的州，也是全美第二大州，仅次于阿拉斯加州
[43] United States Census Bureau 美国人口普查局

New Words

1. **contiguous** /kən'tɪgjuəs/ *adj.* very close or connected in space or time 邻近的，连续的
—California and Mexico are contiguous.
加利福尼亚和墨西哥相邻。
2. **archipelago** /ˌɑːkɪ'peləgəu/ *n.* a group of islands in a large body of water 群岛，多岛海
3. **insular** /'ɪnsjulə/ *adj.* relating to or characteristic of or situated on an island 岛的，岛民的，岛特有的
4. **ethnically** /'eθnɪkli/ *adv.* with respect to ethnicity 人种上，民族上
5. **ratification** /ˌrætɪfɪ'keɪʃən/ *n.* making something valid by formally ratifying or confirming it 批准，认可
6. **annex** /'æneks/ *n.* 附加物，附属建筑 **annexed** *adj.* 附加的，附属的
7. **agrarian** /ə'greəriən/ *adj.* relating to rural matters 土地的，耕地的，有关土地的
—The agrarian reform enabled us to form an alliance with the peasants on the basis of democracy and enabled them to obtain land.
土地改革使我们在民主主义的基础上同农民结成了联盟，使农民得到了土地。
8. **dissolution** /ˌdɪsə'luːʃən/ *n.* separation into component parts 分解
—The President announced the dissolution of Parliament.
总统宣布解散议会。
9. **peninsula** /pə'nɪnsjələ/ *n.* a large mass of land projecting into a body of water 半岛
—Pray for newly established Churches to be a great blessing to this Arabian Peninsula nation.
祈求新成立的教会能成为这个阿拉伯半岛国家的极大祝福。
10. **hinge** /hɪndʒ/ *n.* a joint that holds two parts together so that one can swing relative to the other 铰链
—The door is joined by hinge.
这扇门是用铰链连接的。
11. **precipitation** /prɪˌsɪpɪ'teɪʃən/ *n.* the quantity of water falling to earth at a specific place within a specified period of time 坠落，沉淀，降水，降雨
—There will be precipitation on northern hills tonight.
今夜北部山区有降雪。
12. **diminish** /dɪ'mɪnɪʃ/ *vt.* decrease in size, extent, or range 使减少，使变小
—No man and nothing can interfere with your use of this power or diminish your spare of it.
没有什么人也没有什么事情能干涉你使用这种权力或对你的使用进行限制。
13. **sapped** /sæpt/ *adj.* 受冰川作用侵蚀（或碎裂）的
14. **monsoon** /mɒn'suːn/ *n.* a seasonal wind in southern Asia; blows from the southwest (bringing rain) in summer and from the northeast in winter 季风
—Heavy rains occur during a summer monsoon.

暴雨出现在夏季季风期。

15. **elevation** /ˌelɪˈveɪʃən/ *n.* a height above the level of the sea 海拔
—Mountaineers sometimes have to use oxygen at this elevation.
登山者在这个海拔有时会用到氧气。

16. **vegetation** /vedʒɪˈteɪʃ(ə)n/ *n.* all the plants in a particular region or period 植被，草木
—The lake is now extinct, but our ancestors would have depended on the water and vegetation that grew around it.
湖泊现在干涸了，但是我们的祖先可能曾经依赖湖水和湖周围生长的植被。

17. **drainage** /ˈdreɪnɪdʒ/ *adj.* the system or process by which water or other liquids are drained from a place 排水，排水系统
—Line the pots with pebbles to ensure good drainage.
在这些花盆里铺上一层卵石以确保良好的排水性。

18. **tributary** /ˈtrɪbjʊt(ə)rɪ/ *n.* a branch that flows into the main stream 支流
—Napo River is a tributary of the Amazon.
纳波河是亚马逊河的一个支流。

19. **meander** /mɪˈændə/ *n.* a bend or curve, as in a stream or river 曲流

20. **embayment** /emˈbeɪm(ə)nt/ *n.* an indentation of a shoreline larger than a cove but smaller than a gulf 海湾
—The great majority of earthquakes in this region occur beneath the northern portion of the embayment.
这个地区的绝大多数地震都发生在该海湾北部。

21. **nutrient** /ˈnjuːtrɪənt/ *n.* any substance that can be metabolized by an organism to give energy and build tissue 营养物，滋养物
—In her first book she explained the role of vegetable fibers, vitamins, minerals, and other essential nutrients.
在她的第一本书中，她解释了植物纤维、维生素、矿物质和其他重要营养物质的作用。

22. **interconnected** /ˌɪntəkəˈnɛkt/ *adj.* connected to or with each other 连通的，有联系的
—The causes are many and may interconnect.
原因很多，而且还可能互相关联。

23. **hydrological** /ˌhaɪdrəˈlɑdʒɪkəl/ *adj.* 水文学的
—We have a strong focus on Africa in our International Hydrological Programme.
非洲是我们国际水文学项目的重中之重。

24. **biodiversity** /ˌbaɪə(ʊ)daɪˈvɜːsɪtɪ/ *n.* the existence of a wide variety of plant and animal species living in their natural environment 生物多样性
—There should be no national boundaries in biodiversity protection.
生物多样性的保护应该跨国界。

25. **sculpt** /skʌlpt/ *vt.* create by shaping stone or wood or any other hard material 造型，雕刻
—An artist sculpted a full-size replica of her head.

一位艺术家雕塑了一尊她头部的全幅像。

26. **fertility** /fə'tɪlɪtɪ/ *n.* the state of being fertile; capable of producing offspring 多产，肥沃
—It symbolizes growth, harmony, freshness, and fertility.
它象征着成长、和谐、新鲜和富饶。

27. **quadruple** /'kwɒdrʊp(ə)l/ *v.* If someone quadruples an amount or if it quadruples, it becomes four times bigger 使成四倍，成为四倍
—In order to succeed, you have to double, triple or even quadruple your failure rate.
为了成功，你必须以两倍、三倍甚至四倍于过去的失效率学习。

28. **pronouncement** /prə'naʊnsm(ə)nt/ *n.* public or official statements on an important subject 公告
—Here are the President's latest pronouncements about the protection of minorities.
这是总统最近发布的保护少数民族的声明。

Exercises

1. Choose the correct answer.

1) The United States has________ states all together.
A. 48 B. 49 C. 50 D. 52

2) 2) The Declaration of Independence was issued on ________.
A. July 4, 1776 B. July 5, 1776 C. July 4, 1775 D. July 4, 1777

3) By land area (exclusive of waters), the United States is the world's ________ largest country.
A. first B. second C. fourth D. fifth

4) ________was one of the main routes for the westward expansion of the United States during the 19th century.
A. Great Lakes B. the Missouri River
C. Mississippi River Waterway D. Saint Lawrence River

5) The New York State ratified the United States Constitution on July 26, 1788 to become the ________ state.
A. 10th B. 11th C. 12th D. 13th

2. Decide whether the following statements are True or False.

1) The Mississippi River is the longest river in the United States, with a length of 2,320 miles (3,730 km).

2) The Rocky Mountains (or Rockies) are a major mountain range in eastern North America.

3) The Great Lakes began to form at the end of the last glacial period around 14,000 years ago, as retreating ice sheets exposed the basins they had carved into the land which then filled with melt water.

4) In US, English is the primary language used for legislation, regulations, executive orders, treaties, federal court rulings, and all other official pronouncements.

5) The biggest city in the U.S. is Washington D. C., which has over 8 million people.

3. Fill in the blanks according to the passage.

1) The United States is a country in________.

2) The United States is the _____ most populous country in the world with an estimated population of 328,285,992 as of January 12, 2019.

3) Much of California consists of a _________, with sometimes excessive rainfall from October to April and nearly no rain the rest of the year.

4) The United States shares land borders with ________ (to the north) and ________ (to the south), and a territorial water border with ________ in the northwest.

5) The Great Lakes are the ________ group of freshwater lakes on Earth by total area, and ________ by total volume, containing 21% of the world's surface fresh water by volume.

4. Explain the following terms according to the passage.

1) Declaration of Independence

2) The Rocky Mountains

3) Missouri River

4) Washington D.C.

5) The Great Lakes

5. Answer the following questions according to the passage.

1) Please introduce the topography of America.

2) Please introduce the climate of California.

3) Try to introduce the Rocky Mountains.

6. Discussion.

1) Read the story of "Uncle Sam". Try to describe the characteristics of American people.

On this day in 1813, the United States gets its nickname, Uncle Sam. The name is linked to Samuel Wilson, a meat packer from Troy, New York, who supplied barrels of beef to the United States Army during the War of 1812.Wilson (1766-1854) stamped the barrels with "U.S." for United States, but soldiers began referring to the grub as "Uncle Sam's". The local newspaper picked up on the story and Uncle Sam eventually gained widespread acceptance as the nickname for the U.S. federal government.

In the late 1860s and 1870s, political cartoonist Thomas Nast (1840-1902) began popularizing the image of Uncle Sam. Nast continued to evolve the image, eventually giving Sam the white beard and stars-and-stripes suit that are associated with the character today. The German-born Nast was also credited with creating the modern image of Santa Claus as well as coming up with the donkey as a symbol for the Democratic Party and the elephant as a symbol for the Republicans. Nast also famously lampooned the corruption of New York City's Tammany Hall in his editorial cartoons and was, in part, responsible for the downfall of Tammany leader

William Tweed.

Perhaps the most famous image of Uncle Sam was created by artist James Montgomery Flagg (1877-1960). In Flagg's version, Uncle Sam wears a tall top hat and blue jacket and is pointing straight ahead at the viewer. During World War I, this portrait of Sam with the words "I Want You For The U.S. Army" was used as a recruiting poster. The image, which became immensely popular, was first used on the cover of Leslie's Weekly in July 1916 with the title "What Are You Doing for Preparedness?" The poster was widely distributed and had subsequently been re-used numerous times with different captions.

In September 1961, the U.S. Congress recognized Samuel Wilson as "the progenitor of America's national symbol of Uncle Sam." Wilson died at age 88 in 1854, and was buried next to his wife Betsey Mann in the Oakwood Cemetery in Troy, New York, the town that calls itself "The Home of Uncle Sam".

2) Why is America called the melting pot?

Stay Positive

1. If you want the best the world has to offer, offer it your best.
2. Storms make trees take deeper roots.

Chapter 2

History of the United States

I am a slow walker, but I never walk backwards.

—Abraham Lincoln, American president

1. The Discovery of the New World

The first group of people to reach North America were Asian hunters and **nomads**. Following game along the Siberian[1] coast, they crossed the Bering Strait[2] that connected the two continents about 30,000 to 34,000 years ago. Once in Alaska[3], it took these first North Americans, the ancestors of Native American tribes, thousands of years to work their way south to what is now the United States. People there lived on hunting, cultivating corn and beans. In 1492 with the idea of finding a new route to the Far East to get enough wealth, Christopher Columbus[4] made his first voyage of discovery. When Columbus arrived at the Caribbean in 1492, the New World[5] was far from an empty wilderness. It was home to as many people as lived in Europe—perhaps 60 or 70 million. They were not a single, **homogeneous** population.

Another important figure in the process of discovering the New World was Amerigo Vespucci[6]. He was not the discoverer of the new continents, but it was he who first confirmed the fact that a new continent rather than Asia had been discovered.

2. The Colonial Period (1600–1763)

Most modern American citizens consider Great Britain to be their European "parent" country. However, by the time British arrived in the New World and established their first permanent settlement at Jamestown in 1607, much of the continent had already been claimed by other European nations, especially Spain and France. The failure of Spain in the battle with England in 1588 marked the beginning of the end of Spain's domination of Europe and the Western Hemisphere. More importantly for England, it marked the dawn of the era of permanent English settlement in the New World.

2.1 The Northern Colonies

The northern colonies also called New England[7] today including Massachusetts, Connecticut, New Hampshire, Vermont, Maine and Rhode Island in the northeast of the United States.

During the religious turmoil of the 16th century, a body of men and women called Puritans[8]sought to reform the Established Church[9]of England to purify the rituals and structures associated with Roman Catholicism. Their reformist ideas, by destroying the unity of the state church, threatened to divide the people and to undermine royal authority.

In 1620, a group of 102 Puritans set out for Virginia[10] on board the ship named Mayflower[11]. A storm sent them far north and they landed in New England. Believing themselves outside the reign of any organized government, the men drafted a formal agreement—the *Mayflower Compact*, which was signed aboard the ship on its way from England to the New World, acknowledged their loyalty to the King and pledged their obedience to such just and equal laws as would be necessary to the general good of the colony to be established after landing. This document represents the first example of a written constitution in North America. In December the Mayflower reached Plymouth harbor, the Pilgrims[12] began to build their settlement during the winter. Nearly half the colonists died of exposure and disease, but neighboring Indians provided information that would remain their lives: how to grow maize. By the next fall, the Pilgrims had a plentiful crop of corn, and a growing trade based on furs and wood. Later each year the Plymouth Pilgrims will celebrate survival, as well as the hopes of good fortune in the years that lay ahead in a certain day, and it was President Lincoln who declared Thanksgiving[13] a national celebration in 1863 which was celebrated on the fourth Thursday of November.

New England in the northeast has generally thin, stony soil, relatively little level land, and long winters, making it difficult to make a living from farming. Turning to other pursuits, the New Englanders harnessed water power and established grain mills and sawmills. Good stands of wood encouraged shipbuilding. Excellent harbors promoted trade, and the sea became a source of great wealth. One of the most enterprising trading practices of the time was the so-called "triangular trade[14]." Merchants and shippers would purchase slaves off the coast of Africa for New England rum, and then sell the slaves in the West Indies where they would buy molasses to bring home for sale to the local rum producers.

2.2 The Middle Colonies

The middle colonies contained New York, New Jersey, Delaware and Pennsylvania.

Society in the middle colonies was far more varied and tolerant than in New England. In many ways, Pennsylvania and Delaware owed their initial success to William Penn[15]. Under his guidance, Pennsylvania functioned smoothly and grew rapidly. By 1685 its population was almost 9,000. The heart of the colony was Philadelphia, a city soon to be known for its broad, tree-shaded streets, substantial brick and stone houses, and busy docks. By the end of the colonial period, nearly a century later, 30,000 people lived there, representing many languages, creeds and trades. Their talent for successful business enterprise made the city one of the thriving centers of colonial America.

Though the Quakers[16] dominated in Philadelphia, elsewhere in Pennsylvania others were well represented. Pennsylvania was also the principal gateway into the New World for Germans and the Scots-Irish. As mixed as the people were in Pennsylvania, New York best illustrated the **polyglot** nature of America. By 1646 the population along the Hudson River[17] included peoples from more than 13 different countries.

2.3 The Southern Colonies

In contrast to New England and the middle colonies the southern colonies were the predominantly rural southern settlements: Virginia, Maryland, North and South Carolina, and Georgia.

The first of the British colonies to take hold in North America was Jamestown in Virginia. Under the order of King James I[18], a group of about 100 men set out for Virginia in 1607. The group was made up of townsmen and adventurers more interested in finding gold and they chose a site near the James River to settle.

It was not long before a development happened that changed Virginia's economy. In 1612 John Rolfe[19] began **crossbreeding** imported tobacco seed from the West Indies with native plants and produced a new variety that was pleasing to European taste. The first shipment of this tobacco reached London in 1614. Within a decade it had become Virginia's chief source of revenue. The first blacks were brought to Virginia in 1619, just 12 years after the founding of Jamestown. Initially, many were regarded as indentured servants who could earn their freedom. By the 1660s, however, as the demand for **plantation** labor in the southern colonies grew, the institution of slavery began to harden around them, and Africans were brought to America and forced to be slaves for a lifetime.

2.4 The Seven Years' War

France and Britain engaged in a succession of wars in Europe and the Caribbean at several intervals in the 18th century. Though Britain secured certain advantages, the struggles were generally indecisive, and France remained in a powerful position in North America at the beginning of the Seven Years' War[20] in 1754.

By that time France had established a strong relationship with a number of Indian tribes in Canada and along the Great Lakes, taken possession of the Mississippi River and, by establishing a line of forts and trading posts, marked out an empire stretching from Quebec[21]to New Orleans[22]. Thus, the British were confined to the narrow belt east of the Appalachian Mountains. The French threatened not only the British Empire but the American colonists themselves, for in holding the Mississippi Valley, France could limit their westward expansion.

An armed clash took place in 1754 at the site where Pittsburgh[23], Pennsylvania, is now located, between a band of French regulars and Virginia militiamen under the command of 22-year-old George Washington, a Virginia planter and surveyor.

England's superior strategic position and her competent leadership to American colonies ultimately brought victory in the Seven Years' War, only a modest portion of which was fought in the Western Hemisphere.

In the *Peace of Paris*, signed in 1763, France passed all of Canada, the Great Lakes and the upper Mississippi Valley to the Britain. The dream of a French empire in North America was over.

In North America alone, British territories had more than doubled. Defense and administration of the new territories, as well as of the old, would require huge sums of money and increased personnel. The old colonial system was obviously inadequate to these tasks.

3. The Independence War of America

The Seven Years' War nearly doubled Britain's national debt. The British government, which needed more money to support its growing empire, started a new financial policy. Money for the colonies' defense was to be extracted from the colonists through a stronger central administration. This would come at the expense of colonial self-government. The colonists resisted the new taxes and regulations imposed by England, such as *the Sugar Act*, the *Stamp Act*[24]. They insisted that they could be taxed only by their own colonial assemblies, and the colonists rallied behind the slogan "no taxation without representation". On April 19, 1775, the first shot was fired in the village of Lexington near Boston. Thus the American War of Independence began. The conflict intensified and King George III[25] issued a declaration on August 23, 1775, declaring the colonies to be in a state of rebellion. On May, a second Continental Congress met in Philadelphia, at which a Continental Army and Navy was founded under the command of George Washington[26]. On July 4, 1776, the Continental Congress adopted a *Declaration of Independence*, drafted by Thomas Jefferson[27] of Virginia with the assistance of John Adams[28] and Benjamin Franklin[29]. Armed conflict between America and England lasted until 1783. Known as the *Treaty of Paris*, the peace settlement acknowledged the independence, freedom and sovereignty of the 13 former colonies, now states, to which Great Britain granted the territory west to the Mississippi River, north to Canada and south to Florida, which was returned to Spain.

4. Territory Expansion and the Westward Movement

The United States grew from 13 colonies along the Atlantic coast to a nation spanning across the continent to the Pacific coast. During the 13 years of Indian wars after the War of Independence, the Americans forced England to give up the Old Northwest (present-day Ohio, Indiana, Illinois, Michigan, and Wisconsin) and they forced Spain to open the Mississippi River.

Their crossing of the Mississippi in the 1790s helped persuade Napoleon to sell the Louisiana Territory to the United States for only 15 million dollars. Since then the territory owned by the United States almost doubled. Their move southward, forced Spain to cede Florida and the Gulf coast.

4.1 The War of 1812

Under the *Treaty of Paris*, Britain had agreed to withdraw its troops from the Ohio Valley and to respect American shipping. In practice, though, British troops remained stationed in British forts on US territory, and Royal Navy captains continued to seize American merchant ships to prevent America from trading with France. When diplomatic efforts failed to resolve the crisis peacefully, the United States declared war, thus the war of 1812 between Britain and the United States began. The war ended in 1814. This was a war in which nothing changed—no territory was lost nor gained by either side. To Americans, the battle proved once and for all that the United States was an independent nation, not just a rouge colony. For this reason, many historians refer to the war of 1812 as America's second war for independence.

4.2 The Mexican War

The Americans in Texas, supported by volunteers from the United States, staged an armed uprising and defeated the Mexican army, and Texas won independence in 1836. In 1845, Texas was added to the Union. The war with Mexico started in 1846 and ended in 1848. As a result of the peace treaty, Mexico was forced to sign over California, Utah, and Nevada as well as parts of New Mexico, Arizona, Wyoming and Colorado in exchange for $15 million dollars and exoneration of about $3 million more in previous liability. In 1853 another 30,000 square miles of Mexican land (now the southern part of Arizona and New Mexico) were added to the territory of the United States; in return, the United States paid 10 million U.S. dollars.

With the territorial expansion towards the west, the problem of whether slavery should be allowed to spread into these areas arose again. It became a serious political issue because it might tip the balance of power in the Senate. By the middle of 19th century the differences between the North and the South had increasingly extended, especially in terms of economic foundation. The North firmly established as an industrial society, free labor was desperately needed; the South as plantation, slaved people, opposed high tariffs or taxes that placed on imported goods, which triggered the Civil War.

5. The Civil War

In the early 19th century, slavery began to assume greater importance as a national issue. In the early years of the republic, many leaders had supposed that slavery would die out. As late as 1808, when the international slave trade was abolished, many thought that slavery would soon end. But during the next generation, the South became solidly united behind the institution of slavery as new economic factors made slavery far more profitable than it had been before 1790.

The country was divided into states permitting slavery and states prohibiting it. In the presidential election of 1860, the Republican Party, led by Abraham Lincoln[30], had campaigned against the expansion of slavery beyond the states in which it already existed. The Republican

Abraham Lincoln

victory caused that 11 states left the Union and proclaimed themselves an independent nation, the Confederate States of America: South Carolina, Mississippi, Florida, Alabama, Georgia, Louisiana, Texas, Virginia, Arkansas, Tennessee, and North Carolina. They fought against the U.S. federal government (the Union), which was supported by all the free states and the five border slave states in the north. Both the outgoing and incoming U.S. administrations rejected secession, considering it rebellion. The American Civil War began.

Hostilities began on April 12, 1861. The American Civil War was the deadliest war in American history, causing 620,000 soldier deaths and an undetermined number of civilian casualties. It put an end to slavery; it also made clear that the country was not a collection of semi-independent states but an indivisible whole. In December 1865, Congress ratified the 13th Amendment to the U.S. Constitution, which abolished slavery. The social, political, economic and racial issues of the war decisively shaped the Reconstruction Era that lasted to 1877 and brought changes that helped make the country a united superpower.

5.1 Reconstruction

Reconstruction (1865-1877) took place for most of the decade following the Civil War. At the end of the war, the South was a region destroyed by war, burdened by debt and losing hope with racial warfare. As time passed, it became obvious that the problems of the South were not being solved by radical reconstruction, harsh laws and continuing hatred against former Confederates. During this era, the "Reconstruction Amendments" were passed to expand civil rights for black Americans. In response to Reconstruction, the Ku Klux Klan (KKK)[31] emerged around the late 1860s as an organization opposed to black civil rights, which was classified as a terrorist group in 1870. Reconstruction ended in 1876, and the South soon re-entered the national political scene. The failure of Reconstruction meant that the struggle of African Americans for equality and freedom was deferred until the 20th century—when it would become a national, and not a Southern issue.

5.2 Rise of Industry

In the late 19th century there had been a dramatic expansion of American industry which was described as the Gilded Age by Mark Twin. During this period great factories and steel mills, flourishing cities and vast agricultural holdings marked the land. The first transcontinental railroad was completed in 1869, and by 1900, the United States had longer rail than all of Europe. The petroleum, steel and textile industries prospered. An electrical industry flourished as Americans made use of a series of inventions: the telephone, the light bulb and the phonograph.

After the Gilded Age came the Progressive Era, whose followers called for reform over perceived industrial corruption. Viewpoints taken by progressives included greater federal regulation of anti-trust laws and the industries of meat-packing, drugs, and railroads. Four new constitutional amendments—the Sixteenth through Nineteenth—resulted from progressive activism. The Era lasted from 1900 to 1918, the year marking the end of World War I.

6. US Imperialism and World War I

By 1890 the frontier had disappeared. The last decades of the 19th century were a period of imperial expansion for the United States, as it extended its influence, and at times its domain, over widely scattered areas in the Atlantic and Pacific Oceans and into Central America. In 1867, America purchased Alaska from Russia. Within a few years after the end of the Spanish-American War in 1898, the United States was exercising control or influence over islands in the Caribbean Sea, the mid-Pacific and close to the Asian mainland. When the Hawaiian royal government announced its intention to end foreign influence in 1893, American businessmen joined with influential Hawaiians to install a new government, and in July 1898 the islands were attached.

6.1 War and Neutral Rights

To the American public of 1914, the outbreak of war in Europe came as a shock. At first the encounter seemed remote, but its economic and political effects were swift and deep. By 1915 U.S. industry, which had been mildly depressed, was prospering again with **munitions** orders from the Western Allies. Both sides used propaganda to arouse the public passions of Americans. Moreover, Britain and Germany both acted against U.S. shipping on the high seas, bringing sharp protests from President Woodrow Wilson[32]. The disputes between the United States and Germany grew increasingly worse.

President Wilson warned that the United States would not forsake its traditional right, as a neutral, to trade on the high seas—a view of neutral rights not shared by Germany or Great Britain.

The neutral policy helped Wilson win the reelection in 1916. As late as January 1917, in a speech before the Senate, Wilson called for a "peace without victory," which, he said, was the only kind of peace that could last.

President Woodrow Wilson declared U.S. entry into World War I in April 1917, and American participation in the war proved essential to the Allied victory on November 11, 1918.

6.2 The Great Depression

It is a common misunderstanding that the stock market crash of October 29, 1929, known as Black Tuesday, was the cause of the Great Depression. The two events were closely related, but both were the results of deep problems in the modern economy that were building up through the "prosperity decade" of the 1920s.

As is typical of post-war periods, Americans in the Roaring Twenties turned inward, away from international issues and social concerns and toward greater individualism. The self-centered attitudes of the 1920s seemed to fit nicely with the needs of the economy. Modern industry had the capacity to produce vast quantities of consumer goods, but there was an underlying economic problem: unequal distribution of wealth, high tariffs and war debts, over production in industry and agriculture, stock market crash and financial panic.

The stock market crash was just an announcement of the beginning of the Great Depression but the deep economic problems of the 1920s had already converged a few months earlier to start the downward spiral. Conditions continued to worsen for the next three years till 1932.

However, with the outbreak of World War II in Europe in September 1939, the U.S. government began expanding the national defense system. This stimulated industrial growth and unemployment declined rapidly. After the United States entered the war in December 1941, all sectors of the economy were mobilized to support the war effort. Industry greatly expanded, and unemployment was replaced by a shortage of workers.

7. World War II

After the outbreak of war in Europe the President Franklin Roosevelt[33] proclaimed a limited emergency and authorized increases in the size of the Regular Army and the National Guard. Congress amended the *Neutrality Act*[34]to permit munitions sales to the French and British, and large orders from them stimulated retooling and laid the basis for the expansion of war production in the future. The Army concentrated on equipping its regular forces as quickly as possible and in 1940 held the first large-scale corps and army maneuvers in American history.

7.1 United States Enters the War

On December 7, 1941 Japan launched a surprise attack on the American naval base in Pearl Harbor, citing America's recent trade embargo as justification. The following day, Franklin D. Roosevelt successfully urged a joint session of Congress to declare war on Japan. Four days later Nazi Germany declared war on the United States, drawing the country into a two-theater war. The Western Allies decided that their essential military effort was to be concentrated in Europe, where the core of enemy power lay, while the Pacific theater was to be secondary.

7.2 Battle against Germany

Upon entering the war, the United States and its allies decided to concentrate the bulk of their efforts on fighting Hitler in Europe, while maintaining a defensive position in the Pacific until Hitler was defeated. The United States' first step was to set up a large airforce in Britain to concentrate on bombing raids into Germany itself.

By early 1944, a planned invasion of Western Europe was underway. On June 6, 1944, the largest war armada ever assembled landed on the beaches of Normandy and began the penetration of Western Europe that eventually overthrew Hitler and Nazi Germany. On May 8, 1945, the war with Germany was over, following its unconditional surrender to the Allied forces.

7.3 Battle against Japan

Due to the United States commitment to defeating Hitler in Europe, the first years of the war against Japan was largely a defensive battle with the United States Navy attempting to prevent the Japanese Navy from asserting dominance of the Pacific region. Initially, Japan won the majority of its battles in a short period of time. On April 12, 1945, President Franklin Delano Roosevelt died and Vice President Harry S. Truman[35]was sworn in as the 33rd President of the United States. The use of atomic weapons against Japan was subsequently authorized. The decision to use nuclear weapons to end the conflict has been one of the most controversial decisions of the war. The first bomb was dropped on Hiroshima on August 6, 1945, and the second bomb was dropped on Nagasaki on August 9, 1945. On August 15, 1945, the Japanese surrendered unconditionally, ending World War II.

8. Post World War II

After World War II, the world enter into another war, the Cold War (1947-1991), which was the continuing state of political conflict, military tension, and economic competition existing, primarily between the USSR[36]and the United States. Since the primary participants' military forces never officially clashed directly, it was called the Cold War. In 1960, John F. Kennedy was elected president. At 43, he was the youngest man ever to win the presidency. In October 1962, he was faced with what turned out to be the most drastic crisis of the Cold War: the Cuban Missile Crisis[37]. When the Soviet Union installed nuclear missiles in Cuba, Kennedy decided on isolation to prevent Soviet ships from bringing additional missiles to Cuba, and he demanded publicly that the Soviets remove the weapons. After several days of tension, the Soviets backed down.

His successor, Lyndon B. Johnson[38], enacted a number of new laws from the Kennedy agenda, establishing social reform programs. The struggle of black Americans for equality reached its peak in the mid-1960s. Although civil rights legislation was enacted, some blacks became impatient with the pace of progress. Violence accompanied militant calls for reform. Unrest in the cities erupted, as black leaders criticized the nonviolent tactics of Dr. Martin Luther King[39]. Martin Luther King, who had won the Nobel Prize for his efforts to achieve equality of the races, was assassinated in 1968, which triggered race riots in over 100 cities.

During President Johnson's six years in office, the United States involved in the Vietnam War[40]. Although politicians tended to view the war as part of a necessary effort to check communism on all fronts, a growing number of Americans saw no vital American interest in Vietnam. Demonstrations protesting American involvement in the undeclared war broke out on college campuses.

Increasingly unpopular, President Johnson decided not to run for a second full term. Richard Nixon was elected president in 1968. Nixon negotiated a peace treaty with North Vietnam and a number of other diplomatic breakthroughs. He opened ties to the People's Republic of China and successfully pursued a policy of detente with the Soviet Union. On August 8, 1974, becoming the first President to do so, Nixon resigned the office as it became clear that Congress was about to **impeach** him for White House involvement in the Watergate

Scandal[41].

In the 1980s, the United States increased diplomatic, military, and economic pressures against the USSR, which had already suffered severe economic **stagnation**. The Cold War ended after the Soviet Union collapsed in 1991, leaving the United States as the dominant military power, and Russia possessing most of the Soviet Union's nuclear arsenal. The Cold War and its events have had a significant impact on the world today, and it is commonly referred to in popular culture as fiction.

9. Toward the 21st Century

Shifts in the structure of American society, which began years or even decades earlier, had become apparent by the time the 1980s arrived. The composition of the population and the most important jobs and skills in American society had undergone major changes. The dominance of service jobs became undeniable. For many Americans, the economic, social and political trends of the previous two decades caused a mood of disillusionment. In 1980 Ronald Reagan was elected president.

The central theme of Reagan's domestic policy was that the federal government had become too big and federal taxes too high. During his first term, the administration increased spending on defense expenditures. After the reelection in 1984, Reagan softened his rigid position on arms control. A **recession** marked the early years of Reagan's presidency, but conditions started to improve in 1983 as the United States entered one of the longest periods of sustained economic growth since World War II.

In 1988, George Bush, Reagan's vice president, was elected the 41st president of the United States. As the Cold War ended after 40 bitter years, Bush faced a dramatically changing world. While Bush hailed the march of democracy, he insisted on restraint in U.S. policy toward the group of new eastern European nations. In foreign policy, President Bush's greatest test came when Iraqi President Saddam Hussein[42] invaded Kuwait[43], and then threatened to move into Saudi Arabia[44]. At home, Americans faced some deep and familiar problems as the United States again found itself in recession.

In 1992, voters elected Bill Clinton president. Clinton represented a new generation in American political leadership. For the first time in 12 years both the White House and Congress were held by the same party. But that political edge was brief; the Republicans won both houses of Congress in 1994. In 1998, as a result of his loving affair with a young woman White House intern, Clinton was the second U.S. president to be impeached by the House of Representatives. He was trialed in the Senate and found not guilty of the charges brought against him.

10. The 21st Century

George W. Bush is the 43rd President of the United States. He was sworn into office on January 20, 2001 after one of the most tightly contested presidential campaigns in U.S. history.

Bush expected to focus on domestic issues such as education, the economy, and social security. But his presidency was certainly stopped on September 11, 2001, when the United States suffered the most devastating foreign attack ever against its mainland.

That morning, Middle Eastern terrorists simultaneously **hijacked** four passenger airplanes and used two of them as suicide vehicles to destroy the twin towers of the World Trade Center in New York City; the third crashed into the Pentagon building[45], the Defense Department headquarters just outside of Washington D.C., the fourth, probably meant for the U.S. capital, crashed into the Pennsylvania countryside as passengers fought the hijackers. The death toll, most of it consisting of civilians at the World Trade Center, was approximately 3,000, exceeding that of the Japanese attack on Pearl Harbor in 1941. The world community met the threat posed by global terrorism with an unprecedented worldwide coalition to fight the War on Terror. The North Atlantic Council[46] according to Article 5 of the *North Atlantic Treaty*[47], thereby classified the 9/11 terrorist attacks as an attack on all member states, and pledged any necessary assistance. Both the U.N. General Assembly and Security Council passed by acclamation resolutions condemning the terrorist attacks on the United States.

The United States attributed responsibility for 9/11 to Osama bin Laden[48] and the Al Qaeda[49] organization. A full-scale campaign was launched against Al Qaeda and its associates and support structures. A total of 136 countries offered a range of military assistance to the United States. As a result, the Taliban was removed from power and the first election in more than 40 years took place in Afghanistan.

To coordinate the fight against domestic terrorist attack, the Bush administration introduced new laws, which broadened the search, seizure, and **detention** powers of the federal government. A new Department of Homeland Security, which consolidated 22 federal agencies, was also established. By 2004, with the United States facing a violent insurgency in Iraq and considerable foreign opposition to the war there, the country appeared as sharply divided as it had been four years earlier. President Bush was sworn in for a second term on January 20, 2005. His administration continued to face many challenges.

Global terrorism remains a serious threat. There are important challenges to be faced in Iraq and Afghanistan. In addition, the full impact of globalization is making itself felt in full force. In December 2007, the United States entered the longest post-World War II recession. That prompted the Bush administration to take more direct control of the economy, enacting multiple economic programs intended to preserve the country's financial structure. Though Bush was a popular president for much of his first term, his popularity declined sharply during his second term. After leaving office, Bush returned to his home state Texas.

The former President Barack Hussein Obama[50] began his run for the presidency in February 2007. After a close campaign in the 2008 Democratic Party presidential primaries against Hillary Clinton, he won his party's nomination. In the 2008 general election, he defeated Republican nominee John McCain and was inaugurated as President on January 20, 2009.

Obama is also the 2009 Nobel Peace Prize laureate.

Donald John Trump (born June 14, 1946) is the 45th and current President of the United States. Before entering politics, he was a businessman and television personality. Trump was elected president in a surprise victory over Democratic nominee Hillary Clinton in 2016. After his inauguration in 2017, he became the oldest and wealthiest person ever to assume the presidency, the first without prior military or government service, and the fifth to have won the election while losing the popular vote. His election and policies have sparked numerous protests.

The long-term effects of events and trends occurring at the beginning of the 21st century have yet to be fully understood. In the past, the United States has thrived on such challenges. From its origins as a set of obscure colonies hugging the Atlantic coast, the United States has undergone a remarkable transformation into what political analyst Ben Wattenberg has called "the first universal nation", a population of more than 300 million people representing virtually every nationality and ethnic group on the globe. It is also a nation where the pace and extent of change—economic, technological, cultural, demographic, and social is unceasing. The United States is often the harbinger of the modernization and change that inevitably sweep up other nations and societies in an increasingly interdependent, interconnected world.

Joyful Moment

Expensive Price

Dentist: I'm sorry, madam, but I'll have to charge you 25 dollars for pulling your son's tooth.
Mother: Twenty-five dollars! But I thought you only charged five dollars for an extraction.
Dentist: I usually do. But your son yelled so loud, he scared four other patients out of the office.

Notes

[1] Siberia 西伯利亚
[2] Bering Strait 白令海峡，将西伯利亚最东端和阿拉斯加分开的狭窄海洋通道
[3] Alaska 阿拉斯加，美国最大的州，1959 年成为美国第 49 个州
[4] Christopher Columbus 克里斯托弗·哥伦布（1451—1506），意大利探险家
[5] New World 新大陆，即美洲大陆，是针对欧洲大陆而言的新大陆
[6] Amerigo Vespucci 阿美利哥·韦斯普奇，据说美洲即得名于其名
[7] New England 新英格兰，美国东北的一个沿海地区
[8] Puritan 清教徒，英国 16 世纪末和 17 世纪基督教新教徒中的一派
[9] Established Church 国教，英国国教，也称英格兰圣公会
[10] Virginia 弗吉尼亚（州），1607 年英格兰在北美的第一个永久定居点
[11] Mayflower 五月花号，清教徒先辈们由英国去美洲所乘的船的名字

[12] Pilgrim 清教徒移民，特指 1620 年乘五月花号去美洲的清教徒
[13] Thanksgiving 感恩节，每年十一月的第四个星期四
[14] triangular trade 三角贸易，18、19 世纪将商品从英国运到西非以换取奴隶，然后将他们运至西印度群岛以交换当地的蔗糖及其他货物，再将这些货物运回英国的贸易
[15] William Penn 威廉•佩恩（1644—1718），宾夕法尼亚殖民地的开拓者
[16] Quaker 贵格会教徒
[17] Hudson River 哈德逊河，又称哈德孙河、哈德森河，美国纽约州的一条河
[18] King James I 詹姆斯一世，英格兰国王，1603—1625 年在位，同时还是苏格兰的国王，1567—1625 年在位，称詹姆斯六世
[19] John Rolfe 约翰•罗尔夫（1585—1622），英国在弗吉尼亚州的殖民者
[20] Seven Years' War 七年战争，欧洲主要国家争夺殖民地和领土的战争
[21] Quebec 魁北克省，1867 年成为加拿大联邦最早的四省之一
[22] New Orleans 新奥尔良，1718 年由法国人建立
[23] Pittsburgh 匹兹堡，美国宾西法尼亚州西南部城市，是美国的钢铁工业中心
[24] *Stamp Act*《印花税法案》，1765 年英国议会通过的税收法案
[25] King George III 乔治三世，英国国王，1760—1820 年在位
[26] George Washington 乔治•华盛顿，美国首任总统，1789—1797 年在任
[27] Thomas Jefferson 托马斯•杰斐逊，美国第三任总统，1801—1809 年在任
[28] John Adams 约翰•亚当斯（1735—1826），1797—1801 年任美国第二任总统
[29] Benjamin Franklin 本杰明•富兰克林（1706—1790）
[30] Abraham Lincoln 亚伯拉罕•林肯，美国第 16 任总统，1861—1865 年在任
[31] Ku Klux Klan (KKK) 三 K 党，美国历史最悠久、最庞大的恐怖主义组织
[32] Woodrow Wilson 伍德罗•威尔逊，美国第 28 任总统，1913—1921 年在任
[33] Franklin Roosevelt 富兰克林•罗斯福，美国第 32 任总统，1933—1945 年在任
[34] Neutrality Act《中立法案》
[35] Harry S. Truman 哈里•杜鲁门，美国第 33 任总统，1945—1953 年在任
[36] USSR Union of Soviet Socialist Republics 苏维埃社会主义共和国联盟（苏联）
[37] Cuban Missile Crisis 古巴导弹危机，被看作是冷战的顶峰和转折点
[38] Lyndon B. Johnson 林登•贝恩斯•约翰逊，美国第 36 任总统，1963—1969 年在任
[39] Martin Luther King 马丁•路德•金，美国民权运动领袖，1968 年被谋杀
[40] the Vietnam War 越南战争，从 1955 年起到 1975 年，前后历时 20 年，分为五个阶段。其中第二、三、四阶段（1961—1975 年）为美国助越战争时期
[41] Watergate Scandal 水门事件，美国政治丑闻，此事导致尼克松总统辞职
[42] Saddam Hussein 萨达姆•侯赛因，1979 年任伊拉克总统，1990 年入侵科威特
[43] Kuwait 科威特，波斯湾西北海岸国家
[44] Saudi Arabia 沙特阿拉伯
[45] Pentagon building 五角大楼，美国国防部所在地
[46] North Atlantic Council 北大西洋公约理事会，北大西洋组织的一个机构

[47] North Atlantic Treaty《北大西洋公约》
[48] Osama bin Laden 奥萨马·本·拉登，曾是恐怖组织“基地组织”的首领
[49] Al Qaeda　1988 年本·拉登在阿富汗建立的“基地组织”
[50] Barack Hussein Obama 贝拉克·侯赛因·奥巴马，美国第 44 任总统

New Words

1. **nomad** /'nəʊmæd/ *n.* a member of a people travelling from place to place to find fresh pasture for its animals and having no permanent home 游牧民
—Nomads have inhabited this region for thousands of years.
游牧民族在这地区居住已有数千年了。
2. **homogeneous** /ˌhɒmə'dʒiːniəs/ *adj.* of the same kind; alike 同种的；相似的
—They are homogeneous people.
他们是同类人。
3. **polyglot** /'pɒliglɒt/ *adj.* knowing or using several languages 懂得（或使用）多种语言的
4. **crossbreed** /'krɒsbriːd/ *v.* (of an animal or plant) breed with a different breed, species, or variety 异种交配；杂交
5. **plantation** /plæn'teɪʃən/ *n.* an estate on which crops such as coffee, sugar, and tobacco are grown（种植咖啡、甘蔗、烟草等作物的）种植园，种植场，大农场，庄园
—His father-in-law is a plantation manager.
他岳父是个种植园经营者。
6. **munitions** /mjuː'nɪʃənz/ *n.* [复数形式] military weapons, ammunition, equipment, and stores 军火（包括弹药、装备及库藏）
7. **impeach** /ɪm'piːtʃ/ *v.* charge (the holder of a public office) with misconduct 弹劾（官员）
—Elected officials can be impeached.
选举产生的官员可以被弹劾。
8. **stagnation** /stæg'neɪʃən/ *n.* cease developing; become inactive or dull 不发展；死气沉沉，呆滞，停滞
—Poor economic policies led to a long period of stagnation and decline.
糟糕的经济政策导致了长时间的经济萧条和下滑。
9. **recession** /rɪ'seʃən/ *n.* a period of temporary economic decline during which trade and industrial activity are reduced, generally identified by a fall in GDP in two successive quarters（经济的）衰退（期）
—It was the worst recession since the war.
这是战争以来最萧条的时期。
10. **hijack** /'haɪdʒæk/ *vt.* illegally seize (an aircraft, ship, or vehicle) while in transit and force it to go to a different destination or use it for one's own purposes 劫持（行驶中的飞机、轮船、车辆）

—Three armed men hijacked a white van.
三名武装男子劫持了一辆白色厢式货车。

11. **detention** /dɪ'tenʃən/ *n.* the action of detaining someone or the state of being detained in official custody, especially as a political prisoner（尤指政治犯的）拘留
—He committed suicide while in police detention.
他在被警方拘留期间自杀。

Exercises

1. Choose the correct answer.

1) In the *Peace of Paris*, signed in 1763, France passed all of_______, the Great Lakes and the upper Mississippi Valley to the British.
A. Canada B. New Zealand C. Australia D. Hawaii

2) In December 1865, _______ratified the 13th Amendment to the U.S. Constitution, which abolished slavery.
A. Parliament B. Congress C. Cabinet D. Government

3) When was the *Declaration of Independence* adopted by the Continental Congress?
A. On July 2, 1776. B. On July 4, 1776. C. In May 1775. D. In December 1781.

4) The principle author of the *Declaration of Independence* was _______.
A. Benjamin Franklin B. George Washington
C. Thomas Jefferson D. John Adams

5) "No taxation without representation" was the rallying cry of _______.
A. the settlers of Virginia
B. the people of Pennsylvania
C. the colonists in New England
D. the people of the 13 colonies in the eve of the American Revolution

2. Decide whether the following statements are True or False.

1) When Columbus arrived at the Caribbean in 1492, the New World was an empty wilderness.
2) The Declaration of Independence represents the first example of a written constitution in North America.
3) Though the Quakers dominated in Philadelphia, elsewhere in Pennsylvania others were well represented.
4) After the War with Mexico, Mexico was forced to sign over California, Utah, and Nevada as well as parts of New Mexico, Arizona, Wyoming and Colorado in exchange for $15 million dollars and exoneration of about $3 million more in previous liability.
5) In response to Reconstruction, the Ku Klux Klan (KKK) emerged around the late 1860s as an organization opposed to black civil rights, which was classified as a terrorist group in 1870.

3. Fill in the blanks according to the passage.

1) The first group of people to reach North America were _______and _______. Following game along the coast, they crossed the _______that connected the two continents about 30,000 to 34,000 years ago.

2) Another important figure in the process of discovering the New World was _______. And America was named after him.

3) _______ was the first colony established by England in 1607.

4) In _______ Elizabeth's ships defeated _______ and became the power on the sea.

5) American President _______ opened ties to the People's Republic of China.

4. Explain the following terms according to the passage.

1) The New World

2) War of 1812

3) Thanksgiving

4) Cuban Missile Crisis

5) 9/11 terrorist attacks

5. Answer the following questions according to the passage.

1) It was not long, however, before a development happened that changed Virginia's economy. And what was it that changed Virginia's economy?

2) What was the cause of Great Depression?

3) What did people do to fight with the terrorism after the 9/11 terrorist attacks?

6. Discussions

1) Comparing American culture with Chinese Culture, American culture is characterized by its individualism and religious believes. And a lot of American films and novels are inspired by its religious believes especially by Puritanism, which is also one of the roots of American individualism. Maybe we can get some explanations from the history of Puritans in America.

2) Describe the relationship between America and China under Obama administration.

Stay Positive

1. Gratitude is not only the greatest of virtues, but the parent of all the others.
2. If you don't build your dream, someone will hire you to build theirs.

Chapter 3

Politics of the United States

When I was a boy I was told that anybody could become President; I'm beginning to believe it.

—Clarence Darrow

1. Why Government

What is the proper role of government? While many people have a general philosophy about what government should and should not do, they often struggle to answer the question when faced with specific policy problems.

Think about what life would really be like if we lived in the "state of nature". You would have absolute, limitless individual liberty. You could go where you wanted to go, eat what you wanted to eat, and hang out with whomever you wanted. There would be no laws against drug use, speeding or even stealing.

But you would not be the only one with absolute freedom. Everyone around you would be similarly free to do whatever they chose to do. Consequently, when someone wanted something you had in your possession, they could simply take it, **assuming** they were stronger and faster than you. And if they ended up injuring or killing you to get what you had, or if you hurt or killed them protecting your life and property, that would be the end of the conflict. No police officers would come, there would be no charges filed, there would be no trial, no punishment. In the state of nature, each individual is the "police force" that protects his or her own life, liberty and property.

The role of government, then, is to secure the liberties enjoyed in the state of nature by limiting individual behavior when it harms others. Exactly what those limits should be and what kinds of behavior should remain unregulated are the subjects of intense political debate. Adjusting the continually tipping balance between liberty and order is the primary business of government and politics.

2. The United States Constitution[1]

The United States Constitution was groundbreaking in numerous ways. Indeed, the very features which made it unique have also contributed to its **longevity**. These features also define the framework of American government and politics, establishing the United States of America, its national government and outlining the relationships among the government, the people and the states.

The most significant features of the U.S. Constitution are the establishment of the rule of law, the creation of a federal system with a supreme national government, the separation of governmental powers into three branches that check and balance each other, its flexibility and the establishment of a republican form of government.

The Constitution is considered the supreme law of the land both because of its content and because its authority is derived from the people. The concepts and ideas of the Constitution are the "higher law" in the United States of America, things which a government cannot create or destroy. Among these concepts and ideas is the notion that the people are sovereign and that legitimate governments must be based on popular consent. Because the Constitution was ratified by the representatives of the people, it is a document, in both word and deed, created by and for "the people".

While the Constitution is the supreme law of the land, most of the specific, day-to-day rules and regulations that bring order to American society are not included in the Constitution itself. These "ordinary" laws are creations of the Congress[2], state legislatures and city councils. But the notion that laws are more important than the opinions of individual people—even important people—applies to these laws as well. In America, no one is considered to be above the law. In fact, deliberately trying to avoid the law through deception or bribery are crimes in and of themselves. Even a president who violates the law can be held accountable for doing so.

To all Americans, another basic foundation in their Constitution is the Bill of Rights, adopted in 1791. This consists of 10 very short paragraphs which guarantee freedom and individual rights and forbid interference with lives of individuals by the government. Each paragraph is an Amendment to the original Constitution.

In the Bill of Rights, Americans are guaranteed the freedom of religion, of speech and of the press. They have the right to assemble in public places, to protest government actions and to demand change. They have the right to own weapons if they wish. Because of the Bill of Rights, neither the police nor soldiers can stop and search a person without good reason. They also cannot search a person's home without legal permission from a court.

The Bill of Rights guarantees Americans the right to a speedy trial if accused of a crime. The trial must be by a jury and the accused person must be allowed representation by a lawyer and must be able to call in witness to speak for him or her. Cruel and unusual punishment is forbidden.

3. Federalism[3]

3.1 Why a Federal System?

The framers of the Constitution created a federal system with a national government strong enough to unify the states in their pursuit of common goals without completely robbing the states of their independence. If they had not done so, it is unlikely that the ratifying conventions in the several states would have approved the Constitution. Indeed, the inclusion of the federal principle in the Constitution was a critical factor in its ratification. The benefits of federalism, however, have reached far beyond the ratification debates.

3.2 Protecting Rights and Liberties

Federalism contributes significantly to the protection of individual rights and liberties in this nation. While many of the opponents of the Constitution were fearful that the national government would not respect the rights of the people, there have been several instances in which the national government stepped in to stop the abuse of individual rights at the state level.

While the times when the national government intervened to stop abuses in the states tend to receive comparatively more attention, there have been a number of cases in which it fell upon the states to protect their residents from the **encroachments** of the national government. Some prominent examples are the protection of land use rights, especially in western states, and countless state efforts to minimize the influence and intrusiveness of the national government.

Another significant benefit of federalism is that it keeps many political leaders, the decisions they make and the implementation of public policy close to the people. Imagine that there was only one school board for the entire nation, and not the tens of thousands that exist. Finding someone in Washington who would listen to the concerns of a mother or father from Flagstaff or Little Rock or Topeka would be next to impossible. The school boards and school board members in each of these cities and those in other towns and cities across America, however, can be responsive to the comparatively much smaller number of people they serve. Federalism, with its multiple levels of government, keeps government much closer to the people than would otherwise be possible.

4. The United States Congress

The framers of the Constitution created a republican form of government, one in which the people elect representatives to make public policy decisions for them. At the national level, the people vote directly to choose members of the House of Representatives and the Senate. Members of Congress, both House members and Senators, provide the people of this nation with their most direct link to the decisions and policies made by the national government. Because members of Congress are chosen directly by the people, the Congress is often referred to as the "People's Branch".

There are 435 members of the House of Representatives. Each member represents a Congressional District with roughly the same population. The voters living in each district select the person that represents them in the House.

There are 100 Senators in the United States Senate. The people of each of the 50 states select two Senators to represent them in the Senate. Both of the Senators from a state represent the entire state—they do not divide the state in half geographically, along party lines or on any other basis.

4.1 The Number of Members

Why are there 435 members in the House of Representatives? The Constitution originally set the number at 65, leaving the future size of the House up to the Congress. The only condition was that the number of representatives was not to exceed one for every thirty-thousand people. As the nation grew and more states were added to the Union, the Congress expanded the number of House members to its current size of 435, where it has remained since 1912. Every ten years, a national census is conducted and the seats in the House are "reapportioned," allotting each state a proportion of seats roughly equal to its proportion of the entire national population.

According to the 1910 Census, the population of this nation was about 92 million people. With 435 representatives, there was a House member for every 210,000 people. In the 2000 Census, with a national population of 281 million, there is only one representative for every 647,000 people. There is no reason that the size of the House cannot be expanded. All it would take is an act of Congress.

4.2 Constitutional Offices

The Constitution establishes three specific congressional leadership positions and leaves the creation of other offices to the Congress. The three constitutionally created positions are the Speaker of the House, the President of the Senate and the President Pro Tempore of the Senate.

The Speaker of the House is elected by members of the House and is generally recognized as the leader of the majority party in the House. There is no requirement that the Speaker actually is a member of the House, but every Speaker chosen by the House has been. The importance and power of the Speakership has varied widely over time. Today, the Speaker of the House has a privileged position among House members, with the ability to heavily influence the agenda and priorities of the House.

The Constitution establishes that the Vice President of the United States of America shall be the President of the Senate. However, the President of the Senate is only authorized to break tie votes in the Senate. Furthermore, because it was anticipated that the official duties of the Vice President would prevent daily attendance in the Senate, the Constitution also provides for a President Pro Tempore, or temporary President, to preside when the Vice President is absent. The President Pro Tempore is selected by members of the Senate and is generally one of the more senior members of the majority party. The President Pro Tempore, however, is not the most powerful leader of the Senate. The real power in the Senate is in the hands of party leaders.

5. The Executive Branch

5.1 Office of the President

Most children in this nation have heard the saying that "Anyone can grow up to become the President." Indeed, America's presidents have come from all walks of life, some from the most humble of circumstances. Abraham Lincoln[4]was born in a log cabin. Harry Truman[4]was less than successful in the clothing business. Jimmy Carter[5]was a peanut farmer. Ronald Reagan co-starred with a monkey in one of his biggest motion pictures.

Most of the men who have become President of the United States of America, however, have had distinguished business, political or military careers before assuming the highest office in the land. Donald Trump[6] is the 45th and current President of the United States. Before entering politics, he was a businessman and television personality. He took charge of his family's real estate business in 1971, renamed it The Trump Organization, and expanded it from Queens and Brooklyn into Manhattan. The company built or renovated skyscrapers, hotels, casinos, and golf courses. Trump later started various side ventures, including licensing his name for real estate and consumer products. He managed the company until his 2017 inauguration[7].

5.2 The Presidency in the Separated System

The Constitution of the United States does not grant to the President unlimited authority to run the national government. In fact, it gives only limited powers to the President and grants both the legislative and judicial branches powers that allow them to check and frustrate Presidential power.

While many observers and political scientists have suggested that the Presidency has grown so much in importance and power that the United States political system is presidential-centered and dominated. Indeed, presidential authority is exercised in the context of a separated system, in which the powers of the national government are divided among three branches, each branch holding "checks" against the others.

Presidential elections are every four years, Senate elections every six and House elections every two. Because only one third of Senate seats are contested every two years, it is impossible for all of the members of Congress and the President to be elected at the same time. The voters who select the President, the members of the House and one-third of the Senate in one election are not likely to have the same concerns and preferences as the voters who select new House members and another third of the Senate two years later. Moreover, because the President is elected by the entire nation while members of Congress are elected by the voters in the states or districts from which they come, members of Congress and the President do not represent the same **constituencies**.

The President of the United States of America, by virtue of formally granted constitutional powers, has several significant leadership roles. While these roles are varied and diverse, they can generally be divided into two large areas of authority and responsibility: domestic policy and foreign affairs. So distinct are the two realms of presidential activity and so different are the degrees of success within each that political scientists generally refer to these two subdivisions as the "two presidencies".

6. The Federal Judiciary

The federal courts often are called the guardians of the Constitution because their rulings protect rights and liberties guaranteed by it.

Through fair and impartial judgments, the federal courts interpret and apply the law to resolve disputes. The courts do not make the laws. That is the responsibility of Congress. Nor do the courts have the power to enforce the laws. That is the role of the President and the many executive branch departments and agencies.

The founding fathers of the nation considered an independent federal judiciary essential to ensure fairness and equal justice for all citizens of the United States. The Constitution they drafted promotes judicial independence in two major ways. First, federal judges are appointed for life, and they can be removed from office only through impeachment and conviction by Congress of "Treason, Bribery, or other high Crimes and Misdemeanors." Second, the Constitution provides that the compensation of federal judges "shall not be diminished during their continuance in office" which means that neither the President nor Congress can reduce the salary of a federal judge. These two protections help an independent judiciary to decide cases free from popular passion and political influence.

6.1 United States Supreme Court[8]

The Supreme Court of the United States of America is established in Article III of the Constitution. While the Constitution formally provides for a "Chief Justice" of the Court, it leaves the actual size of the Court up to the Congress. The United States Supreme Court consists of the Chief Justice of the United States and eight associate justices. At its discretion, and within certain guidelines established by Congress, the Supreme Court each year hears a limited number of the cases it is asked to decide. Those cases may begin in the federal or state courts, and they usually involve important questions about the Constitution or federal law.

The size of the Supreme Court is determined by the Congress. When a vacancy opens on the Court, the President nominates a new justice who is then confirmed or rejected by the Senate. If confirmed, the nominee becomes a member of the Court and holds that office "during good behavior". In other words, short of committing an impeachable offense, Supreme Court justices serve for life or until they voluntarily retire.

6.2 The United States District Courts

The United States district courts are the trial courts of the federal court system. Within limits set by Congress and the Constitution, the district courts have jurisdiction to hear nearly all categories of federal cases, including both civil and criminal matters. Every day hundreds of people across the nation are selected for jury duty and help decide some of these cases.

There are 94 federal judicial districts, including at least one district in each state, and the District of Columbia and Puerto Rico. Three territories of the United States—the Virgin Islands, Guam, and the Northern Mariana Islands—have district courts that hear federal cases, including bankruptcy cases.

7. The Legislative Process

The United States Congress is the chief legislative or law-making body in the land. Through the laws it passes, it defines crimes and punishments, establishes levels of taxation and spending and creates the programs and policies that shape American government and politics.

The legislative process can be long, tedious, complex and frustrating. Indeed, it is much more difficult to pass a bill than it is to kill one. There are numerous times and places during the legislative process at which a bill can die. Only a very few survive to become law.

The chief function of Congress is the making of laws. The legislative process comprises a number of steps.

The work of Congress is initiated by the introduction of a proposal in one of four principal forms: the bill, the joint resolution, the concurrent resolution, and the simple resolution.

A bill is the form used for most legislation, whether permanent or temporary, general or special, public or private. A bill originating in the House of Representatives is designated by the letters "H.R.", signifying "House of Representatives", followed by a number that it retains throughout all its parliamentary stages. Bills are presented to the President for action when approved in identical form by both the House of Representatives and the Senate.

8. Voting in America

The formal requirements for voting in the United States are simple. Anyone who is a citizen of the United States of America and at least 18 years of age is **eligible** to vote. Additionally, every state but one (North Dakota) requires voters to register to vote a reasonable number of days before the election (usually thirty days). The primary objective of the registration requirement is to prevent **fraudulent** voting. A secondary effect of requiring voters to register, however, is that only those who are interested and attentive are likely to vote. A month or more before Election Day, a voter must find out where to register and then go there and register or he or she will not be able to vote on Election Day.

8.1 People that Can Vote

The right to vote is sometimes referred to as "**suffrage**". Suffrage in the United States is currently enjoyed by all citizens over the age of 18, as noted. However, this has not always been the case. In the early years of the republic, the eligible electorate consisted primarily of white, male and property owners. States gradually relaxed property-ownership requirements until all males of 21 years or more were allowed to vote. After the Civil War, the right to vote was extended to all citizens, regardless of race, by the 13th Amendment to the Constitution. The Women's Suffrage Movement succeeded with the 19th Amendment and the extension of the right to vote to women (some states already allowed women to vote, but the Amendment required all states to do so). The 23rd Amendment allotted electoral votes to the District of Columbia, thereby giving its residents the right to vote in presidential elections. And the 26th Amendment, ratified in 1971, granted the right to vote to every citizen who is 18 years or older.

Voting rights are extended by the Constitution. However, this does not mean they are exercised. Most notably, black voters did not fully enjoy the right to vote for many years after the ratification of the 13th Amendment because of intimidation, discrimination and tactics such as literacy tests and poll taxes. Moreover, many people who have the right to vote simply choose not to exercise it. Millions of eligible voters have not even registered to vote.

8.2 Electoral College

Unlike members of Congress, Presidents are not elected directly by the people. Instead, they are chosen by the Electoral College, one of the least-understood institutions in American politics. The framers of the Constitution were fearful of direct democracy and the "tyranny of the majority" it might produce. Consequently, they created a complex "filtering" process known as the Electoral College which was intended to insulate the selection of the President from the **whim**s of the people. The Electoral College is comprised of "electors", individuals who cast the electoral votes for their states. Originally, electors were free to cast their votes as they chose. Today, electors are "bound" or "committed" by state law to vote for the candidate who received the most popular votes in their state. With the exceptions of Maine and Nebraska, states give all of their electoral votes to the candidate who wins a majority of votes in the state. (The procedure for electing the President is outlined in Article II, Section 1 of the Constitution.)

Each state has a number of electoral votes equal to the number of Senators and House Members that it is eligible to send to the Congress. For example, the state of New York elects two Senators (as every other state does) and 31 Members of the House. New York, then, has 33 electoral votes. The total number of electoral votes in the Electoral College is 538—one for each of the 100 Senators and 435 House Members plus the three allotted to the District of Columbia by the 23rd Amendment to the Constitution.

Electors are chosen by the political parties in each state. When voters cast their ballots in favor of a presidential candidate they are actually voting for the electors of the same party as that candidate. When a candidate wins the popular vote in a state, he or she wins that state's electoral votes. Those votes are formally cast by the electors chosen to represent the winning candidate's party in each state.

Under the original rules of the Electoral College, as established by the Constitution, electors cast separate votes for President and Vice-president. Whoever received a majority of electoral votes would be the President and the runner-up would become the Vice-President.

Given the distribution of electoral votes across the nation, it is possible for a presidential candidate to be elected President by winning less than one-fourth of the states. Out of 538 electoral votes, a candidate must win 270 to have a majority and the largest 11 states control 270 electoral votes. When candidates campaign for the Presidency then, they tend to spend most of their time in large states with large blocks of electoral vote—smaller states tend to get overlooked.

In theory, Congress and the President are independent of each other. Their relationship is one of the "checks and balances", that is, the powers of one limit those of the other. But in reality, there is close cooperation between the two branches of government. Only when they have different tactics or measures, may they sometimes find themselves in conflict with each other.

Under the Constitution, a sitting President may be removed from office before his term expires only by an impeachment process whereby the House of Representatives, upon sufficient evidence, brings a "bill of impeachment" approved by two-thirds of its membership. Next there comes a trial in the Senate, with the Chief Justice of the Supreme Court as the judge and the Senate as the jury. This power has been used only twice and no President has ever been actually impeached in American History. In 1868, Congress tried to impeach President Andrew Johnson but failed. In 1974 a proposal was passed in a committee of the House to impeach President Nixon over the Watergate Scandal. But before the proposal went to the House for debate, Nixon resigned office, and Gerald R. Ford, the Vice-President, succeeded him.

9. Political Parties

The Republican Party is one of the two major political parties in the United States, the other being its historic rival, the Democratic Party. Republicans emphasize the role of free market decision making in fostering economic prosperity. They support the idea of individuals being economically responsible for their own actions and decisions. They favor a laissez-faire free market, policies supporting business, economic liberalism, and **fiscal** conservatism but with higher spending on the military. Historically, the Democratic Party has favored farmers, laborers, labor unions, and religious and ethnic minorities; it has opposed unregulated business and finance, and favored progressive income taxes. Once dominated by unionized labor and the working class, the Democratic base currently consists of a large number of well-educated and relatively affluent liberals as well as those in the socially more conservative working class. Today, Democrats advocate more social freedoms, affirmative action, balanced budget, and a free enterprise system tempered by government intervention (mixed economy). The party believes that the government should play a role in **alleviating** poverty and social injustice, even if such requires a large role for government and progressive taxation.

9.1 The Democratic Party

The Democratic Party is one of the major contemporary political parties in the United States, along with the Republican Party. It is the oldest political party in continuous operation in the United States and it is one of the oldest parties in the world. The Democratic Party traces its origin to the Democratic-Republican Party, founded by Thomas Jefferson, James Madison, and other influential opponents of the Federalists in 1792. The economically activist philosophy of Franklin D. Roosevelt, has shaped much of the party's economic agenda since 1932, and served to tie the two regional factions of the party together until the late 1960s. In fact, Roosevelt's New Deal coalition usually controlled the national government until the 1970s. Since the 2008 general elections, the Democratic Party is the majority party for the 111th Congress; the party holds an outright majority in the House of Representatives and the Democratic caucus (including two independents) constitutes a majority in the United States Senate. Democrats also hold a majority of state governorships and control a majority of state legislatures.

9.2 The Republican Party

The party's founding members chose the name "Republican Party" in the mid-1850s in part as in homage to Thomas Jefferson (it was the name initially used by his party). The name echoed the 1776 republican values of civic virtue and opposition to aristocracy and corruption. It is the second-oldest continuing political party in the United States. The term "Grand Old Party" is a traditional nickname for the Republican Party, and the initialism "G.O.P" (or GOP) is a commonly used designation. Founded in Ripon, Wisconsin, in 1854 by anti-slavery expansion activists and modernizers, the Republican Party quickly surpassed the Whig Party as the principal opposition to the Democratic Party. It first came to power in 1860 with the election of Abraham Lincoln to the presidency and presided over the American Civil War and Reconstruction. Today, the party supports a conservative and/or center-right platform, with further foundations in supply-side fiscal policies and social conservatism. There have been 19 Republican Presidents. Republicans currently fill a minority of seats in both the United States Senate and the House of Representatives, hold a minority of state governorships, and control a minority of state legislatures. In the Presidential election of 2008, the party's nominees were Senator John McCain of Arizona for President and Alaska Governor Sarah Palin for Vice President.

Donald Trump, the current President of the United States, is the 12th Republican to hold that office. On June 16, 2015, Trump announced his candidacy for President of the United States at Trump Tower in Manhattan. He announced his campaign slogan: "Make America Great Again".Trump said his wealth would make him immune to pressure from campaign donors. In the 2016 Republican Party presidential primaries, Trump entered a field of 17 major candidates who were vying for the 2016 Republican nomination; this was the largest presidential field in American history. Trump's campaign was initially not taken seriously by political analysts, but he quickly rose to the top of opinion polls. On Super Tuesday, Trump won the plurality of the vote, and he remained the front-runner throughout the remainder of the primaries. By March 2016, Trump became poised to win the Republican nomination. After a landslide win in Indiana on May 3, 2016—which prompted the remaining candidates to suspend their presidential campaigns—RNC Chairman Reince Priebus declared Trump the presumptive Republican nominee. After becoming the presumptive Republican nominee, Trump shifted his focus to the general election. Trump began campaigning against Hillary Clinton, who became the presumptive Democratic nominee on June 6, 2016. On July 15, 2016, Trump announced his selection of Indiana Governor Mike Pence as his running mate. Four days later on July 19, Trump and Pence were officially nominated by the Republican Party at the Republican National Convention. The list of convention speakers and attendees included former presidential nominee Bob Dole, but the other prior nominees did not attend. Two days later, Trump officially accepted the nomination in a 76-minute speech. On September 26, 2016, Trump and Clinton faced off in their first presidential debate, which was held at Hofstra University in Hempstead, New York. The TV broadcast was the most watched presidential debate in United States history. The second presidential debate was held at Washington University in Saint Louis, Missouri. The final presidential debate was held on October 19 at the University of Nevada, Las Vegas. On November 8, 2016, Trump received 306 pledged electoral votes versus 232 for Clinton. The official counts were 304 and 227 respectively, after defections on both sides. Trump's victory marked the return of a Republican White House combined with control of both chambers of Congress.

Joyful Moment

Mrs. Brown went to visit one of her friends and carried a small box with holes punched in the top.

"What's in your box?" asked the friend. "A cat," answered Mrs. Brown.

"You see I've been dreaming about mice at night and I'm so scared! This cat is to catch them."

"But the mice are only imaginary," said the friend.

"So is the cat," whispered Mrs. Brown.

Notes

[1] The United States Constitution 美国宪法，美国的根本大法，奠定了美国政治制度的法律基础，是世界上第一部成文宪法。

[2] Congress 国会，美国最高立法机关，由参议院和众议院组成

[3] federalism 联邦制，是若干个单位联合组成的统一国家，国家整体与组成部分之间是一种联盟关系，联邦政府行使国家主权，是对外交往的主体。

[4] Harry Truman 哈里 • 杜鲁门，第 33 任总统，1884 年出生于密苏里州拉马尔

[5] Jimmy Carter 吉米 • 卡特，第 39 任总统，1924 年 10 月 1 日生于美国佐治亚州普兰

[6] Donald Trump 唐纳德 • 特朗普，第 45 任美国总统，1946 年 6 月 14 日生于纽约

[7] Inauguration of Donald Trump 唐纳德 • 特朗普于当地时间 2017 年 1 月 20 日中午在美国首都华盛顿宣誓就职，正式成为美国第 45 任总统。

[8] Supreme Court 联邦最高法院是美国联邦法院系统的最高审级和最高审判机关。1869 年根据国会法令规定，由一位首席法官和八位法官组成。

New Words

1. **assume** /ə'suːm/ *vt.* to take to be the case or to be true 假定

   —I assumed you could speak French fluently.

   我以为你能讲流利的法语。

2. **longevity** /lɒn'dʒevəti/ *n.* the property of being long-lived 长命，长寿

   —Her longevity as a star is very long.

   她当明星的时间很长。

3. **encroachment** /ɪn'krəʊtʃmənt/ *n.* entry to another's property without right or permission 侵占

   —I resent the encroachment on my time.

   我讨厌别人侵占我的时间。

4. **constituency** /kən'stɪtʃuənsi/ *n.* a district that elects its own representative to parliament 选区

   —The Conservative Party is losing ground in that constituency.

   保守党正逐渐失去该选区的支持者。

5. **eligible** /'elɪdʒəbəl/ *a.* qualified for or allowed or worthy of being chosen 有资格当选的，合格的

   —Anyone with an annual income of under £5,000 may be eligible to apply.

   凡年收入在 5 000 英镑以下者均可申请。

6. **fraudulent** /'frɔːdʒələnt/ *a.* intended to deceive 欺诈的，不诚实的

   —She got the job of science teacher by fraudulent means; she pretended she'd studied at university.

她用欺骗手法取得了理科教员的职位，谎称曾在大学读过书。

7. **suffrage** /'sʌfrɪdʒ/ *n.* the right to vote 投票，选举权

—In that country, women have no suffrage.

在那个国家，妇女没有选举权。

8. **whim** /wɪm/ *n.* a sudden desire; an odd or fanciful or capricious idea 一时的兴致，冲动；怪念头

—He is guided by whim without regard to the facts.

他一时冲动，忽视了事实。

9. **fiscal** /'fɪskəl/ *a.* involving financial matters 财政的，国库的

—We are trying to get a thorough understanding of the government's fiscal policy.

我们正努力对政府的财政政策进行全面的了解。

10. **alleviate** /ə'liːvieɪt/ *vt.* provide physical relief, as from pain; make easier 减轻，使缓和

—The doctor gave her an injection to alleviate the pain.

医生给她注射以减轻疼痛。

Exercises

1. Choose the correct answer.

1) Which of the following is the only branch that can make federal laws, and levy federal taxes?

A. The Executive. B. The Legislative.
C. The Judicial. D. The President.

2) Which of the following is NOT a power of the President?

A. The President can veto any bill passed by Congress.
B. The President has the authority to appoint federal judges when vacancies occur.
C. The President can make laws.
D. The President has broad powers, with the executive branch, to issue regulation and directives regarding the work of the federal department.

3) The Bill of Rights consists of __________.

A. 10 very short paragraphs in an amendment
B. 10 amendments adopted in 1787
C. 10 amendments added to the Constitution in 1791
D. the amendments concerning the freedom of speech, the freedom of the press and the freedom of religion

4) Which of the following is NOT guaranteed in the Bill of Rights?

A. The freedom of religion.
B. The freedom of searching a person's home by police.
C. The freedom of press and speech.

D. The right to own weapons if one wishes.

5) There are __________ members of the House of Representatives.

A. 425 B. 435 C. 352 D. 423

2. Decide whether the following statements are True or False.

1) Today, the United States has two major political parties. One is the Democratic Party; the other is the Republic Party.

2) The U.S. Constitution set up a federal system with a strong central government.

3) The main duty of the Congress is to make laws, including those which levy taxes that pay for the work of the federal government.

4) Americans have to join a political party in order to be a candidate for public office.

5) In the Bill of Rights, Americans are guaranteed the freedom of religion, of speech and of the press.

3. Fill in the blanks according to the passage.

1) The Supreme Court is composed of ________ Chief Justice and ________ associate justices.

2) A federal system is one in which power is shared between ________ and ________ with some rights reserved to each.

3) The U.S. federal government consists of the following three branches: the executive, ________ and ________ .

4) The Congress is divided into ________ with 435 members who serve two years, and ________ with 100 lawmakers who serve six-year terms.

5) The two major political parties are ________ and ________, the former is thought to be more liberal, and the latter is believed to be more conservative.

4. Explain the following terms according to the passage.

1) a federal system

2) the executive

3) bill

4) Constitution

5) congress

5. Answer the following questions according to the passage.

1) What are the two political parties in the United States? What is the difference between them?

2) Why is a government necessary?

3) What is the relationship between the President and the Congress?

6. Discussion.

1) What are some of the major powers of each of the three branches of the U.S. government? How are the three branches supposed to check and balance each other?

2) Summarize the main advantages of the federal system.

Stay Positive

1. The outer world you see is a reflection of your inner self.
2. Happiness isn't getting all you want. It's enjoying all you have.

Chapter 4

Economy of the United States

Economy, the poor man's mints; extravagance, the rich man's pitfall.

—Martin Tupper, American economist

1. Introduction

1.1 Overview of the US Economy

The economy of the United States is a highly developed mixed economy. It is the world's largest economy by nominal GDP and the second-largest by purchasing power parity (PPP). In 2017, its gross domestic product (GDP) was $19,555.87 billion, it also enjoys a high rank of GDP per capita of No. 8 in the world. The US economy has maintained a stable overall GDP growth rate, a low unemployment rate, and high levels of research and capital investment funded by both national and foreign investors. The following table shows the top 10 countries with highest GDP in 2017 by the World Bank. Their GDP per capita and rank is also given respectively.

Table 4.1 2017 World's GDP and GDP per capita List by the World Bank

Rank by GDP	Country	GDP (millions of USD)	GDP per capita	Rank by GDP per capita
1	United States	19,555,874	59,532	8
2	China	13,173,585	8,827	74
3	Japan	4,342,160	38,428	27
4	Germany	3,595,406	44,470	19
5	United Kingdom	3,232,281	39,720	24
6	India	2,607,409	1,940	143
7	France	2,586,568	38,477	26
8	Italy	1,932,938	31,953	28
9	Brazil	1,759,267	9,821	70
10	Canada	1,682,368	45,032	18

1.2 The US Economic System

The United States declared its independence in the same year, 1776, that Scottish economist Adam Smith [1] wrote *The Wealth of Nations* [2], a book that has had an enormous influence on American economic development. In his book, Smith argued that "An invisible hand" (the market) guides them to enrich and improve all of society". Most Americans believe that the rise of their nation as a great economic power could not have occurred under any system except capitalism, also known as free enterprise after a conclusion to Smith's thinking: that government should interfere in commerce as little as possible.

Adam Smith would easily recognize the bright aspects of American business, but other aspects he would not. As we have seen, American industrial development in the 19th century took a toll on working men and women. Factory owners often required them to put in long hours for low wages, provided them with unsafe and unhealthy workplaces, and hired the children of poor families. Entrepreneurs took full advantage of the lack of government oversight to enrich themselves by forming monopolies, eliminating competition, setting high prices for products, and selling poor-qualified goods.

In response to these evils and at the **insistence** of labor unions and the Progressive Movement [3], in the late 19th century Americans began to modify their faith in free capitalism. In 1890, the Sherman Antitrust Act [4] took the first steps toward breaking up monopolies.

The sum total of these laws and regulations has changed American capitalism, in the words of one writer, from a "freely running horse to one that is bridled and saddled". However, political conservatives believe there is too much government regulation of business. They argue that some of the rules that firms must follow are unnecessary and costly. In response to such complaints, the government has tried to reduce the paperwork required of businesses and to set overall goals or standards for businesses to reach, as opposed to dictating detailed rules of operation.

1.3 Basic Ingredients of the US Economy

The first ingredient of a nation's economic system is its natural resources. The United States is rich in mineral resources and fertile farm soil, and it is blessed with a moderate climate. It also has extensive coastlines on both the Atlantic and Pacific Oceans, as well as on the Gulf of Mexico.

The second ingredient is labor, which converts natural resources into goods. The number of available workers and, more importantly, their productivity help determine the health of an economy.

The quality of available labor—how hard people are willing to work and how skilled they are—is at least as important to a country's economic success as the number of workers. In the early days of the United States, frontier life required hard work, and what is known as the Protestant Work Ethic[5] reinforced the characteristic. The Protestant Work Ethic, sometimes called the Puritan Work Ethic, is a sociological, theoretical concept. It is based upon the notion that the Calvinist emphasis on the necessity for hard work is proponent of a person's calling and worldly success is a sign of personal salvation. A strong emphasis on education, including technical and vocational training, also contributed to America's economic success, as did willingness to experiment and to change.

1.4 Sino-US Economic Relationships

The PRC (People's Republic of China) and the US started trade relations in 1972 and 1973. US direct investment in China covers a wide range of manufacturing sectors, several large hotel projects, restaurant chains, and petrochemicals. US companies have entered agreements establishing more than 20,000 equity joint ventures, contractual joint ventures, and wholly foreign-owned enterprises in China. Some of the factors that influence the US trade deficit with China include:

- a shift of low-end **assembly** industries to mainland China from the newly industrialized countries in Asia, mainland China has increasingly become the last link in a long chain of value-added production;
- US demand for labor-intensive goods exceeds domestic output;
- The undervaluation of the Renminbi relative to the United States dollar.

2. Economic Performance of the US since the 21th century

2.1 The Early 2000s

Like a four-wheel-drive vehicle crossing rough places, the US economy **cruised** along in the early 2000s, even while hitting some big rocks: a stock market crash, terrorist attacks, wars in Iraq and Afghanistan, corporate accounting scandals, widespread hurricane destruction, surging energy prices, and sliding real estate values.

After a mild recession in March, November 2001, the US economy resumed expanding, an average 2.9% during 2002-2006, while price inflation, unemployment and interest rates remained relatively low.

2.2 The Great Recession period

The Great Recession was a period of general economic decline observed in world markets during the late 2000s and early 2010s. The scale and timing of the recession varied from country to country. In terms of overall impact, the International Monetary Fund concluded that it was the worst global recession since the Great Depression in the 1930s. The causes of the recession largely originated in the United States, particularly the real estate market, though policies of other nations contributed as well.

According to the US National Bureau of Economic Research, the recession began in December 2007 and ended in June 2009, thus extending over 19 months. The Great Recession was related to the financial crisis of 2007-2008 and US subprime mortgage crisis of 2007-2009. The Great Recession resulted in the scarcity of valuable assets in the market economy and the collapse of the financial sector in the world economy. Many mortgage companies and other investment banks faced a worsening crisis from 2007-2008, with the bankruptcy of Lehman Brothers and **bailouts** of several other financial institutions.

2.3 Global Financial Crisis Impacts upon the US

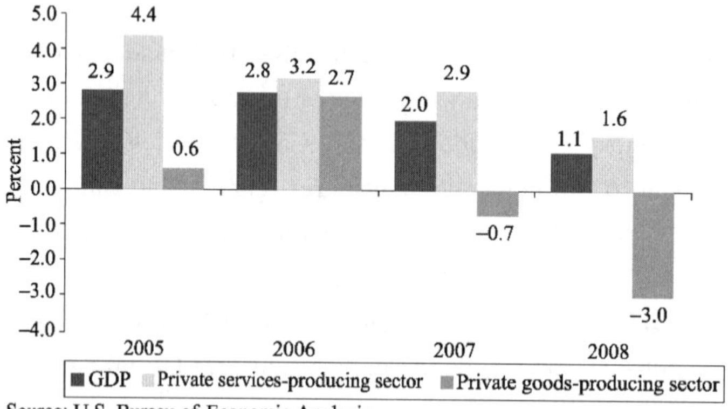

Source: U.S. Bureau of Economic Analysis

Figure 4.1 Annual Growth of US Economy in Real GDP

Real gross domestic product—the output of goods and services produced by labor and property located in the United States—decreased at an annual rate of approximately 6% in the fourth quarter of 2008 and first quarter of 2009, versus activity in the year-ago periods. The US unemployment rate increased to 9.5% by June 2009, the highest rate since 1983 and roughly twice the pre-crisis rate. The average hours per work week declined to 33, the lowest level since the government began collecting the data in 1964.

Initially the companies affected were those directly involved in home construction and mortgage lending such as Northern Rock and Countrywide Financial, as they could no longer obtain financing through the credit markets. Over 100 mortgage lenders went bankrupt during 2007 and 2008. The crisis hit its peak in September and October 2008. Several major institutions failed, were acquired under duress, or were subject to government takeover. These included Lehman Brothers [6], Merrill Lynch [7], Fannie Mae [8], Freddie Mac [9], and AIG [10].

2.4 Emergency and Shortterm Responses

Various actions had been taken since the crisis became apparent in August 2007. In September 2008, major instability in world financial markets increased awareness and attention to the crisis. Various agencies and regulators, as well as political officials, began to take additional, more comprehensive steps to handle the crisis. Government agencies had committed or spent trillions of dollars in loans, asset purchases, guarantees, and direct spending.

A number of commentators suggested that if the **liquidity** crisis continued, there could be an extended recession or worse. The continuing development of the crisis prompted fears of a global economic collapse. Investment bank UBS [11] stated that 2008 would see a clear global recession, with recovery unlikely for at least two years. UBS economists announced that the "beginning of the end" of the crisis had begun, with the world starting to make the necessary actions to fix the crisis: capital injection by governments; injection made systemically; interest rate cuts to help borrowers. The world's central banks were cutting interest rates. UBS emphasized the United States needed to implement systemic injection. UBS further emphasized that this could only fix the financial crisis, but "the worst is still to come".

At the end of October 2008, UBS revised its outlook downwards: the forthcoming recession would be the worst since the Reagan recession of 1981 and 1982 with negative growth for the US, Euro zone, the UK and Canada in 2009; very limited recovery in 2010; but not as bad as the Great Depression (1929-1933), and soon the economy world recover as it always did after recessions.

2.5 Recent Economic Development After the Recession

The Bush administration (2001–2009) and Obama administrations (2009–2017) applied banking bailout programs and Keynesian stimulus via high government deficits, while the Federal Reserve maintained near-zero interest rates. These measures helped the economy recover.

Real GDP regained its pre-crisis (late 2007) peak by 2011, household net worth by the second quarter of 2012, non-farm payroll jobs by May 2014, and the unemployment rate by September 2015. Each of these variables continued into post-recession record territory following those dates, with the US recovery becoming the second longest on record in April 2018.

By various measures the United States remains the world's most productive, competitive, and influential large economy. Yet more and more the US economy is itself influenced by dynamic economies overseas. And it faces challenges both at home and abroad.

3. Economic Sectors

3.1 International Trade

3.1.1 Import and Export

The United States is the most significant nation in the world when it comes to international trade. For decades, it has led the world in imports while simultaneously remaining as one of the top three exporters of the world. Besides, the governments of the United States, Canada, and Mexico signed North American Free Trade Agreement (NAFTA), which has created a trilateral trade bloc in North America. The agreement came into force on January 1, 1994.

There has been an unfavorable balance of trade since the 1970s. The American government therefore began to pursue a protectionist policy in trade to encourage its export and limit its import. China has become America's No.1 trading partner in its importing field, followed by Canada, Mexico, Japan and Germany. According to the General Administration of Customs of China (GACC), in 2017 the US's imports from China were 429.8 billion dollars, while its exports to China were 153.9 billion dollars.

3.1.2 Investment in the United States

Foreign direct investment (FDI) plays a major role in the US economy, both as a key driver of the economy and an important source of innovation, exports and jobs. The United States has always provided foreign investors a stable and welcoming market. As a place to do business, the United States offers a predictable and transparent legal system, low taxes, outstanding infrastructure, and access to the world's most profitable consumer market.

Broadly speaking, the US has a fundamentally "open economy" and low barriers to foreign direct investment. During the 2008-2009 global economic recession, direct foreign investment shrank dramatically in 2009, dropping by more than half from a year earlier. Foreign direct investment to the US inflows rallied in 2010, posting gains over the previous year.

Foreign direct investment in the US shrank by 28 percent in 2012 to $166 billion over the previous year. President Barack Obama said in 2012, "In a global economy, the United States faces increasing competition for the jobs and industries of the future. Taking steps to ensure that we remain the destination of choice for investors around the world will help us win that competition and bring prosperity to our people."

In September 2013, the United States House of Representatives voted to pass the Global Investment in American Jobs Act of 2013, a bill which would direct the United States Department of Commerce to "conduct a review of the global competitiveness of the United States in attracting foreign direct investment". Supporters of the bill argued that increased foreign direct investment would help job creation in the United States.

Foreign direct investment in the United States increased by 45,701 million dollars in the first quarter of 2018. Foreign direct investment in the United States averaged 24,494 million dollars from 1994 to 2018, reaching an all time high of 48,155 million dollars in the first quarter of 2018 and a record low of –9,988 million dollars in the fourth quarter of 2001.

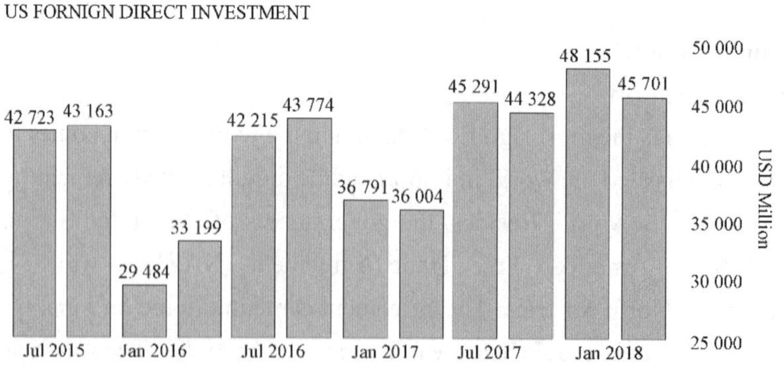

Figure 2 Foreign Direct Investment in the United States from 2015 to 2018

3.2 Manufacturing

The US is the leading manufacturer in the world. Its main industries are petroleum, steel, motor vehicles, aerospace, telecommunications, chemicals, electronics, food processing, consumer goods, and mining.

The petroleum industry includes the global processes of exploration, extraction, refining, transporting (often by oil tankers and pipelines), and marketing petroleum products. The largest volume products of the industry are fuel oil and gasoline (petrol). Petroleum is also the raw material for many chemical products, including pharmaceuticals, fertilizers, pesticides, and plastics.

The automotive industry designs, develops, manufactures, markets, and sells the world's motor vehicles. In 2017, more than 97.3 million motor vehicles, including cars and commercial vehicles were produced worldwide, of which 11.19 million motor vehicles were manufactured in the United States, the second largest in the world after China. Some world-leading automobile makers have factories in the US, such as Ford, Chrysler, Daimler AG, BMW, Navistar, Volvo, Toyota, Nissan, and Honda, etc.

The United States builds millions of computers each year and ranks second in the world in the production of electronic components. High-technology research and the production of software are mainly in the Silicon Valley of California, Boston, North Carolina, Austin in Texas, and Seattle Washington which is the home of the headquarters of Microsoft.

3.3 Service Industry

The largest sector of the US economy in terms of output and employment is service, or tertiary industry. Service industries can be very different from each other, ranging from hospitals to vacation resorts and automobile repair shops. Most of the service industry jobs are classified as white-collar jobs, and many of them require advanced education. These include many high-paying jobs in high technology field, financing, banking, education, health services, communications, entertainment, and tourism. They also include lower-paying positions that require little educational background, such as retail store clerks, and fast-food restaurant workers. In 2017, the output of US service industry was 15,521.9 billion dollars, accounting for 80.05% of US economic output and a similar proportion of employment.

Financial services make up an important section of the service industry because the large US economy needs a large financial market. Financial services refer to services provided by the finance industry. The finance industry contains a broad range of organizations that deal with the management of money. Among these organizations are banks, credit card companies, insurance companies, consumer finance companies, stock brokerages, investment funds and some government sponsored enterprises.

The major types of financial services include bank services, foreign exchange services, investment services, insurance and others. Banking in the United States is regulated by both the federal and state governments.

The bank makes profit in the form of the interest it charges on loans made to governments, businesses, and private individuals. Large banks in the United States include Chase Manhattan Corporation [12], Citibank [13], Morgan Guaranty Trust [14] (all headquartered in New York City);

Bank of America [15] (headquartered in San Francisco); and NationsBank (headquartered in Charlotte, North Carolina).

The United States also has a large insurance industry. Insurance companies provide insurance as well as a variety of other services, including deposit accounts, **pension** management, **mutual funds**, and other investments.

Tourism in the United States is a large industry that serves millions of international and domestic tourists yearly. Tourists visit the US to see natural wonders, cities, historic landmarks and entertainment venues. Americans seek similar attractions, as well as **recreation** and vacation areas. The most visited tourist attraction in the US is the Times Square in Manhattan, New York City which attracted approximately 62 million visitors from home and abroad in 2017.

American people like to move from place to place and they are known as "a nation on the move" or "a nation on wheels". As a result, the United States has a large transportation industry. In comparison to most of the Western world, the United States relies much more heavily on its roads both for commercial and personal transit. Car ownership is nearly universal except in a few of the largest cities where extensive mass transit systems have been built.

With the creation of the Eisenhower Interstate [16] in the 1950s, both long-distance trips and daily commutes became dominated by private automobile usage. This network of freeways meets federal standards and receives substantial federal funding and is particularly well-developed. The entire system is both the largest expressway system in the world and the largest public works project in US history.

Due to the size of the United States and the generally large distance between major cities, air transportation is the preferred method of travel for trips over 300 miles, such as for business travelers and long distance vacation travelers.

Air cargo comprises a large number of daily flights in the United States and is operated by private parcel companies such as FedEx [17] and United Parcel Service (UPS) [18]. These organizations operate some of the largest fleets in the world. Most air cargo moved by these organizations is time sensitive overnight and 2nd day parcels. The UPS also moves much of its letters and time sensitive parcels via air, but on regularly scheduled passenger flights.

3.4 Major Cities and Industries

The United States is actually an urban nation with more than 97% of its people relying on cities for a living. The main traditional industries of the US economy used to include steel, automobile, housing and military. Now America's industrial structure is undergoing changes with more and more emphasis being laid on electronics and chemistry.

Due to historical as well as geographical reasons, America's industries are not evenly distributed all over the country. New England developed its commerce and industry in colonial time by making use of its fine harbors and dense forests. It was often called "the workshop of the nation" by Americans.

The Midwest is America's leading center of heavy industry. It is most important in the production of motor vehicles and other transportation equipment, fabricated metals and nonelectrical machinery. America's heavy industries near the Great Lakes depend heavily upon three resources: iron ore from the Lake Superior area, coal deposits in Western Pennsylvania and Western Virginia, and cheap water transportation across the Great Lakes. They constitute the pillars of the development of heavy industries here in this region.

The American South is a newly developed industrial region. Historically, the South relied heavily on agriculture, and was highly rural until after 1945. It has since become more industrialized and urban and has attracted national and international migrants. The American South is now among the fastest-growing areas in the United States. Houston is the largest city in the Southern United States.

3.4.1 Washington, D.C.

Washington has a growing, diversified economy with an increasing percentage of professional and business service jobs. The GDP of the Washington Metropolitan Area was \$531.3 billion in 2017, making it the fifth-largest metropolitan economy in the United States. Between 2009 and 2016, GDP per capita in Washington D.C had consistently ranked the very top among U.S. states.

In December 2017, 25% of the employees in Washington D.C. were employed by a federal governmental agency. This is thought to immunize Washington D.C. to national economic downturns because the federal government continues operations even during recessions. Many organizations such as law firms, non-profit organizations, **lobbying** firms, trade unions, industry trade groups, and professional associations have their headquarters in or near D.C., to be close to the federal government.

3.4.2 New York City

New York City is a global center of international business and commerce. The city is a major center for banking and finance, retailing, world trade, transportation, tourism, real estate, new media, traditional media, advertising, legal services, accountancy, insurance, theater, fashion, and art in the United States.

Many Fortune 500 corporations are headquartered in New York City, as are a large number of multinational corporations. One out of ten private sector jobs in the city is with a foreign company. New York City has been ranked first among cities across the globe in attracting capital, business, and tourists.

In February 2017, New York City's unemployment rate fell to 4.3%, the lowest in the city's recorded history, with the city achieving the status of what many economists refer to as "full employment".

Lower Manhattan is the third largest central business district in the United States, and is home to the New York Stock Exchange, located on Wall Street, and the NASDAQ, representing the world's first and second largest stock exchanges respectively, when measured by average daily trading volume and overall market capitalization. Financial services account for more than

35% of the city's employment income. Real estate is a major force in the city's economy. The Time Warner Center is the property with the highest-listed market value in the city.

3.4.3 Chicago

Chicago is the largest city in the state of Illinois and the third largest city in the United States with over 2.7 million people. It has the third-largest metropolitan GDP in the United States—about $670.5 billion in 2017. The city has also been rated as having the most balanced economy in the United States, due to its high level of diversification.

It is a major world financial center, with the second largest central business district in the US. The city is also home to major financial and futures exchanges, including the Chicago Stock Exchange, the Chicago Board Options Exchange (CBOE) [19], and the Chicago Mercantile Exchange [20], which is owned, along with the Chicago Board of Trade by Chicago's CME Group. The CME Group, in addition, owns the New York Mercantile Exchange (NYMEX), the Commodities Exchange Inc. (COMEX) and the Dow Jones Indexes [21].

Chicago is the largest food-processing center of the United States. It has large stockyards and meat-packing plants which rely on cattle, pigs and poultry from the Middle West. Some American novels, such as *The Jungle* [22] and *Sister Carrie* [23], provide vivid descriptions of American workers' life in Chicago during America's industrialization. Chicago is also a center of clothing industry.

3.4.4 Detroit

Detroit is located in southeastern Michigan and separated by the Detroit River from the Canadian province of Ontario. Detroit's metropolitan region is the home of the headquarters of General Motors, Ford Motor Company, and Chrysler Corporation. The automobile industry has given Detroit its nickname, "The Motor City".

Several major corporations are based in the city, including three Fortune 500 companies. The most heavily represented sectors are manufacturing (particularly automotive), finance, technology, and health care. About 80,500 people work in downtown Detroit, comprising one-fifth of the city's employment base.

The state governor declared a financial emergency in March 2013, appointing an emergency manager. On July 18, 2013, Detroit filed the largest municipal bankruptcy case in US history. It was declared bankrupt by US judge Stephen Rhodes on December 3, who cited its $18.5 billion debt and declared that negotiations with its thousands of creditors were unfeasible.

On May 21, 2014, J.P. Morgan Chase announced that it was injecting $100 million over five years into Detroit's economy, providing development funding for a variety of projects that would increase employment. It is the largest commitment made to any one city by the nation's biggest bank. On May 19, 2015, J.P. Morgan Chase announced that it has invested $32 million for two redevelopment projects in the city's Capitol Park district, the Capitol Park Lofts and the Detroit Savings Bank building. Those investments are separate from Chase's five-year, $100-

million commitment. On May 10, 2017, Chase & Co. announced a $50 million increase in the $100 million investment the firm committed to economic development and neighborhood stabilization in Detroit by 2019. Half of the $150 million will be grants and the other half is going to a variety of loan funds for small business growth, mixed-use real estate development and residential housing projects.

3.4.5 Los Angeles

The economy of Los Angeles is driven by international trade, entertainment (television, motion pictures, video games, music recording, and production), aerospace, technology, petroleum, fashion, apparel, and tourism.

Other significant industries include finance, telecommunications, law, healthcare, and transportation. In the 2017 Global Financial Centres Index, Los Angeles was ranked as the 19th most competitive financial center in the world, and sixth most competitive in United States.

Two of the six major film studios, Paramount Pictures and 20th Century Fox, are located within the city limits, their locations being part of the so-called "Thirty-Mile Zone" of entertainment headquarters in Southern California. Some of the major companies headquartered in the cities of Los Angeles county are Hilton Hotels (Beverly Hills) [24], The Walt Disney Company[25], Warner Bros.[26], Sony Pictures Entertainment (parent of Columbia Pictures, located in Culver City)[27], DreamWorks (Glendale)[28], etc. Hollywood is a neighborhood in the central region of Los Angeles, California, which is notable as the home of the U.S. film industry. It is the largest district for television and film industry in America.

Los Angeles is the largest manufacturing center in the western United States. The contiguous ports of Los Angeles and Long Beach together comprise the fifth-busiest port in the world and the most significant port in the Western Hemisphere and is vital to trade within the Pacific Rim.

Joyful Moment

Secret for a Long, Happy Life

A woman walks up to a little old man rocking in a chair on his porch.

"I couldn't help noticing how happy you look," she says. "What's your secret for a long, happy life?"

"I smoke three packs a day, drink a case of whiskey a week, eat fatty foods and never, ever exercise."

"Wow, that's amazing," says the woman. "How old are you?"

"Twenty-six."

Notes

[1] Adam Smith 亚当·斯密（1723—1790），经济学的主要创立者

[2] *The Wealth of Nations* 外文全称为 *An Inquiry Into the Nature and Causes of the Wealth of Nations*《国富论》，亚当·斯密的著作

[3] Progressive Movement 美国进步运动，美国史学界一般把 1900 至 1917 年间美国所发生的政治、经济和社会改革运动统称进步运动

[4] Sherman Antitrust Act 谢尔曼反托拉斯法, 美国国会制定的第一部反托拉斯法，还是美国历史上第一个授权联邦政府控制、干预经济的法案，该法因由参议员约翰·谢尔曼提出而得名。

[5] Protestant work ethic 新教工作道德，以专注的现世目标、克俭的生活作风、负有责任感的勤劳工作和合理的行为算计为特征。

[6] Lehman Brothers 雷曼兄弟公司

[7] Merrill Lynch 美林集团，世界最著名的证券零售商和投资银行之一，总部位于美国纽约

[8] Fannie Mae 房利美公司，联邦国民抵押房贷款协会(Federal National Mortgage Association)的昵称，成立于 1938 年。

[9] Freddie Mac 房地美公司, 全球知名金融机构, 联邦住房抵押贷款公司(Federal Home Loan Mortgage Corp.)的昵称

[10] American International Group（AIG）美国国际集团，美国一家跨国金融和保险公司

[11] UBS（United Bank of Switzerland）瑞士联合银行集团，简称瑞银，是瑞士最大的金融机构

[12] Chase Manhattan Corporation 大通曼哈顿公司，总部设在纽约

[13] Citibank 花旗银行，花旗集团下的一家银行，最古老的商业银行之一

[14] Morgan Guaranty Trust 摩根保证信托公司，世界大型商业银行之一

[15] Bank of America 美国银行

[16] Eisenhower Interstate 艾森豪威尔州际公路系统，是美国公路系统的一部分，大多属高速公路，标志为蓝底警徽形，白字书写公路编号。

[17] FedEx 联邦快递，是一家国际性速递集团，总部设于美国田纳西州。2018 年 7 月 19 日，《财富》世界 500 强排行榜发布，联邦快递位列 155 位。

[18] United Parcel Service（UPS）联合包裹服务公司，是美国的快递承运商与包裹递送公司，总部设于乔治亚州的亚特兰大。2018 年 7 月 19 日，《财富》世界 500 强排行榜发布，UPS 快递位列 138 位。

[19] Chicago Board Options Exchange 芝加哥期权交易所，成立于 1973 年 4 月 26 日。它的正式成立，标志着期权交易进入了标准化、规范化的全新发展阶段。

[20] Chicago Mercantile Exchange 芝加哥商品交易所，成立于 1898 年，其前身为农产品交易所。2007 年芝加哥商品交易所（CME）和芝加哥期货交易所（CBOT）合并成全球最大的衍生品交易所——CME 集团。

[21] Dow Jones Index 道琼斯指数，一种算术平均股价指数，它是世界上历史最为悠久的股票指数。

[22] *The Jungle*《屠场》是作家兼记者厄普顿·辛克莱于 1906 年出版的一部小说，旨在强调工人阶级的困境并描述 20 世纪初美国肉类加工行业的腐败现象。

[23] *Sister Carrie*《嘉莉妹妹》是德莱塞在 1900 年出版的一部小说，本书通过年轻的乡下姑娘嘉莉的坎坷遭遇，反映了 19 世纪末期美国社会失业、贫困、饥饿的阴暗面。

[24] Hilton Hotels 希尔顿国际酒店集团

[25] The Walt Disney Company 华特·迪士尼公司，简称迪士尼，是大型传媒娱乐企业。

[26] Warner Bros. 全称为 Warner Bros. Entertainment Inc.，华纳兄弟娱乐公司，1923 年成立

[27] Sony Pictures Entertainment 索尼影视娱乐有限公司

[28] DreamWorks 梦工厂，美国一家影视公司

New Words

1. **insistence** /ɪn'sɪstəns/ *n.* continual and persistent demands 坚持，强调，坚决主张

— It is her insistence on personal privacy that left me a deep impression.

她对个人隐私权的坚持给我留下了深刻的印象。

2. **assembly** /ə'sembli/ *n.* a group of machine parts that fit together to form a self-contained unit 装配

—The production is greatly increased due to a new assembly line installed.

由于安装了新装配线，生产量大大提高。

3. **cruise** /kru:z/ *v.* travel at a moderate speed 巡航

—Several privateer often cruise near the entrance of the channel.

几只武装民船经常在这个海峡的进口附近巡航。

4. **bailout** /'beɪlaʊt/ *n.* a bailout of an organization or individual that has financial problems is the act of helping them by giving them money 紧急财政援助

—It is one of the biggest government bailouts of a private company in years.

这是政府近年来对私人公司最大的紧急财政援助之一。

5. **liquidity** /lɪ'kwɪditi/ *n.* being in cash or easily convertible to cash; debt paying ability 流动性；偿债能力

—The bank has progressively increased its liquidity.

银行逐渐地增加其流动资产。

6. **pension** /'penʃən/ *n.* a regular payment to a person that is intended to allow them to subsist without working 退休金

—A pension is often commutable into a lump sum.

养老金通常可换成一次性总付款。

7. **mutual funds** *n.* a regulated investment company with a pool of assets that regularly sells

and redeems its shares 共同基金

—Usually individuals invest through money market mutual fund.

通常个人通过货币共有基金来进行投资。

8. **recreation** /ˌrekri'eɪʃən/ *n.* an activity that diverts or amuses or stimulates 消遣，娱乐

—Sport and recreation have always been part of university life.

运动和娱乐活动一直是大学生活的一部分。

9. **lobby** /'lɒbi/ *v.* try to persuade that a particular law should be changed or that a particular thing should be done 游说

—The Wilderness Society lobbied Congress to authorize the Endangered Species Act.

荒野协会游说国会批准《濒危物种法》。

Exercises

1. Choose the correct answer.

1) Who is the author of *The Wealth of Nations*, a book that has had an enormous influence on American economic development?

A. Adam Smith. B. Samuel Osgood. C. Fannie Mae. D. Abraham Lincoln.

2) Which of the following took the first step toward breaking up monopolies?

A. Environmental Protection Agency. B. The Progressive Movement.

C. Congress Law. D. The Sherman Antitrust Act.

3) Which state of the following was often called "the workshop of the nation" by Americans?

A. Western Pennsylvania. B. Western Virginia.

C. New England. D. Wisconsin.

4) Which of the following is the largest district for television and film industry in America?

A. New York City. B. Chicago. C. Hollywood. D. Los Angeles.

5) Which country has become America's No.1 trading partner in its importing field?

A. Britain. B. Canada. C. China. D. Japan.

2. Decide the following statements are True or False.

1) US GDP per capita is No.1 in the world.

2) US economy is enjoying fast growth since early 2000s.

3) Smith thinks that government should interfere in commerce as little as possible.

4) The number of labor is important to a country's economic success, rather than the quality of it.

5) The largest sector of the US economy in terms of output and employment is service industry.

3. Fill in the blanks according to the passage.

1) ________state is called "the workshop of the nation" by Americans.

2) ________ is the financial and business center of America.

3) ________ (trade agreement) is created by the governments of the United States, Canada, and Mexico.

4) Microsoft company was founded by ________.

5) ________ is nicknamed as "The Motor City".

4. Explain the following terms according to the passage.

1) trade bloc

2) IMF

3) real gross domestic product

4) Protestant work ethic

5) financial services

5. Answer the following questions according to the passage.

1) What are the factors that influence the US trade deficit with mainland China?

2) Which are the basic ingredients of the US Economy?

3) What are the main types of financial services?

6. Discussion.

1) What did the US do to create a stable and welcome market to attract investors?

2) What measures have government agencies taken to fight against the crisis?

Stay Positive

1. The best way to predict the future is to create it.
2. The pessimist complains about the wind; the optimist expects it to change; and the realist adjusts the sails.

Chapter 5

Military of the United States

My fellow Americans, ask not what your country can do for you; ask what you can do for your country. My fellow citizens of the world, ask not what America will do for you, but what together we can do for the freedom of man.

—John Kennedy, American President

1. Overview

As of 2018, the U.S. Armed Forces consist of the Army, Marine Corps, Navy and Air Force, all under the command of the United States Department of Defense. There also is the United States Coast Guard, which is controlled by the Department of Homeland Security. The President of the United States is the commander in chief of each branch of the Armed Forces. The Secretary of Defense is the "Principal Assistant to the President in all matters relating to the Department of Defense".

In addition, each state has a National Guard commanded by the state's governor and coordinated by the National Guard Bureau [1]. The President of the United States has the authority during national emergencies to assume control of individual state National Guard units.

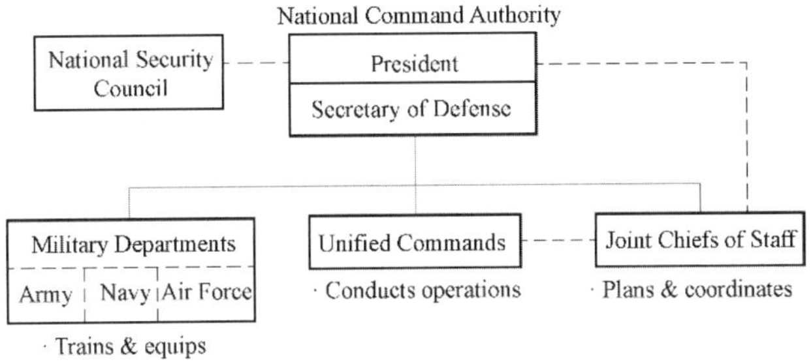

Figure 1 National Command System of the U.S. Armed Forces

The President and the Secretary of Defense exercise authority and control of the Armed Forces through two distinct branches of the chain of command. One branch runs from the President, through the Secretary of Defense, to the combatant commanders for missions and forces assigned to their commands. The other branch, used for purposes other than operational direction of forces, runs from the President through the Secretary of Defense to the Secretaries of the Military Departments, i.e., the Secretary of the Army, the Secretary of the Navy, and the Secretary of the Air Force. The Military Departments, organized separately within the Department, operate under the authority, direction, and control of the Secretary of each Military Department.

2. History

The military history of the United States spans a period of over two centuries. During the course of those years, the United States **evolved** from an alliance of 13 British colonies without a professional military to the world's sole remaining superpower of the late 20th and early 21st centuries.

2.1 The Colonial Wars

The beginning of the United States military lies in civilian **frontiersmen**, armed for hunting and basic survival in the wilderness. They relied on the support of the British regular army and navy for any serious military operation.

In the early years of the British colonization of North America, military action in the colonies that would become United States was the result of conflicts with Native Americans. Beginning in 1689, the colonies also frequently became involved in a series of wars between Great Britain and France for control of North America, the most important of which were Queen Anne's War, in which the British annexed French Acadia, and the final French and Indian War (1754-1763). This final war was to give thousands of colonists, including George Washington, military experience which they put to use during the American Revolution.

2.2 The War of Independence

Ongoing political tensions between Great Britain and 13 colonies became a crisis in 1774 when the British placed the province of Massachusetts under martial law. While shooting began at Lexington and Concord in 1775, the Continental Congress appointed George Washington as commander-in-chief of the newly created Continental Army. General Washington was not the greatest battlefield **tactician**, but his overall strategy proved to be sound: keep the army intact, wear down British resolve, and avoid decisive battles except to exploit enemy mistakes. A French naval victory in the Chesapeake led to the surrender of a British army at Yorktown in 1781, resulting in the Treaty of Paris in 1783, which recognized the independence of the United States.

2.3 The American Civil War

Daring American Civil War, eleven Southern slave states declared their secession from the United States and formed the **Confederate** States of America (the Confederacy). Led by Jefferson Davis [2], they fought against the United States (the Union), which was supported by all the free states and the five border slave states. Union states were loosely referred to as "the North".

Sectional tensions had long existed between the states located north of the Mason-Dixon

Line [3] and that south of it, primarily centered on the "peculiar institution" of slavery and the ability of states to overrule the decisions of the national government. During the 1840s and 1850s, conflicts between the two sides became more violent.

The American Civil War caught both sides unprepared. Both the Union and the Confederacy had to build their armies practically **from scratch**. Both sides sought a quick victory focused on the respective nearby capitals of Washington, D.C. and Richmond, Virginia, but neither side would surrender their national identity cheaply. Even after the First Battle of Bull Run [4], many were slow to accept that war would last much longer than a single campaign. However, it spilled across the continent, and even to the high seas.

The American Civil War is sometimes called the "first modern war" due to the use of mass conscription, military railroads, **trench** warfare, submarines, ironclads, **aerial** reconnaissance, rifles, and machine guns. It introduced the modern world to the horrors of total war.

2.4 The World War I

The United States originally wished to remain neutral when World War I broke out in August 1914. However, it insisted on its right as a neutral party to immunity from German submarine attack. On April 6, 1917, the United States declared war on Germany. The Odenwald, built in 1903, was an armed German supply ship which tried to force its way out of the bay and deliver supplies to the German submarines waiting in the Atlantic Ocean. Lt. Marxuach gave the order to open fire on the ship from the walls of the fort. In 1917 ex-President Theodore Roosevelt was authorized by Congress to raise four divisions of volunteers to fight in France; however Woodrow Wilson [5] refused this offer. By summer 1918, a million American soldiers of the American Expeditionary Force were in Europe under the command of John J. Pershing, with 25,000 more arriving every week. The failure of Germany's spring offensive meant they had exhausted their manpower reserves and were unable to launch attacks or even defend their lines. Meanwhile the German home front revolted and a new German government signed a conditional surrender, ending the war on November 11, 1918.

2.5 The World War II

The war in Europe began in earnest on September 1, 1939 with the invasion of Poland by Nazi Germany, and concluded on September 2, 1945, with the official surrender of the last Axis nation [6] — Japan. However, in Asia the war began earlier with Japanese invasions of China, and in Europe, the war ended earlier with the unconditional surrender of Germany on May 8, 1945.

It was the largest armed conflict in history, spanning the entire world and involving more countries than any other war, as well as introducing powerful new weapons, introducing the first use of nuclear weapons. The war ravaged civilians more severely than any previous conflict and served as a background for tremendous killings by Nazi Germany as well as several other mass slaughters of civilians which, although not technically **genocide**, were significant. In total, World War II produced about 70 million deaths, more than any other war to date.

US involvement in World War II was initially limited to providing war material and financial support to the United Kingdom, the Soviet Union, and Republic of China. The US entered officially on December 8, 1941 following the Japanese attack on Pearl Harbor, Hawaii the previous day. On December 11, the remaining Axis powers, Germany and Italy, declared war on the US, drawing the US firmly into the war and removing all doubts about the global nature of the conflict. The loss of battleships and sailors and airmen at Pearl Harbor forced the US to rely on its remaining aircraft carriers, which won a major victory over Japan, and its growing submarine fleet. Bloody battles at Iwo Jima and Okinawa in 1945 led the US to look for a way to end the war with minimal loss of lives. The U.S. used atomic bombing of Hiroshima and Nagasaki [7] to shock the Japanese leadership, which quickly brought about the surrender of Japan.

Despite the crippling effects of the Great Depression, the United States was able to mobilize quickly, eventually becoming the dominant military power in most theaters of the war (excepting only eastern Europe and mainland China), and the industrial might of the US economy is widely cited as a major factor in the Allies' eventual victory in the war.

World War II holds a special place in the American psyche as the country's greatest triumph, and the soldiers of World War II are frequently referred to as "the greatest generation" for their sacrifices in the name of liberty. Over 16 million served (about 13% of the population), and over 400,000 were killed during the war; only the American Civil War saw more Americans killed (although the majority of soldier deaths that were directly caused by the war were the result of disease). The US entered the war, like many other nations, as a country struggling with economic and social problems and unsure of its identity. It emerged as one of the two undisputed superpowers along with the Soviet Union, and unlike the Soviet Union, the US homeland was virtually untouched by the ravages of war. The importance of US military and political power in world affairs since 1945 cannot be overstated; the outcome of the war and the fortunes of the victors have shaped world events to this day.

During and following World War II, the United States and the United Kingdom developed an increasingly strong defense and intelligence relationship. Examples of this include extensive basing of US forces in the UK, shared intelligence, shared military technology (e.g. nuclear technology), shared procurement (mainly British purchases of American weapon systems, but increasingly the opposite in recent years).

2.6 The Cold War

Following the Second World War, the United States emerged as a global superpower against the Soviet Union in the Cold War. In this period of some 40 years, the United States provided foreign military aid and direct involvement in **proxy** wars against the Soviet Union. It was the principal foreign actor in the Korean War and Vietnam War during this era. Nuclear weapons were held in ready by the United States under a concept of mutually assured destruction with the Soviet Union.

◆ The Vietnam War

The Vietnam War, also known as the Second Indochina War, was a war fought between

1955 and 1975 on the ground in South Vietnam and bordering areas of Cambodia and Laos and In Vietnam, the conflict is known as the "American War." Although a small US presence had existed in Vietnam since the late 1950s, major US involvement is generally considered to have begun in 1964.

Fighting on one side was a coalition of forces including the Republic of Vietnam (South Vietnam), the United States, South Korea, Thailand, Australia, New Zealand, and the Philippines. Participation by the South Korean military was financed by the United States, but Australia and New Zealand fully funded their own involvement. Other countries normally allied with the United States in the Cold War, including the United Kingdom and Canada, refused to participate in the coalition, although a few of their citizens volunteered to join the U.S. forces. The U.S. and its allies fought against the North Vietnamese Army (NVA) as well as the National Liberation Front [8], or "VC", a guerrilla force within South Vietnam. The NVA received substantial military and economic aid from the Soviet Union, turning Vietnam into a proxy war.

Even today, "Vietnam" is a politically controversial subject in the U.S. Some Americans view the Second Indochina War as a noble, if not perfect, cause which limited and delayed communist expansion and conquest of Vietnam, Laos, and Cambodia. Others see the conflict as a **quagmire**, a waste of American blood and treasure in a conflict that did not concern US interests. Military service during Vietnam is still an issue in U.S. presidential campaigns more than 30 years after US troops left the country, and fears of another "quagmire" have been major factors in U.S. military planning since 1975.

2.7 Post-Cold War Era

◆ The Gulf War

The Persian Gulf War was a conflict between Iraq and a coalition force of 34 nations led by the United States. The lead up to the war began with the Iraqi invasion of Kuwait in August 1990 which was met with immediate economic sanctions by the United Nations against Iraq. The coalition began **hostilities** in January 1991, resulting in a decisive victory for the U.S. led coalition forces, which drove Iraqi forces out of Kuwait with minimal coalition deaths. Despite the low death toll, over 180,000 US **veterans** would later be classified as "permanently disabled" according to the US Department of Veterans Affairs. The main battles were aerial and ground combat within Iraq, Kuwait and bordering areas of Saudi Arabia. Land combat did not expand outside of the immediate Iraq/Kuwait/Saudi border region, although the coalition bombed cities and strategic targets across Iraq, and Iraq fired missiles on Israeli and Saudi cities.

Following the Gulf War, in order to protect minority populations, the US, Britain, and France declared and maintained no-fly zones in northern and southern Iraq, which the Iraqi military frequently tested. The no-fly zones persisted until the 2003 invasion of Iraq, although France withdrew from participation in **patrolling** the no-fly zones in 1996, citing a lack of humanitarian purpose for the operation.

"Operation Desert Storm" was the U.S. name of the air and land operations and is often incorrectly used to refer to the entire conflict; although the U.S. Postal Service issued a postage stamp reflecting Operation Desert Storm in 1992 and the U.S. military awarded campaign ribbons for service in Southwest Asia.

2.8 War on Terrorism

The War on Terrorism is a global effort by the governments of several countries to neutralize international terrorist groups and ensure that **rogue** nations no longer support terrorist activities. It has been adopted as a response to the September 11, 2001 attacks on the United States.

◆ **Iraq War**

The Iraq War or the Occupation of Iraq, referred to by the U.S. military as Operation Iraqi Freedom and by the British military as Operation Telic, is an ongoing military campaign which began on March 20, 2003 with the invasion of Iraq by a multinational force led by troops from the United States and the United Kingdom. Approximately 250,000 United States troops, with support from 45,000 British, 2,000 Australian and 200 Polish combat forces, entered Iraq primarily through their staging area in Kuwait. After approximately three weeks of fighting, Hussein and the Ba'ath Party were forcibly removed, followed by an extended period of military occupation.

◆ **Syrian and Iraqi Intervention**

With the emergence of ISIL [9] and its capture of large areas of Iraq and Syria, a number of crises resulted that sparked international attention. ISIL had perpetrated sectarian killings and war crimes in both Iraq and Syria. Gains made in the Iraq War were rolled back as Iraqi army units abandoned their posts. Cities were taken over by the terrorist group which enforced its brand of Sharia law. The kidnapping and decapitation of numerous Western journalists and aid-workers also garnered interest and outrage among Western powers. The US intervened with airstrikes in Iraq over ISIL-held territories and assets in August, and in September a coalition of US and Middle Eastern powers initiated a bombing campaign in Syria aimed at degrading and destroying ISIL and Al-Nusra-held territory. By December 2017, ISIL had no remaining territory in Iraq, following the 2017 Western Iraq campaign. Airstrikes by US and Coalition forces have continued in Syria against the Assad government especially after the Douma chemical attack in 2018.

3. The US Military Departments

3.1 The US Army

The United States Army serves as the land-based branch of the U.S. Military. It is made up of three components: one active component, the Regular Army; and two reserve components, the Army National Guard and the Army Reserve. Both reserve components are primarily composed of part-time soldiers who train once a month, and conduct two to three weeks of annual training each year.

The Army National Guard is organized, trained and equipped as a component of the U.S. Army. When it is not in federal service it is under the command of individual state and territorial governors. However the National Guard can be federalized by presidential order and against the governor's wishes.

The US Army is led by a civilian Secretary of the Army, who reports to the Secretary of Defense, and serves as civilian oversight for the U.S. Army Chief of Staff [10]. The Army Chief of Staff is a member of the Joint Chiefs of Staff, a body composed of the service chiefs from each service who advise the President and Secretary of Defense on military matters under the guidance of the Chairman and Vice Chairman of the Joint Chiefs of Staff.

The US Army is the largest military branch within the country and has troops deployed around the globe. In 2017, the Regular Army had 476,000 soldiers, the Army National Guard had 343,000 soldiers, and the United States Army Reserve had 199,000 soldiers, forming a combined military strength of 1,018,000 soldiers.

3.2 The US Navy

The United States Navy is the naval service branch of the United States Armed Forces and one of the seven uniformed services of the United States. It is the largest and most capable navy in the world, with the highest combined battle fleet and the world's largest aircraft carrier fleet, with eleven in service, and two new carriers under construction.

The Navy is administratively managed by the Department of the Navy, which is headed by the civilian Secretary of the Navy. The Department of the Navy is itself a division of the Department of Defense, which is headed by the Secretary of Defense. The Chief of Naval Operations is the most senior naval officer serving in the Department of the Navy.

With 319,421 personnel on active duty and 99,616 in the Ready Reserve, the Navy is the third largest of the service branches. It has 282 deployable combat vessels and more than 3,700 operational aircraft as of March 2018, making it the second largest and second most powerful air force in the world.

As of 2018, the navy operates over 460 ships, including vessels operated by the Military Sealift Command crewed by a combination of civilian contractors and a small number of uniformed Naval personnel, 3,650 aircraft, 50,000 non-combat vehicles and owns 75,200 buildings on 3,300,000 acres (13,000 km^2).

3.2 The US Air Force

The United States Air Force is the aerial and space warfare service branch of the United States Armed Forces. It is one of the five branches of the United States Armed Forces, and one of the seven American uniformed services. Along with conducting independent air and space operations, the US Air Force provides air support for land and naval forces and aids in the recovery of troops in the field.

As of 2017, the service operates more than 5,369 military aircraft, 406 ICBMs and 170 military satellites. It has a $161 billion budget and is the second largest service branch, with 318,415 active duty personnel, 140,169 civilian personnel, 69,200 Air Force Reserve personnel, and 105,700 Air National Guard personnel.

4. Recruitment Culture of the US Military

The US military is famous for its **synchronized** multi-conscription **propaganda**. In this year's "Fleet Week" period, in addition to routine fleet parade, the Coast Guard life-saving performance, the major branches also seize this good opportunity to spread recruitment advertisements. The Air Force recruitment leaflets strongly promote that the Air Force can provide a variety of skills courses, and generous salaries and benefits, claiming that soldiers retired from the Air Force will be "very competitive" in the job market, which is a tempting option.

US military always pay attention to the military recruitment propaganda. The regular practices include mailing promotional materials to school-age young people each year; offering free magazines with instructions to the military profession to high school students nationwide; carrying out public welfare activities to enhance the public image of the military and so on. In recent years, the U.S. military campaign also requires a new **guise**, weird measures one after another. For example, the military cooperate with television stations, newspapers and websites to engage "military life experience" activities, lucky people will have the opportunity to live in the barracks a few days, or even have the opportunity to learn to operate F-15 fighter jets. In the first half of this year, the famous West Point [11], designed a kind of game software called "the United States Army" in order to attract young people. This online game allows players to accept a variety of basic military training, in order to complete a variety of difficult tasks in the virtual battlefield.

Interestingly, economic survey shows it's harder for the military to recruit when the economy is better, unemployment rate is lower. Statistics said that for every 1% decline in the U.S. unemployment rate, the Army's recruiting is to reduce about 9%. For example, compared with the average annual unemployment rate of 4% in 1990s, the U.S. unemployment rate has risen to 7.4% in July 2013. It is not bad for the military because it means that there will be more pressure on young people in employment and they may turn to defect to the barracks. With the economic recovery in recent years, however, the unemployment rate has fallen to 3.8% by the end of May, 2018. It will be more difficult to recruit new soldiers for the military departments.

US Armed Forces Recruiting Station

Joyful Moment

What to Expect and What Missed

My father, brother and I visited West Point to see a football game between Army and Boston College. Taking a stroll before kickoff, we met many cadets in neatly pressed uniforms. Several visiting fans asked the recruits if they would pose for photographs, "to show our son what to expect if he should attend West Point."

One middle-aged couple approached a very attractive female cadet and asked her to pose for a picture. They explained, "We want to show our son what he missed by not coming to West Point."

Notes

[1] National Guard Bureau 国民警卫局，美国国民警卫队（United States National Guard）的管理机构

[2] Jefferson Davis 杰佛逊 • 戴维斯（1808—1889），美国军人、政治家，在美国内战期间担任南部邦联首任及唯一一任总统。

[3] Mason-Dixon Line 美国宾夕法尼亚州和马里兰州的分界线，也是南北战争之前美国的南北区域分界线。

[4] First Battle of Bull Run"第一次牛奔河战役"(1861)，是美国南北战争东部战区中，联邦（北军）的主要军团波多马克军团（Army of the Potomac）参与的主要战役之一。

[5] Woodrow Wilson 伍德罗 • 威尔逊（1856—1924），美国第 28 任总统。

[6] the Axis nation 二战中的轴心国，也称为 Axis powers，是指在第二次世界大战中结成的法西斯国家联盟，主要成员是纳粹德国、意大利和日本及与他们合作的一些国家和占领国。

[7] Hiroshima and Nagasaki 广岛和长崎

[8] National Liberation Front 越南南方民族解放阵线

[9] ISIL (Islamic State of Iraq and the Levant) “伊拉克和黎凡特伊斯兰国”，逊尼派恐怖组织，原名为统一圣战组织。

[10] Army Chief of Staff 陆军参谋长

[11] West Point 西点军校，美国军事学院（The United States Military Academy），美国第一所军事学校，因为学院位于纽约州西点（哈德逊河西岸），所以常被称为西点军校。

New Words

1. **evolve** /ɪ'vɒlv/ *v.* to develop gradually（使）逐渐形成，逐步发展，逐渐演变
   —The group gradually envolved into a political party.
   该团队逐步发展成了一个政党。
2. **frontiersmen** /frʌn'tɪəzmən/ *n.* a man who lives on the frontier 边境地带的居民
3. **tactician** /tæk'tɪʃən/ *n.* a person who is very clever at planning the best way to achieve something 有策略的人，手段高明的人
   —He is very shrewd, a good tactician and it will be nice to talk to him.
   他非常精明，是睿智的战术家，与他交谈一定会非常的愉快。
4. **confederate** /kən'fedərət/ *adj.* belonging to a confederacy 联盟的，同盟的，邦联的
5. **from scratch** without any previous preparation or knowledge 从头开始，从零开始
   —We should all start from scratch, so that new life can be beyond the realm.
   我们要从零开始，才能跨越人生新的境界。
6. **trench** /trentʃ/ *n.* a long deep hole dug in the ground in which soldiers can be protected from enemy attacks 战壕
   —World War I was characterized by trench warfare.
   第一次世界大战的主要特征是战壕式地面战。
7. **aerial** /'eəriəl/ *n.* a piece of equipment made of wire or metal rods for receiving or sending radio and television signals 天线
   —On the receiving instrument he also used an elevated aerial.
   在接收装置上，他也采用了高架天线。
8. **genocide** /'dʒenəsaɪd/ *n.* the murder of a whole race or a group of people 种族灭绝，大屠杀
   —The genocide of the Holocaust made many doubt tenets of European modernity. 大屠杀的种族灭绝，使很多人怀疑欧洲现代性的原则。
9. **proxy** /'prɒksi/ *n.* the authority that you give to somebody to do something for you when you cannot do it yourself 代理权，代表权
   —How do I enter my proxy information?
   我怎么输入我的代理服务器信息？
10. **quagmire** /'kwɒgmaɪə/ *n.* a difficult or dangerous situation 困境，险境
    —We have no intention of being drawn into a political quagmire.
    我们无意卷入一场政治困境。

11. **hostility** /hɒ'stɪlɪtɪ/ *n.* unfriendly or aggressive feelings or behavior 敌意；对抗
—If a child lives with hostility, he learns to fight.
小孩如果活在仇恨里，就学会斗争。
12. **veteran** /'vɛtərən/ *n.* a person who was a soldier, sailor, etc. in a war 退伍军人，老兵
—The veteran worker has two apprentices working with him.
这位师傅是退伍军人，现在带着两个徒弟一起工作。
13. **patrol** /pə'trəʊl/ *v.* to drive or walk around a particular area, especially in a threatening way to go around aifferent parts of an area at regular times to check that there is no trouble or danger.（尤指威胁性地）逛荡，闲逛；巡逻
—Police patrol the streets at night.
警察晚间在街道上巡逻。
14. **rogue** /rəʊg/ *adj.* behaving differently from other similar people or things, often causing damage 行为失常的
—Computer systems throughout the country are being affected by a series of mysterious rogue programs.
全国的计算机系统正受到一系列神秘的异常程序的影响。
15. **infantry** /'ɪnfəntri/ *n.* infantries are soldiers who fight on foot rather than in tanks or horses 步兵团
—He signed on for nine years on this infantry.
他签署了志愿书要在步兵服役九年。
16. **echelon** /'eʃəlɒn/ *n.* a rank or position of authority in an organization or a society 等级；阶层
—If you are in the lower income echelon, you will go broke and become homeless.
你如果是低收入者，会破产无家可归。
17. **mortar** /'mɔːtər/ *n.* a heavy gun that fires bombs and shells high into the air 迫击炮
18. **battalion** /bə'tæliən/ *n.* a large group of soldiers that form part of a brigade（军队的）营
—A whole battalion of soldiers surrounded us in a tight ring.
整个军队把我们紧紧地包围在包围圈中。
19. **synchronize** /'sɪŋkrənaɪz/ *v.* to happen at the same time or to move at the same speed as something; to make something do this（使）同步，在时间上一致，同速进行
—The sound on a film must synchronize with the action.
影片中的声音必须与动作配合一致。
20. **propaganda** /ˌprɒpə'gændə/ *n.* ideas or statements that may be false or exaggerated and that are used in order to gain support for a political leader, party, etc.宣传，鼓吹
—The publication of this book may be of some help to our propaganda work.
这本书的出版，对于这一次宣传工作，可能是有些帮助的。
21. **guise** /gaɪz/ *n.* a way in which somebody/something appears, different from usual or that hides the truth about them/it 外貌，伪装

—One of the robbers went under the guise of a respectable dealer in antiques.
一个强盗装扮成有声望的古董商。

Exercises

1. Choose the correct answer.

1) In the War of Independence, ________ is the commander in chief.
A. Benjamin Franklin B. George Washington
C. Dwight Eisenhower D. Jefferson Davis

2) In American Civil War, the Confederacy is led by ________.
A. Jefferson Davis B. George Washington
C. Eisenhower D. Wilson

3) Which war was the largest armed conflict in history?
A. The War of Independence. B. The American Civil War.
C. The World War I. D. The World War II.

4) Which of the following is not a component of the United States Army?
A. The Regular Army. B. The Army National Guard.
C. The Army Reserve. D. Royal Navy.

5) Which war is called "the first modern war"?
A. The World War II. B. The American Civil War.
C. The World War I. D. The War of Independence.

2. Decide whether the following statements are True or False.

1) The President of the United States is the commander in chief of each branch of the Armed Forces.
2) The beginning of the United States military lies in civilian frontiersmen.
3) The United States joined the war as soon as the World War I broke out in August 1914.
4) The United States military is the largest in the world.
5) The U.S. used atomic bombing of Hiroshima and Nagasaki to shock the Japanese leadership, which quickly brought about the surrender of Japan.

3. Fill in the blanks.

1) The World War II concluded in 1945, with the official surrender of ________, the last Axis nation.
2) ________ is currently the nation's largest military branch in America.
3) In American Civil War, the two parties involved were________ and ________.
4) The Republican Party, led by ________, had campaigned against the expansion of slavery in 1860.
5) The soldiers of World War II are frequently referred to as "________" for their sacrifices in the name of liberty.

4. Explain the following terms.

1) The Odenwald

2) Cold War

3) Iraq War

4) Korean War

5) Vietnam War

5. Answer the following questions.

1) How was the US drawn into the World War II?

2) Why is World War II significant for the US?

3) Name three propaganda methods that US uses for army recruitment.

6. Discussion.

1) How do people view Vietam War domestically in US?

2) Why has the world entered the era of War on Terrorism?

Stay Positive

1. Life is an onion and one cries while peeling it.
2. Better to light one candle than to curse the darkness.

Chapter 6

Culture and Education of the United States

Give a man a fish and he will eat for a day. Teach a man how to fish and he will eat for the rest of his life.

—Chinese proverb

1. Introduction

Often referred to as a melting pot, the United States is characterized by variety. Foreigners usually have different views of it. Some foreigners describe America as hell by pointing to its unemployment, poverty line, the gap between the rich and the poor, racial discrimination, high crime rate, high divorce rate, political scandals and wastefulness. Some others try to cover up America's social problems by citing its large wealth, tens of millions of cars, spacious living quarters, high standard of life, large consumption, efficiency and high technology, high productivity and low birth rate, universal education, direct election and freedom.

2. Culture

Surface characteristics of culture (e.g. clothing styles and music) change rapidly, deeper characteristics of culture (e.g. values and beliefs) change slowly. Below are general descriptions of key cultural characteristics of the U.S., which may help you interpret and understand the behavior that you observe.

2.1 Mainstream U.S. Culture

2.1.1 Individual Freedom

Uncle Sam

U.S. Americans are known for their strong sense of **individualism**. It means that people mainly concern about themselves, rather than their family, community, etc. This may appear selfish to people of other cultures. However, the motive for this characteristic is a belief that each person has individual, unique gifts and talents, and that it is right and proper to develop these. Americans also generally believe that they are responsible for their own happiness and fulfillment. For example, some give up highly paying careers to follow lower-paying, service-oriented work because they find it more personally fulfilling. Americans usually feel that their identity comes from what they have accomplished in life, rather than who their parents are or what socioeconomic level they come from.

2.1.2 Self-reliance

Self-reliance is valued from the days of their pioneers. Back then, people had to be self-reliant, or they could not survive! As a result, it has become an admired characteristic in this country. The greeting "How are you today?" is more of a ritual than a meaningful exchange; the expected reply is "Fine", even if you do not feel fine. This characteristic also manifests in peoples' **inclination** to "do it yourself (DIY)". Many people repair their own plumbing, do their own sewing, painting, fence repair, car repair, etc., even though they could afford to hire someone to do it for them. There is even a well-known joke about some Americans (especially men) refusing to ask for directions when lost!

Statue of Liberty

2.1.3 Egalitarianism

Egalitarianism—the notion of equality before the law and in public encounters—is closely related to the characteristics of openness, friendliness, and informality. Related to this is the idea that any person who breaks a law should be punished according to the law, even if the person is important, famous, or rich. Of course, in practice, this is not always true, but one can see in the news that when public officials or powerful people are suspected of wrongdoing, there is intense interest in the proper legal processes being carried out. Egalitarianism is based on the belief that even when people have differences in their status, which are external and often self-accomplished, one person is not inherently better than another because of family, finances, etc.

2.1.4 Explicitness

Have you ever seen a society that talks so much about freedom yet has so many rules, regulations, laws, contracts, applications and forms, forms and more forms? While some cultures value meanings expressed by implication (suggesting that the inner understanding of people is in agreement), Americans value the clarity of explicitness (suggesting that inner understanding and outer behavior are in agreement).

2.1.5 Equality of Opportunity and Competition

Equality is one of their most cherished values. This concept is so important for Americans that they have even given it a religious basis. They say all people have been "created equal". American legal and institutional heritage prescribes equal rights for every citizen and condemns privileges. Civil Rights and women's liberation movements of the 1960s are good examples of this. To most Americans, equality means that every individual should have an equal chance for success. Life is seen as a race in which everyone compete in order to win. Americans believe that competition brings out the best in any individual. They think that it challenges or forces each person to develop their potential and to display their talents.

2.1.6 Material Wealth and Hard Work

The rich resources in the United States and its development in technology and growth in economy have created large amount of material goods and modern comforts. Americans enjoy material comfort and convenience brought by fine cars, fancy homes, various foods, and expensive clothing and furniture. Material wealth is the most widely accepted measure of social status in the United States. Driven by the desire to make more money and own more material goods, Americans find themselves pressured to work harder. They believe that all people can enjoy these material comforts if they are as industrious and hard-working as possible.

2.2 Cuisine

As a multicultural country, America has different types of foods. Mainstream American culinary arts[1] are similar to those in other Western countries. Wheat is the primary cereal grain. Traditional American cuisine uses ingredients such as turkey, venison, potatoes, sweet potatoes, corn, squash, and maple syrup. Slow-cooked pork and beef barbecue, crab cakes, potato chips, and chocolate chip cookies are American styles. The foods of immigrants are also popular in United States as it is a large country with huge population. Iconic American dishes such as apple pie, fried chicken, pizza, hamburgers, and hot dogs derive from the recipes of various immigrants and domestic innovations. Americans generally prefer coffee to tea, with more than half of the adult population drinking at least one cup a day. Orange juice and different drinks made with milk are also liked at larger scale. The sweet soft drinks with high quantity of sugar are taken as a source of energy by most of the Americans.

2.3 National Holidays

The holidays celebrated in America are derived from significant events in US history and religious traditions.

As a legacy of colonization, Thanksgiving has become a traditional American holiday which evolved from the will of English pilgrims[5] to "give thanks" for their welfare. Today, Thanksgiving is generally celebrated as a family reunion with a large afternoon feast. European colonization has led to many traditional Christian holidays such as Easter, Lent[6], St. Patrick's Day, and Christmas, although they are celebrated in a **secular** manner by many people today.

Independence Day (known as the Fourth of July) celebrates the anniversary of the country's Declaration of Independence from the Kingdom of Great Britain. It is generally observed by parades throughout the day and fireworks at night.

Halloween is thought to have evolved from the ancient Celtic festival of Samhain[7] which was introduced to the American colonies by Irish settlers. It has become a holiday that is widely celebrated by children and teens who traditionally dress up in costumes and go door to door saying "Trick or Treat" in exchange for candy. It also brings about eerie and frightening urban legends and movies.

Table 1　　Federally Recognized Holidays in the US

Date	Official Name	Remarks
January 1	New Year's Day	Celebrating the beginning of the Gregorian calendar year. Festivities include counting down to midnight (12:00 AM) on the preceding night, New Year's Eve.
Third Monday in January	Martin Luther King, Jr. Day	Honoring Martin Luther King, Jr., Civil Rights leader, who was actually born on January 15, 1929; combined with other holidays in several states.
January 20, the first January 20 following a Presidential election	Inauguration Day[8]	Observed only by federal government employees in Washington D.C., and the border counties of Maryland and Virginia, in order to relieve congestion that occurs with this major event. Celebrating the swearing-in of President of the United States and Vice President of the United States. Celebrated every fourth year.
Third Monday in February	President's Day	Many people consider it a day of honoring all American presidents.
Last Monday in May	Memorial Day	Honoring the nation's war heroes; it marks the unofficial beginning of the summer season.
July 4	Independence Day	Celebrating the Declaration of Independence, also called the Fourth of July.
First Monday in September	Labor Day	Celebrating the achievements of workers and the labor movement; it marks the unofficial end of the summer season.
Second Monday in October	Columbus Day	Honoring Christopher Columbus, traditional discoverer of the America. In some areas it is also a celebration of Italian culture and heritage.
November 11	Veterans Day	Honoring all veterans of the United States armed forces. A traditional observation is a moment of silence at 11:00 a.m. remembering those killed in war.

continued

Date	Official Name	Remarks
Fourth Thursday in November	Thanksgiving Day	Traditionally it's a day of giving thanks for the autumn harvest. It includes the consumption of a turkey dinner. It marks the start of the holiday season.
December 25	Christmas	Celebrating the Nativity of Jesus. People exchange gifts and decorate Christmas trees.

2.4 Media

The media of the United States consist of several different types: television, radio, cinema, newspapers, magazines, and internet-based web sites.

2.4.1 Radio

American radio broadcasts in two bands: FM and AM. Some stations are only talk radio—featuring interviews and discussions—while music radio stations broadcast one particular type of music: hip-hop, country, etc. Radio broadcast companies have become increasingly **consolidated** in recent years. National Public Radio is the nation's primary public radio network, but most radio stations are commercial and profit-oriented.

2.4.2 Newspapers

Newspapers have declined in their influence and penetration into American households over the years. The U.S. does not have a national paper. *The New York Times*[9] and *The Wall Street Journal*[10] are sold in most U.S. cities.

Although its primary audience has always been the people of New York City, *The New York Times* has gradually become the dominant national "newspaper of record". *The Los Angeles Times* and *The Wall Street Journal* are also newspapers of record to a lesser extent. Although *USA Today* has tried to establish itself as a national paper, it has been widely derided by the academic world as the "McPaper"[11] and is not subscribed to (let alone archived) by most libraries.

With a very few exceptions, all the newspapers in the U.S. are privately owned. Most general-purpose newspapers are either being printed once a week, usually on Thursday or Friday, or daily. Probably due to competition from other media, the number of daily newspapers in the U.S. has declined over the past half-century.

2.4.3 Magazines

The United States has a large magazine industry with hundreds of magazines serving almost every interest. The U.S. has three leading weekly newsmagazines: *Time*, *Newsweek* and *U.S. News and World Report*. All three (in theory, at least) strive to provide objective news reporting and limit personal bias to the opinion pages. *Time* is well-known for naming a "Person of the Year" each year, while *U.S. News and World Report* publishes an annual rating of American colleges and universities.

The U.S. also has over a dozen major political magazines, serving every part of the political spectrum from left to right. Besides the hundreds of specialized magazines that serve the diverse interests and hobbies of the American people, there are also dozens of magazines published by professional organizations for their members, such as *Communications of the ACM* (for computer science specialists) and *ABA Journal* (for lawyers).

2.5 Sports

Baseball has been regarded as the national sport since the late 19th century, while American football is now by several measures the most popular spectator sport. Basketball and ice hockey are the country's next two leading professional team sports. These four major sports, when played professionally, each occupy a season at different, but overlapping, times of the year. College football and basketball attract large audiences. Boxing and horse racing were once the most watched individual sports, but they have been eclipsed by golf and auto racing, particularly NASCAR[12]. In the 21st century, televised mixed martial arts has also gained a strong following of regular viewers. While soccer is much less popular in the United States than in many other nations, it is played widely at the youth and amateur levels. Tennis and many outdoor sports are popular as well.

3. Education

Education in the United States is mainly provided by the public sector, with control and funding coming from three levels: federal, state, and local. School attendance is **mandatory** and nearly universal at the primary and secondary levels (known inside the United States as the elementary and high school levels). The ages for compulsory education vary by state, beginning at ages of five to eight and ending at the ages of 14 to 18. A growing number of states are now requiring school attendance until the age of 18. In most public and private schools, education is divided into three levels: elementary school, junior high school (often called middle school), and high school (sometimes referred to as secondary education).

3.1 School Grades

In the U.S. the first year of compulsory schooling begins with children at the age of five or six. Children are then placed in year groups known as grades, beginning with first grade and culminating in 12th grade.

Table 2 Education in the United States

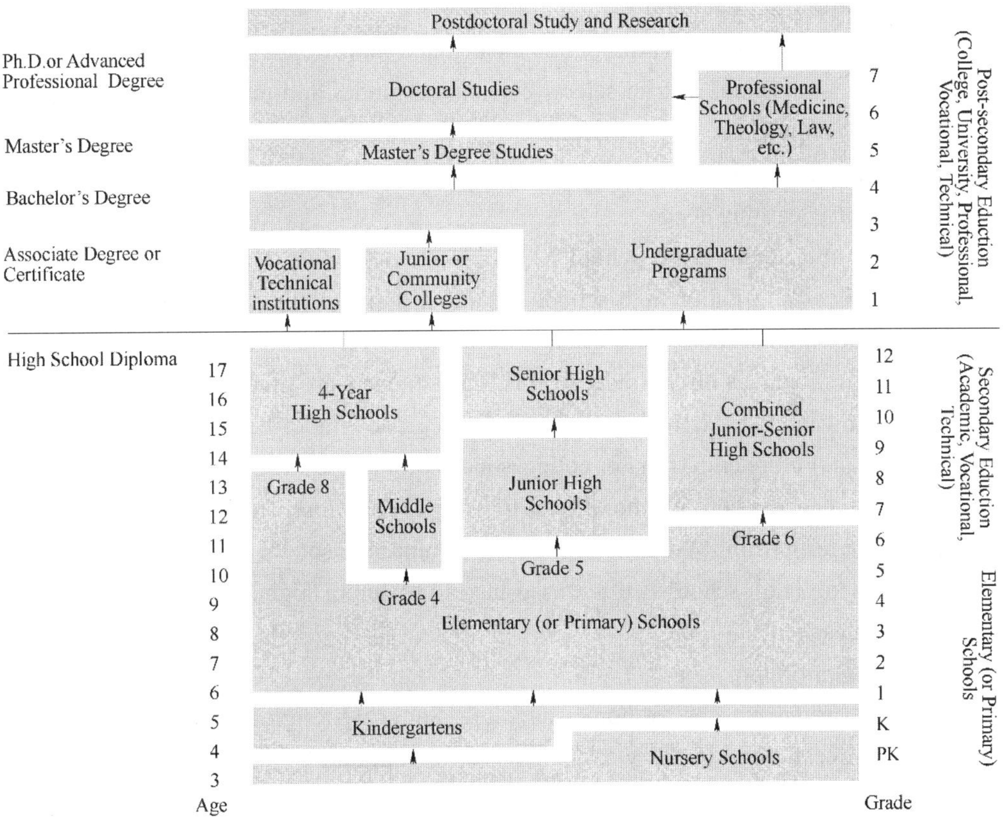

3.2 School System

3.2.1 Preschool

There are no mandatory public prekindergarten in the United States. The federal government funds the Head Start preschool program [13] for children of low-income families, but most families are on their own with regard to finding a preschool or childcare. In large cities, there are sometimes upper-class preschools catering to the children of the wealthy. Because some upper-class families see these schools as the first step toward the Ivy League [14], there are even counselors who specialize in assisting parents and their young children through the preschool admissions process.

3.2.2 Elementary and Secondary Education

Schooling is compulsory for all children in the United States, but the age range for which school attendance is required varies from state to state. Most children begin elementary education with kindergarten (usually five to six years old) and finish secondary education with 12th grade (usually 18 years old). Most parents send their children to either a public or private institution. According to government data, one-tenth of students are enrolled in private schools. Approximately 85% of students enter the public schools, largely because they are free. Parents may also choose to educate their own children at home.

◆ **Elementary School**

Typically, the curriculum within public elementary education is determined by individual school districts. The school district selects curriculum guides and textbooks. School systems vary widely not only in the way curricular decisions are made but also in how teaching and learning take place. Public Elementary School teachers typically instruct between 20 and 30 students of diverse learning needs.

◆ **Junior and Senior High School**

Middle school and junior high school are any school intermediate between elementary school and senior high school. It usually includes sixth, seventh and eighth grade; junior high school sometimes includes ninth grade. At this time, students are given more independence as choosing their own classes. Usually, starting in ninth grade, grades become part of a student's official transcript. Future employers or colleges may want to see steady improvement in grades and a good attendance record on the official transcript. Therefore, students are encouraged to take much more responsibility for their education. Senior high school is a school attended after junior high school. High school is often used instead of senior high school and distinguished from junior high school.

3.2.3 Home Schooling

There are various reasons for home schooling. Some are religious conservatives who see non-religious education as contrary to their moral or religious systems, or who wish to add religious instruction to the educational curriculum (and who may be unable to afford a church-operated private school, or where the only available school may teach views contrary to those of the parents). Others feel that they can more effectively tailor a curriculum to suit an individual student's academic strengths and weaknesses, especially those with singular needs or disabilities. Still some others feel that the negative social pressures of schools (such as bullying, drugs, crime, sex, and other school-related problems) are harmful to a child's proper development. Parents often form groups to help each other in the homeschooling process, and may even assign classes to different parents, similar to public and private schools.

3.2.4 Education of Students with Special Needs

In the United States, education for students with special needs is structured to adhere as closely as possible to the same experience received by typically developing peers. In order to more clearly identify special needs students, the federal government defined 13 categories of special needs. These included autism[15], deaf-blindness, deafness, hearing impairment, mental retardation[16], multiple disabilities, other health **impairment**, and specific learning disability.

The key to overcoming special needs in the mainstream school for students is special classes. These classes are taught by teachers with training in adapting curricula to meet the needs of students with special needs.

3.2.5 Public and Private Schools

The United States has an education system **decentralized** by state. There are no national schools. K-12 students in most areas have a choice between free tax-funded public schools, or privately-funded private schools.

Public school systems are supported by a combination of local, state, and federal government funding. Because a large portion of school revenues come from local property taxes, public schools vary widely in the resources they have available per student. Class size also varies significantly from one district to another. Curriculum decisions in public schools are made largely at the local and state levels; the federal government has limited influence. Admission to individual public schools is usually based on residency. To compensate for differences in school quality based on geography, school systems serving large cities and portions of large cities often have "magnet schools" [17].

Private schools in the United States include parochial schools [18] (affiliated with religious denominations), non-profit independent schools, and for-profit private schools. Private schools charge varying rates depending on geographic location, the school's expenses, and the availability of funding from sources other than tuition. Unlike public school systems, private schools have no legal obligation to accept any interested student. Admission to some private schools is highly selective. Private schools offer the advantages of smaller classes, fewer than 20 students in a typical elementary classroom, a higher teacher/student ratio across the school day, and greater individualized attention.

3.2.6 Colleges and Universities

Post-secondary education in the United States is known as college or university and commonly consists of four years of study at an institution of higher learning. There are over 4,000 colleges, universities, and junior colleges in the country. Like high school, the four undergraduate grades are commonly called freshman, sophomore, junior, and senior years (alternatively called first year, second year, etc.). Admissions criteria involve grades earned in high school courses taken, the students' GPA[19], class ranking, and standardized test scores (Such as the SAT[20] or the ACT[21] tests). The most common method consists of four years of study leading to a Bachelor of Arts (BA), a Bachelor of Science (BS). Five-Year Professional Architecture programs offer the Bachelor of Architecture Degree (B.Arch)

Graduate study leads to a more advanced degree such as a master's degree, which could be a Master of Arts (MA), Master of Science (MS), Master of Business Administration (MBA), or other less common master's degrees such as Master of Education (MEd), and Master of Fine Arts (MFA). After additional years of study and sometimes in conjunction with the completion of a master's degree, students may earn a doctoral degree. Only about 9% of students ever receive postgraduate degrees, and most, after obtaining their bachelor's degree, proceed directly into the workforce.

3.2.7 Famous Universities and Colleges

Harvard University

Harvard University a private university located in Cambridge, Massachusetts, and a member of the Ivy League. Founded in 1636 by the colonial Massachusetts legislature, Harvard is the oldest institution of higher learning in the United States. It is also the first and oldest corporation in North America. Administratively, Harvard University comprises ten primary academic units.

Initially called "New College" or "the college at New Towne", the institution was renamed Harvard College on March 13, 1639. It was named after John Harvard, a young clergyman from the London Borough of Southwark, England. The earliest known official reference to Harvard as a "university" occurs in the new Massachusetts Constitution of 1780. Harvard University has transformed into a modern research university.

Yale University

Yale University is a private research university in New Haven, Connecticut, United States of America, and a member of the Ivy League. Founded in 1701, Yale has produced many notable alumni, including five U.S. presidents, 19 U.S. Supreme Court justices, and several foreign heads of state.

In 1718, the College was renamed Yale College to honor a gift from Elihu Yale, a governor of the British East India Company. In 1861, the Graduate School of Arts and Sciences became the first U.S. school to award the Ph.D. Yale College was transformed beginning in the 1930s through the establishment of residential colleges, 12 of which now exist. All tenured professors teach undergraduate courses, more than 2,000 of which are offered annually. Yale and Harvard have been rivals in academics, athletics, and other activities for most of their history, competing annually in The Game and the Harvard-Yale Regatta.

Stanford University

The Leland Stanford Junior University, commonly referred to as Stanford University or Stanford, is a private research university located in Stanford, California. The university was founded in 1885 by former California governor and senator Leland Stanford and his wife. The Stanfords used their farm lands to establish the university, hoping to create a large institution of higher education in California.

In 2018, Stanford University enrolled about 17,178 students, among which 7,062 are undergraduates. The University is divided into a number of schools such as the Stanford Business School, Stanford Law School, Stanford School of Medicine, and Stanford School of Engineering.

Princeton University

Princeton University is a private research university located in Princeton, New Jersey. The school is one of the eight universities of the Ivy League and is considered one of the Colonial Colleges.

Founded in 1746 at Elizabeth, New Jersey, as the College of New Jersey, it was moved to Newark in 1747, then to Princeton in 1756 and renamed "Princeton University" in 1896.

Princeton University has traditionally focused on undergraduate education. A unique blend of research university and liberal arts, Princeton does not offer professional schooling generally, but it does offer professional master's degrees and doctoral programs in the sciences, humanities, and social sciences, as well as engineering.

Massachusetts Institute of Technology

The Massachusetts Institute of Technology (MIT) is a private research university located in Cambridge, Massachusetts. MIT has five schools and one college, containing a total of 32 academic departments, with a strong emphasis on scientific and technological research.

Founded by William Barton Rogers in 1861 in response to the increasing industrialization of the United States, the university adopted the German university model and emphasized laboratory instruction from an early date. In the past 60 years, MIT's educational programs have expanded beyond the physical sciences and engineering into social sciences like economics, philosophy, linguistics, political science, and management. Its endowment and annual research expenditures are among the largest of American universities.

Joyful Moment

Second Language

A mother mouse was out for a stroll with her babies when she spotted a cat crouched behind a bush. She watched the cat, and the cat watched the mice.

Mother mouse barked fiercely, “Woof, woof, woof!” The cat was so terrified that it ran for its life.

Mother mouse turned to her babies and said, “Now, do you understand the value of a second language?”

Notes

[1] culinary arts 烹饪工艺

[2] tacos 炸玉米饼

[3] burritos 墨西哥卷饼

[4] pasta 意大利面

[5] English pilgrims 1620 年赴美的英国清教徒

[6] Lent（基督教的）四旬斋，也叫大斋节，封斋期一般是四十天，从圣灰星期三（大斋节的第一天）到复活节，基督徒视之为禁食和为复活节做准备而忏悔的节期。

[7] Samhain 萨温节。在古凯尔特人的信仰里，新的一年于 11 月 1 日开始。按照凯尔特人的传统，人们认为转折点具有某种神奇的魔力。萨温节标志着他们一年中最大的转折点——天气的变化，同时也是每个人生活的变化。凯尔特人相信这个神秘时刻打开了生者与亡灵的某种联系。那些灵魂已经跨越最终的转折点，那是生与死的转变。他们认为在萨温节那一天是生死两个世界距离最近的时刻，故人的灵魂会重游人间。萨温节的很多活动都和这种信仰有关，其中许多活动都已演变成了今天万圣节的风俗。

[8] Inauguration Day 美国总统就职日

[9] *The New York Times*《纽约时报》

[10] *The Wall Street Journal*《华尔街日报》

[11] Mcpaper 是“快餐报，速食报”的意思，通常指《今日美国报》，因其以麦当劳快餐的方式处理新闻而获得了 Mcpaper 的绰号。

[12] NASCAR National Association of Stock Car Auto Racing 全国运动汽车竞赛协会，美国最大、最受认可的赛车竞速团体。由 NASCAR 认可三个最大的竞速系列是 Sprint 杯、全国系列和野营世界卡车系列。该协会亦监管 NASCAR 区域竞速、Whelen 改装车巡回竞速和 Whelen 全美系列。

[13] Head Start preschool program 开端计划

[14] Ivy League 常春藤联盟，指的是美国东部八所历史最悠久的名牌大学，因其校舍墙

上常春藤盘蔓而得名。它们是布朗大学、哥伦比亚大学、康奈尔大学、达特茅斯学院、哈佛大学、宾夕法尼亚大学、普林斯顿大学和耶鲁大学)。

[15] autism 自闭症

[16] mental retardation 智力迟钝，智能缺陷（同 mental deficiency）

[17] magnet schools 磁石学校，又称为特色学校。没有学区和入学条件的限制，学生可以自愿申请入学，由电脑编班入学。它办学特点鲜明，针对儿童特殊兴趣爱好，开设富有特色的课程。

[18] parochial schools 教区学校

[19] GPA(grade point average)平均学分绩点，是大多数大学及高等教育院校所采用的一种评估学生成绩的制度。计算方法是把学科所得到的成绩，换算成为一个绩点，再按照各学科的学分比例加权。

[20] SAT 测验在中国俗称“美国高考”，全称为 Scholastic Aptitude Test（学术能力测验）或 Scholastic Assessment Test（学术评估测试），是由美国大学委员会委托美国教育测验服务社定期举办的测验，是美国各大学申请入学的重要参考。

[21] ACT 考试，全称为 American College Testing 美国大学入学考试，亦称“美国高考”

New Words

1. **individualism** /ˌɪndɪ'vɪdʒuəlɪzəm/ *n.* a belief in the importance of the individual and the virtue of self-reliance and personal independence 个人主义

   —The shift toward individualism among Japanese is most pronounced among the young.

   日本人向个人主义的转变在青少年中最为显著。

2. **inclination** /ˌɪnklɪ'neɪʃən/ *n.*an attitude of mind especially one that favors one alternative over others 倾向，意向

   —She showed no inclination to go.

   她没有表现出要走的意向。

3. **egalitarianism** /ɪˌgælɪ'teəriənɪzəm/ *n.* the belief that all people are equal and should have the same rights and opportunities, and to actions that are based on this belief（主张在社会、政治、经济权利方面人人平等的）平等主义

   —Holding to the ideal of “egalitarianism”, the country prides itself on making no distinction of ethnic background or race.

   该国高举“平等”旗帜，为本国在对待种族背景或人种上的无区别做法感到骄傲。

4. **secular** /'sekjələ/ *adj.* concerning those who are not members of the clergy 世俗的

   —The general history tendency of Christian music is becoming secular.

   基督教音乐总的历史趋势是向世俗化不断转变。

5. **consolidate** /kən'sɒlɪdeɪt/ *v.* make firm or secure; strengthen 巩固

   —The army consolidated the position which they had captured.

   部队巩固了他们已占领的阵地。

6. **mandatory** /'mændətərɪ/ *adj.* required by rule 命令的，强制性的
—Although not mandatory, it is certainly the easiest way to manage deployment.
虽然不是强制的，但它是管理部署的最简单的方法。
7. **impairment** /ɪm'peəmənt/ *n.* the condition of being unable to perform as a consequence of physical or mental unfitness 损伤，缺陷
—She did not have any evidence of hearing impairment.
她没有任何听力受损的证据。
8. **decentralized** /ˌdiː'sentrəlaɪzd/ *adj.* withdrawn from a center or place of concentration 分散的
—The balance between centralized and decentralized decision making is sometimes delicate.
在集中决策和分散决策之间进行平衡有时是棘手的。

Exercises

1. Choose the correct answer.

1) ______ and the Thirteenth have long been considered extremely unlucky because it has some bad associations which came from mythology, tale of the Bible, and the customs and habits.

A. Monday B. Tuesday C. Friday D. Sunday

2) _________ adopted the German university model and emphasized laboratory instruction from an early date.

A. Harvard University
B. Yale University
C. The Massachusetts Institute of Technology
D. Princeton University

3) Which school does not belong to Ivy League? __________.

A. Harvard University B. Columbia University
C. Yale University D. Massachusetts Institute of Technology

4) Americans see their material possessions as __________.

A. have nothing to do with their social status
B. the natural reward for their hard work
C. no indication of a person's abilities
D. a gift from parents

5) By vote of Congress, ________, beginning in 1986, is Martin Luther King Day.

A. January 15
B. the first Monday of every January
C. the second Monday of every January

D. the third Monday of every January

2. Decide whether the following statements are True or False.

1) Equality is one of their most cherished values. Americans believe all people have been "created equal".

2) With a very few exceptions, all the newspapers in the U.S. are publicly owned.

3) American radio broadcasts in two bands: FM and AM.

4) *The New York Times* and *Wall Street Journal* which are sold in most U.S. cities are two kinds of national paper.

5) Such American ideals as equality of opportunity and self-reliance are only partly carried out in real life but are still important because people believe in them.

3. Fill in blanks according to the passage.

1) ________is celebrated by children and teens who traditionally dress up in costumes and go door to door saying the words "Trick or Treat" in exchange for candy.

2) ________ (known as the Fourth of July) celebrates the anniversary of the country's Declaration of Independence from the Kingdom of Great Britain.

3) _______________, produced from 1913 to 1938, honored a pair of connected tragedies from the settlement of the American frontier—the destruction of the buffalo herds and the American Indians.

4) To most Americans, equality means that every individual should have an equal chance for _________.

5) _________ has been regarded as the national sport of the United States since the late 19th century.

4. Explain the following terms according to the passage.

1) Independence Day

2) SAT

3) The Statue of Liberty

4) equality

5) Ivy League

5. Answer the following questions according to the passage.

1) Explain the origin of Uncle Sam.

2) Please list reasons for home schooling.

3) Describe the main features of American education system.

6. Discussion.

In American context, what is the meaning of "individualism", "materialism", and "equality"?

Stay Positive

1. Never frown, even when you are sad, because you never know who is falling in love with your smile.
2. Meeting you was fate, and falling in love with you was out of my control.

Chapter 7

Religion of the United States

Without God there is for mankind no purpose, no goal, no hope, only a wavering future, an eternal dread of every darkness.

—Jean Paul (1763-1825), German novelist and humorist

1. General Introduction

America is a highly religious country, and has been since its earliest days. Religion has remained a constant factor in America. A majority of Americans report that religion plays a "very important" role in their lives, which is unusual among developed nations. Even Americans who are members of no established religion are likely to believe in God. Religion in the United States is also characterized by a diversity of religious beliefs and practices. Various religious faiths have flourished within the United States.

2. The Principal American Religions

Christianity is the largest religion in the United States with various Protestant Churches having the most adherents. In 2016, Christians represent the 73.7% of the total population, 48.9% identifying as Protestants, 23.0% as Catholics and 1.8% as Mormons, and are followed by people having no religion with 18.2% of the total population. Judaism is the second largest religion in the U.S., practised by 2.1% of the population, followed by Islam with the 0.8%. Mississippi is the most religious state in the country, with 63% of its adult population described as very religious, saying that religion is important to them and attending religious services almost every week, while New Hampshire, with only 20% of its adult population described as very religious, is the least religious state.

2.1 Protestantism

2.1.1 Protestantism in America at a Glance

The United States as a nation was founded and formed largely by Protestants, who remain a powerful and by far the largest group in the United States. Without some understanding of Puritanism, there is no understanding of America.

At the beginning of the 17th century, when Britain was in the reign of King James, religious persecution became more serious and many people in Britain went to America for religious freedom. One typical group is the Puritan who suffered a lot at that time. In 1620, the "Mayflower" took them from Plymouth in England to the Plymouth[1] colony in New England area, which was followed by more religious people who were attracted by the tolerance of religion in the new land. This is the Puritans' early settlement in America.

The Protestant branch of the Christian faith broke away from the Roman Catholic Church mainly because of their great differences in religious beliefs and religious practice. The Protestants insisted that all individuals must stand alone before God. The Protestant belief that the individual, not the organized church should be the center of religious life is perhaps the major cause of their religious diversity.

2.1.2 Different Denominations

American Protestants are now spread widely among more than 200 different denominations. The largest Protestant group is the Baptists[2]. Next to Baptists, the most numerous Protestants are the Methodists[3]. Both of the two groups have their origins wholly in Britain. Other major Protestant bodies, having memberships in the millions, are the Lutherans[4], Presbyterians[5], and Episcopalians[6].

◆ **Baptism**

Baptists in America concentrated particularly in the southern states. Baptists believe in baptism (by full immersion of the body into water) of believers, rather than of infants. There is, however, no body of official Baptist doctrine, as you might find in other religions.

Baptists hold sway in the Bible Belt[7] region, which is a geographical region in the south and the midsection of the United States—areas that host large groups of fundamentalist[8]. Communities in this region, especially in rural areas, are among the most religious in the country.

◆ **Methodism**

Methodists are the second largest Protestant group in America. While modern Methodism has officially abandoned many of its more conservative views, American Methodism had traditionally been associated with very strict standards of personal living regarding gambling, sex, alcohol, or even card playing and dancing.

Methodists believe in infant baptism, done by **sprinkling** of water rather than by full immersion. Methodism, with its root in 18th century England, is a socially active religion, with a great number of colleges, missions and hospitals to its credit.

◆ **Lutheranism**

Lutheranism began in 1517 with Martin Luther's split from the Catholic Church. It is the oldest Protestant group. Lutherans emphasize that a young person must engage in a long study of the Lutheran Catechism before becoming a full-fledged church member. Lutherans stress spirituality rather than strict living.

Lutheran worship retains many Catholic practices, such as Holy Communion[9], in a simplified form. Holy Communion is something Christians do to remember what Jesus did for them. At Holy Communion there is the breaking and sharing of bread which is a reminder of Jesus' body being broken on the cross, and there is also the sharing of wine which is a reminder of Jesus' blood.

◆ **Mormons and the Christian Scientists**

Another two interesting Protestant groups founded in the United States are the Mormons and the Christian Scientists. The Mormons (officially known as the Church of Jesus Christ of Latter-day Saints) were organized in New York in 1830. It was customary for Mormon men to have more than one wife, so they were forced out of several established communities. They traveled westwards and settled in the unpopulated valley of the Great Salt Lake, where they built a thriving community. Then the federal government passed anti-**polygamy** laws and refused to admit Utah[10] as a state until 1896, after the Mormons had discontinued this practice.

Christian Scientists follow the Bible and teachings of Mary Baker Eddy (1821-1910). The Christian Scientist strives to see his or her true sense as spiritual. Accordingly, disease is a result of the delusions of the body which can be overcome through prayer and spiritual understanding. Because of these beliefs, Christian Scientists do not believe in scientific medicine, but have their own highly trained practitioners[11] who treat illnesses through spiritual means. As a result, they have been the subject of many controversial court cases because they refuse to provide medical treatment for their children.

2.1.3 Puritanism's Influence on American Life

Since Puritans settled in New England area in the 1620s, they have played an important role for a long time. They took with them values, ideas, beliefs and customs, which were gradually modified by the new environment, the new situation, the new conditions and experiences they went through. The wilderness and later the frontier, as well as the resulting hardships, forced them to become not only practical but also adaptable, individualistic and "doers", people of action.

To the Puritans, a person by nature is wholly sinful and can achieve good only by severe and persistent discipline. Emphasis is laid on constant self-examination and self-discipline. According to the views held by the early Puritans, **profanation** of the Sabbath day[12], adultery, drunkenness, playing games of chance, and participation in theatrical performances were serious sins.

Perhaps the greatest influence that Protestantism has had on American life comes from its philosophy regarding a person's relationship to his or her work. This philosophy—commonly called the Protestant work ethic—stresses the moral value of work, self-discipline, and personal responsibility. Puritans have also made a virtue of qualities that made for economic success—self-reliance, **frugality,** industry, and energy—and through them influenced modern social and economic life. The accumulation of wealth is not considered evil unless it leads to a life of idleness and sin. The American emphasis on hard work, financial success, practicality, efficiency, and self-sufficiency has much in common with the Protestant work ethic.

2.2 Catholicism

Roman Catholics are the largest individual religious denomination in the United States. In the latter half of the 19th century, more Catholics stayed near the east coast. They were concentrated especially in New York and Massachusetts, and still a very important element of the population in these two states.

2.2.1 Differences between Catholics and Protestants

Roman Catholicism differs from Protestantism in two critical areas. Protestants believe in private interpretation of the Bible. Catholics believe the Church is appointed by God as protector of the Bible to interpret the scripture. Most Protestants believe in a universal priesthood of all believers, while Catholics have a specially ordained priesthood.

2.2.2 Catholic Dogma

Catholicism runs by a series of rules, originating from the Pope in Rome. Protestants vary on social issues like divorce, abortion and homosexuality, while the Catholic Church has set guidelines on these matters. It also **censor**s certain movies, plays and books, which Catholics may not read or attend. Catholic priests may not marry, and they must be male. Nearly all Americans Catholics express loyalty to their church through support for Catholic school and through a hope that their children will marry Catholics.

2.2.3 Catholic **Parochial** Schools

Since many Catholic would like to send their children to parochial schools, Catholic funds have built thousands of elementary and secondary schools, plus many fine colleges and universities. Catholic school children wear distinctive uniforms, and are taught by nuns and lay teachers in a religious atmosphere. In addition, Catholic charities and hospitals are widespread.

2.2.4 Discrimination against Catholics

Though Catholics have lived in America since its earliest days, they were discriminated against through much of America's history. In early America, Catholicism found other religious groups already established. They were numerically superior and generally looked upon with greater favor. During the early 19th century, when Protestantism was making its gains, Catholicism was struggling to exist. Later, it became strong through immigration. For early Catholic immigrants, who were poor and uneducated, the church gave its members a feeling that they were not alone and foreign. If people had problems, they discussed them with their priest. Catholic immigrants needed this sense of security at a time when anti-Catholic feelings were strong among many Americans. After World War II, the old Catholic immigrant culture began to melt into the larger American society. Catholics became wealthier and better educated.

2.3 Judaism

The third major religion in the United States is Judaism and the United States is home to the second largest Jewish community in the world (after Israel).

2.3.1 Judaism at a Glance

Christianity and Judaism share the same roots. Jews share many concepts with Christians, yet differ in that they believe the Messiah[13] has not yet come. The Jews are awaiting the coming of a Messiah or Saviour, while Christians believe that Jesus Christ was the Saviour and are now waiting for his second coming. Jews believe in the **immortality** of the soul but not in Christian concepts of heaven and hell. Rabbis, meaning teachers, are leaders in the Jewish faith, but any knowledgeable Jewish layman may lead a Jewish service. The Torah, the first five books of the Bible, is kept on a scroll and read aloud every Sabbath (Saturday) during worship. These scrolls are sacred to Jews.

The Jewish holy day, the Sabbath is a special day in Religious Jewish ritual. It starts at sunset on Friday and continues until sunset on Saturday. During the Sabbath, observant Jews will do nothing that might be counted as work. Among the things that they cannot do are driving and cooking. Jewish families will get together Friday nights for special meals on special dishes. They may not work, travel, write, do business or carry money on the Sabbath. Stores run by orthodox or religious Jews are often closed on Saturdays, but open on Sundays.

In Jewish tradition, the family home is a sacred place. It is customary for religious Jewish men to cover their heads with a skullcap (Yarmulke[14]) either all the time or when they pray. Extremely orthodox Jews also wear elaborate costumes, usually in black, that tend to set them apart from other Americans.

Very religious Jews also observe ancient **dietary** laws: no pork or horse meat, no shellfish, no mixing of meat and dairy products. **Kosher** food and meats must be prepared according to certain rituals under rabbinic supervision. Jews cannot eat meat from any animal which does not both chew its cud (food brought up into the mouth by an animal from its first stomach to be chewed again) and has a split hoof[15], such as rabbit or hare, pig, horse, dog or cat. In neighborhoods with large Jewish populations kosher foods are available in special stores, and even in special sections of supermarkets.

2.3.2 Three major divisions

There are three major divisions of American Jews: Reform, Orthodox, and Conservative Judaism[16]. The basis of Orthodoxy was constituted by the Eastern European Jews whose motive for coming to the United States was more to escape from persecution than to make a fortune. Orthodox Jews are the most traditional and observe all the customs strictly, including the separation of men and women in the synagogue.

Reform Jews are of German origin. In the New World, these immigrants saw little reason to retain their old ways. They were encouraged to change the traditional Jewish laws and customs in order to adjust themselves to a new way of life, thus starting what is now called Reform Judaism. Reform Jews do not follow dietary laws, mix the sexes in worship and dress just like everyone else. They follow Jewish tradition with modern forms.

Conservative Judaism offered a compromise, combining the best of Reform Judaism and

Orthodoxy and avoiding their excesses. Conservatism accepted many of the "modern" practices pioneered by Reform while retaining traditional content in its religious services.

2.3.3 Jews in America and Worldwide

The Jewish religion is ancient. The Jewish people have suffered through thousands of years of cruel persecution and oppression. America has served as a great refuge for Jews, who quickly became part of American community.

The Jewish people are few in number in America and worldwide, but their intellectual and cultural contributions have been very great indeed. Among the great 20th-century musicians, for example, many violinists, pianists, and composers are Jewish. American Jews have also been prominent lawyers, judges and doctors. Twentieth-century thought has been greatly influenced by the original ideas of three European-born Jews: Karl Marx (founder of socialism and communism), Albert Einstein (one of the founders of the atomic age), and Sigmund Freud (founder of Psychoanalysis).

3. Characteristics of American Religion

3.1 Religious Freedom

America is remarkable now, as in the past, for its attachment to the principle of freedom of belief and disbelief. It has always been a safer haven for believers and nonbelievers alike.

The roots of religious freedom go back to the settlement of the colonies by the British in the 17th century. Not only England, but also Europe as a whole, were still in a state of religious trouble caused by the Reformation and Counter-Reformation. The desire for religious freedom was one of the strongest reasons why many colonial settlers came to America. As they escaped from religious persecution in their old countries, they were determined that there would be no religious oppression and they would be free to practice their religion and worship as they desired in the home they were building up.

Among the rights that the new nation guaranteed was freedom of religion. The Bill of Rights of the U.S. Constitution provides that there is no state religion and that church and state must be separated. Under these conditions, a variety of different religious groups developed and grew, with each group having a "live and let live" attitude toward the others.

The United States is more than a heaven for religious believers. Non-belief has also been jealously guarded from the beginning. In history, great care has been taken to ensure that non-believers were not made subject to religious laws desired by those who are religious. For example, as long ago as 1810 a rule was made that postal deliveries should take place on Sundays, on the ground that it was wrong that public services should be stopped on Sundays because religious people believed that Christians had a duty to rest on Sundays.

3.2 Diversity

The United States is perhaps the most religiously pluralistic in the world. There are over 220 recognized denominations in the United States and Americans practice nearly every religion found in the world today.

In the early days, several of the colonies were established as refuges for specific sects and denominations. Plymouth Colony was founded by British Separatists. Massachusetts and New Haven (Connecticut) were established by Puritans favoring a reform of the Church of England along Congregationalist lines. Pennsylvania was founded as a Quaker experiment and Maryland as a refuge for Catholics from Protestant England.

As the reputation of the American colonies for religious freedom spread, more religious groups made their way to the colonies. In the 1600s, religious dissidents from Europe made up the majority of the population of the American Colonies. Controversies over biblical issues and religious practice led to new denominations such as the Baptists, who spread throughout America. By the time that the US won its independence from England and established a federal government, it was indeed a land of religious diversity.

During the 19th and 20th centuries, America's tradition of religious diversity continued as the country went through a series of cycles of decline in religious warmth followed by religious revival. Immigrants from throughout the world, many of whom brought distinctive religious traditions with them, have continued to enrich America's faith communities. The United States, a nation of immigrants, is noted as a **potpourri** of faiths, from the international to the extremely privatized.

America has also been a fertile ground for new religions. The Mormon and Christian Science Churches are perhaps the best-known of the faiths that have sprung up on American soil. Because of its tradition of noninterference in religious matters, the United States has also provided a comfortable home for many small sects from overseas. The Amish[17], for example, descendants of German immigrants who reside mostly in Pennsylvania and neighboring states, have lived simple lives, wearing plain clothes and staying away from modern technology, for generations. Some small groups are considered to be religious cults, however, as long as they abide by the law, they are generally left alone. Religious prejudice is rare in America, and interfaith meetings and cooperation are commonplace.

3.3 Non-dogmatism or Religious Tolerance

Most Americans are really religious and tolerant, faithful and open. It is called non-dogmatism or religious tolerance.

Although a majority of Americans say religion is very important to them, nearly three-quarters of them say they believe that many faiths besides their own can lead to **salvation**, according to a survey by the Pew Forum on Religion & Public Life. And almost the same number of Americans believe that there is more than one true way to interpret the teachings of their religion.

The point is not that religion doesn't matter for most people. Actually, it does. It's that as seriously as they take their own religion, they are also tolerant of the view that others can pursue their own path to salvation. Most Americans are diverse in their own views, but united in their tolerance for and acceptance of the religious views of others. It's not the case that Americans don't believe in anything. It's that they believe in everything. They aren't religious purists or dogmatists.

3.4 Religious Cults

Religious cults are still a frightening aspect of modern American life. They usually prey on confused young people, separating them from their families at a time when their judgment is weakest. The cults provide support networks for young people with adjustment problems or low self-esteem. Thousands of young people would go door to door selling flowers and begging for money for the church, sleeping in vans or communal dormitories and preaching the sect's teachings on the street. In controversial cases, parents had to kidnap their own children to save them from the cult.

Cults and movements have from time to time caused shocking events such as mass suicides. In 1997, for example, 39 members of the Heaven's Gate cult[18] in California committed suicide together in an event designed to coincide with the arrival of the Hale-Bopp comet, which they interpreted as their signal to leave the earthly existence.

4. Religion in Today's America

4.1 Religion in Americans Life

Religion plays an important role in American's life in several ways. It provides a personal identity, social contacts, and important rituals. Social groups, close friendships and marriages are often formed with members of one's own religion. In the U.S., religion provides the customs and ceremonies that mark life's most important events—the naming of a baby, coming-of-age ceremonies, weddings, and funerals. Perhaps most importantly, many religions promise the believers some form of eternal life, which is a great comfort, especially to the old and the sick.

The major American religions also provide the comfort of a personal God to turn to in times of trouble. However, Americans have never believed in simply waiting for God to solve their problems. In the U.S., religious faith lives side by side with a strong belief in free will and an admiration of self-reliance. Ben Franklin (the great 18th century writer, inventor, and statesman) said, "God helps them that help themselves." During World War II, this same idea was expressed in the saying, "Praise the Lord, and pass the ammunition." Americans do not believe in accepting misfortunes as God's will. They count on their own actions to improve the quality of life. Some turn to their religious leader for advice in dealing with family problems or making important decisions in their lives.

4.2 New Tendency

4.2.1 Fluid

An extensive new survey by the Pew Forum on Religion & Public Life finds that religious affiliation in the U.S. is extremely fluid.

The survey finds that every religion is losing and gaining members. Catholicism has lost the greatest number of followers to other faiths or no faiths, but the overall Catholic population remains steady due to Catholic Latino immigrants. Catholics, Buddhists, Jehovah's Witnesses and followers of "other faiths" gained the greatest percentages from those who changed childhood affiliation; Hinduism, Catholicism and Judaism gained the fewest adherents from this group.

4.2.2 It's Becoming Less Religious

The new American Religious Identification Survey (ARIS) indicates that the percentage of non-believers has nearly doubled from 8 to 15 percent in the past 18 years (from 1990 to 2008). These results are devastating for those who believe that the US, unlike "secular" Europe, will always be a nation of churchgoers.

Non-believers now outnumber every religious group in America except Catholics and Baptists. This is not a surprise to Americans—though it may surprise British people who insist on portraying Americans as people of simple and sunny faith, whatever form it takes.

One only has to read the blogs to realize that there is a vast number of young Americans out there who share a liberal contempt for religion. It was no coincidence that Sam Harris's frightening book against religion, *The End of Faith*, sat in the *New York Times* best seller lists for 33 weeks.

The trend towards religious indifference was clearly illustrated by the Obama administration and its supporters: never had there been so many young atheists and agnostics working in the White House and on Capitol Hill[19]. At the moment the Democrats have absorbed most of the non-believers, secularization will come to the Republicans, too.

5. Religious Views about Social Issues

5.1 Euthanasia

In the United States, euthanasia, sometimes known as "mercy-killing," is legal in Washington D.C. and the states of California, Colorado[20], Oregon[21], Vermont, Hawaii and Washington. According to a 2017 Gallup Poll, 73% of all Americans feel euthanasia is morally acceptable, while among those who attend religious services weekly, only 55% regarded euthanasia as morally acceptable, and among those who rarely if ever go to church, 87% say it should be allowed. A 74-year-old man from Iowa commented, "Of course, I expect doctors to make patients as comfortable as possible, but only God can take away a life."

5.2 Abortion

Religion has had a major influence on the policies surrounding abortion in America, as shown by differing requirements in states, based on the amount of religious influence in particular states.

Washington, in the case of a minor, does not require consent from one or both of the parents. Also, a waiting period is not required, as opposed to Texas and Louisiana, where one must wait at least 24 hours before having an abortion. Washington is a wonderful example of a state that has a smaller religious influence than most other states and has more liberal policies toward abortion. This is partly because Washington has the largest percentage of people that are unaffiliated with a religion.

Southerners and mid-westerners are more likely to believe abortion should not be permitted, while those in the west and northeast are more likely to think it should be generally available. This is because the "Bible Belt," or the southern and mid-western states of America, has traditionally had more Christians than the rest of the country.

Joyful Moment

The Last Request

A woman in Brooklyn, New York City, decided to prepare her will and make her final requests. She told her rabbi she had two final requests. First, she wanted to be cremated(火葬), and second, she wanted her ashes scattered all over Bloomingdales.

"Why Bloomingdales（布鲁明戴尔百货公司）?" asked the rabbi.

"Then I'll be sure that my daughters would visit me twice a week."

Notes

[1] Plymouth 普利茅斯，位于马萨诸塞州

[2] Baptist 浸礼会教徒，浸礼会是美国新教教派，要求信徒受浸水礼而非点水礼

[3] Methodists 卫理公会教徒，卫理公会是美国新教教派

[4] Lutherans 路德会教徒，路德会是美国新教教派，以马丁·路德宗教思想为依据

[5] Presbyterians 长老会教徒，长老会是新教教派

[6] Episcopalians 美国圣公会教徒

[7] Bible Belt 美国南部和中西部有着较强基督教信仰基础的地区，被称为圣经带，民风非常保守，对宗教非常狂热。

[8] fundamentalist 信奉正统派基督教的人，原教旨主义者

[9] Holy Communion 圣餐礼，基督教的重要仪式

[10] Utah 犹他州，位于美国西部。1847 年由布里格姆·扬格率领的摩门教徒在此地区居住，1896 年它作为第 45 个州被纳入美国。

[11] practitioners（基督教科学派的）信仰疗法术士，坚信通过修正人的人生观，塑造信仰体系，能恢复或者强化其心理能力，以达到治愈疾病的目的。

[12] Sabbath day 安息日，信徒应当按律法要求遵守安息日，停止劳动，并在这一天举行聚会礼拜。

[13] Messiah 弥赛亚，救世主（指耶稣基督）

[14] Yarmulke 亚莫克便帽，犹太男子在祷告、学习、吃饭等时戴的圆顶小帽

[15] split hoof 蹄分两瓣。按《圣经》规定，犹太人只能吃蹄分两瓣又反刍的走兽的肉。

[16] Reform, Orthodox, and Conservative Judaism 犹太教的三大派系——改革派、正统派和保守派

[17] Amish 阿米什人，基督新教再洗礼派门诺会信徒。

[18] Heaven's Gate cult 天堂之门，又称“天门教”，于 1997 年停止活动。

[19] Capitol Hill 美国国会

[20] Colorado 科罗拉多州

[21] Oregon 俄勒冈州

New Words

1. **sprinkle** /'sprɪŋkəl/ *v.* to throw small pieces of something or drops of a liquid on something 撒，洒，把……撒（洒）在……上

   —Grandma sprinkled the flowers with water.

   祖母将水洒在花上。

2. **polygamy** /pə'lɪgəmi/ *n.* the custom of having more than one wife 一夫多妻（制）

   —Eight years later, Mormonism withdrew its support of polygamy.

   八年之后，摩门教取消了对一夫多妻制的支持。

3. **profanation** /ˌprɒfə'neɪʃən/ *n.* behavior or words showing disrespect for religious things 亵渎

   —He felt that it is a profanation to break upon that enchanted strain.

   他觉得打断这迷人的音乐是极不礼貌的。

4. **frugality** /fruː'gæləti/ *n.* the quality of being careful in avoiding waste 节俭

   —Frugality, when all is spent, comes too late.

   花光了才节俭，为时已太晚。

5. **censor**/'sensə/ *v.* to examine books, films/movies, etc. and remove parts which are considered offensive, immoral or politically dangerous 审查，检查，删减

   —It's not constitutional to censor the press.

   审查新闻是违反宪法的。

6. **parochial** /pə'rəʊkiəl/ *a.* connected with a church parish 教区的，堂区的

   —He is very interested in parochial affairs.

   他对教区的事务非常感兴趣。

7. **immortality** /ˌɪmɔː'tæləti/ *n.* the state of being remembered for a long time or forever 永生，永垂不朽

   —He has achieved immortality.

   他获得了永垂不朽的声名。

8. **dietary** /'daɪətəri/ *a.* of or relating to the diet 饮食的

   —Will there be any special dietary requirements?

有什么特殊的饮食方面的要求吗？

9. **kosher** /'kəʊʃə/ *a.* (of food) prepared according to the rules of Jewish law 合乎犹太教教规及礼仪要求的
—All their food is strictly kosher.
他们所有的食物都完全符合犹太教食规。

10. **potpourri** /ˌpəʊpʊ'riː/ *n.* a collection of various different items which were not originally intended to form a group 杂烩，集锦
—It is a potpourri of short stories and humorous verses.
这是本短篇小说及幽默诗句集锦。

11. **salvation** /sæl'veɪʃən/ *n.* the state of being saved from the power of evil 得救，救赎
—Work earns salvation.
劳动即救赎。

Exercises

1. Choose the correct answer.

1) The majority of Americans identify themselves as ________.
A. Christians B. Buddhists C. Muslims D. Baptists

2) Of the 78.4% of Americans with a Christian connection, ________ groups make up about 51%.
A. Protestant B. Roman Catholics
C. Eastern Orthodox D. Christian Scientists

3) The largest Protestant group is the ________.
A. Methodists B. Lutherans C. Baptists D. Episcopalians

4) In the U.S., religious faith lives side by side with a strong belief in free will and an admiration of ________.
A. wealth B. self-reliance C. power D. hard work

5) To the Puritans, a person by nature was wholly ________ and could achieve good only by severe and persistent discipline.
A. powerful B. pure C. ignorant D. sinful

2. Decide whether the following statements are True or False.

1) At the beginning of the 17th century, religious persecution became more serious and many people in Britain went to America for fortune.

2) Methodists believe in infant baptism, done by full immersion.

3) The Mormons were forced out of several established communities because they refused to follow the traditional Catholic practices.

4) The United States is home to the second largest Jewish community in the world.

5) All Catholics would like to send their children to parochial schools.

3. Fill in the blanks according to the passage.

1) It is customary for religious Jewish men to cover their heads with a _______ either all the time or when they pray.

2) ________ are the second largest Protestant group in America.

3) During the Sabbath, observant Jews will do nothing that might be counted as ________.

4) Reform Jews are of ________ origin.

5) America is remarkable now, as in the past, for its attachment to the principle of ________ of belief and disbelief.

4. Explain the following terms according to the passage.

1) Kosher food

2) the Jewish holy day, the Sabbath

3) Bible Belt

4) Holy Communion

5) Conservative Judaism

5. Answer the following questions according to the passage.

1) How is Christianity similar to Judaism?

2) How does Roman Catholicism differ from Protestantism?

3) Why has America always been a safer haven for believers and nonbelievers alike?

6. Discussion.

Care 4 America is a not-for-profit Florida-based counseling network, offering Christian counseling for depression, guilt, anger, teen anger management, anxiety, faith building, etc. The following passage is taken from its website.

"Are you really happy with you and your life? Have you noticed that your life has many of the same ups and downs? As teenagers are we in search of finding who we are? And what is real happiness? As we approach 18 or 21 years old we have had the apron strings cut and have donned our wings to fly to our own unique happiness.

The world tells us that drinking, drugs, parties, girls, boys, and lots of other worldly things make us happy. And when we wake up after those parties and fun events and look back at those times and ask ourselves: What happened? Was I happy? What are the consequences of those moments of adult like happiness?

Sin and things that we know are wrong are fun and we have a lot of pleasure when doing them. Sins and wrongdoings are pleasures for a season, just like spring, fall, winter, summer. But, like the seasons they too will pass. We remember that after the fun stuff is over, we are alone again and wonder if this is the endless circle of having fun, feeling alone and having problems. Most people go through this type of circular thinking process and then may add in information about What Does God Want Me to Be Doing? Some people make a decision to follow God's Path and some continue to follow the Circular Path going from fun and sin to problems and severe consequences. Most times the consequences become more and more severe as they make negative progress toward their goal of finding happiness and fun in the wrong un-Godly manner. God is actually telling you that you have made the choice to seek sinful un-Godly ways to become more social and he sends many wakeup calls (consequences) so that you will make the right path choices next time."

Questions:

1) Think about whether you are really happy with you and your life. Do you think religion can give you directions for a happy life?

2) The following are some quotes. Read them and discuss what do you think about religion?

When I do good, I feel good; when I do bad, I feel bad, and that is my religion.

—Abraham Lincoln

My religion consists of a humble admiration of the illimitable superior spirit who reveals himself in the slight details we are able to perceive with our frail and feeble mind.

—Albert Einstein

I am determined that my children shall be brought up in their father's religion, if they can find out what it is.

—Charles Lamb

It is a fine thing to establish one's own religion in one's heart, not to be dependent on tradition and second-hand ideals. Life will seem to you, later, not a lesser, but a greater thing.

—D. H. Lawrence

Rational arguments don't usually work on religious people. Otherwise, there wouldn't be religious people.

—Doris Egan

Everyone ought to worship God according to his own inclinations, and not to be constrained by force.

—Flavius Josephus

Everybody likes to go their own way—to choose their own time and manner of devotion.

—Jane Austen

Stay Positive

1. Curiosity is one of the permanent and certain characteristics of a vigorous mind.
2. I find that the harder I work, the more luck I seem to have.

Chapter 8

Literature and Arts of the United States

The man who does not read books has no advantage over the man that cannot read them.

—Mark Twain (1835—1910), U.S. humorist, writer and lecturer

1. Literature

Like other national literatures, American literature was shaped by the history of the country that produced it. For almost a century and a half, America was merely a group of colonies. The colonial writings could not count as American literature but merely a branch of British literature. Though America became the United States, a nation, in 1783, its cultural independence did not arrive until the mid-19th century. Therefore, the history of American literature is also the story of the slow emergence of native elements and national characteristics.

1.1 The Colonial Period (1607-1775)

American literature at first was naturally a colonial literature. The early settlers of the New Continent were occupied by the survival concern in the harsh wilderness, and their writings paid particular attention to practical details of settlement. In this sense, the earliest American literature is principally "a literature of travel and description, history and chronicle".

American literature finds its deep root in Puritanism, which stresses predestination, original sin, total depravity, and the salvation of a selected few who would receive God's grace. Its two significant aspects are represented by two figures in this period—Jonathan Edwards stands for the idealistic aspect of Puritanism and Benjamin Franklin for the practical aspect of Puritanism.

Jonathan Edwards (1703-1758) defended his burning belief in the concept that man could attain virtue and salvation only through God's grace most notably in *Freedom of Will* (1754).

Benjamin Franklin (1706-1790) represents the materialist Puritanism. He was born "poor and obscure", and he received little education. But he read widely and became almost everything: printer, publisher, essayist, scientist, inventor, orator, statesman, ambassador and politician. Franklin had a definite gift for writing. His best writing is found in his *Autobiography*, a record of his rise from humble circumstances that offered worldly wise suggestions for future success.

However, this worldly success is in line with Puritanism: hard work is the right way to worship God, and the material success of the believer is evidence of God's love.

1.2 The Revolutionary Period (1775-1790)

The Revolutionary Period refers to the period between 1765 when the Stamp Act was passed and 1790. Thomas Jefferson, an influential political writer, is most representative of this period. He was remembered as the drafter of the *Declaration of Independence*.

1.3 The Romantic Period (1790-1865)

Being one of the most important periods in American literature history, American Romantic Period stretches from the end of 18th century to the outbreak of the Civil War. In America as in Europe, fresh new vision influenced artistic and intellectual circles. Yet there was an important difference: romanticism in America coincided with the period of national expansion and the discovery of a distinctive American voice.

The romantic spirit seemed particularly suited to American democracy: it stressed individualism, affirmed the value of the common person. In New England, romanticism fell upon fertile soil.

During this period, most of American writings placed an increasing emphasis on the free expression of emotions, and they displayed an increasing attention on the spiritual state of their characters. They celebrated America's landscape with its virgin forests, meadows, streams, and vast oceans. Although British influences were strong, American writers began to produce a literature that was truly native and American romanticism exhibited from the very outset distinct features of its own.

1.3.1 Fiction

The history of American fiction starts later than both the prose and poetry. Two pioneers of romanticism, Washington Irving and James Fenimore Cooper, began the age of fiction.

Washington Irving (1783-1859), the first American to achieve the international literary reputation, is regarded as the Father of American Literature. He was the first to write using the local color of America. His most famous stories are *Rip Van Winkle* (1819) and *The Legend of Sleepy Hollow* (1820).

James Fenimore Cooper (1789-1851) is one of the first authors to write about American Westward Movement. He did his best work in the *Leather stocking Tales*, a five-volume series celebrating the career of a great frontiersman. The *Leather stocking Tales* demonstrates Cooper's rich imagination because Cooper has never been to the frontier or lived with any Indians.

History also figured in tales and romances of Nathaniel Hawthorne(1804-1864)[1], the leading New England fictionist of the period. He was a descendant of a long line of Puritan immigrants and a pioneer in psychological description. He tried to find out how men reacted when they found they had done something wrong. In his famous novel *The Scarlet Letter*, he probed into the guilty conscience of two lovers, who committed adultery. The story is not a praise of a sinning woman, but a hymn on the moral growth of her who had been sinned against.

Edgar Allan Poe(1809-1849)[2]is a lonely writer both in life and in literary history. Miserable parentless childhood, suspended college life and the early death of his wife all cast shadow toward his life and resulted in his early mysterious death. Poe achieved greatly in short stories, poetry and literary theory. His masterpieces of terror *The Fall of the House of Usher*, *The Masque of the Red Death* were written according to a carefully worked out psychological method. As a poet, he achieved fame with *The Raven*, a long poem.

Herman Melville (1819-1891), famous as the author of *Moby Dick* in literary world, was neglected and misunderstood in his lifetime. Melville spoke ahead of his time. When most people were highly praising the power of man and the progress of science and life, he presented a bleak view of the world in which the universe is Godless and purposeless and human life meaningless and futile.

1.3.2 Poetry

American poetry can be traced to two founts, Walt Whitman and Emily Dickinson.

Walter Whitman (1819-1892)[3]was a believer in democracy, in the splendor of the common man. He published the first edition of *Leaves of Grass* in 1855. This autobiography in verse was intended to show the ideas, beliefs, emotions, and experiences of the common man in a great period of American individualism.

Emily Dickinson (1830-1886) is different from Whitman in many ways. Whereas Whitman turned to the outer world and embraced society, Dickinson cast her eyes inward to explore the inner feelings of the individual. Remained unmarried for her whole life, Dickinson lived in her father's house for most of her life. Her poems are short. The real world remains invisible in her lines, neither are there people. Beneath her calm appearance, Dickinson buries her fervent yearning for God's help, for love and for good life. Her most famous poems include *My Life Closed Twice Before Its Close*, *Because I Could Not Stop for Death* and *A Narrow Fellow in the Grass*.

1.3.3 Prose

When American romanticism reaches its peak—transcendentalism[4], prose became the major literary genre of creation. The transcendentalist movement was based on a fundamental belief in the unity of the world and God.

Ralph Waldo Emerson(1803-1882)[5]is acclaimed as the chief spokesman of New England transcendentalism. He avoided building a logical intellectual system because such a rational system would have negated his romantic belief in intuition and flexibility. Most of his major ideas are suggested in his *Nature*, *The American Scholar* and *Essays*.

Henry David Thoreau (1817-1862) was a renowned New England transcendentalist. Throughout his life, he reduced his needs to the simplest level and managed to live on very little money, thus maintaining his independence. Thoreau's masterpiece, *Walden*, or *Life in the Woods*, is the result of two years, two months, and two days (from 1845 to 1847) he spent living in a cabin. This is his famous experiment of transcendentalism—to stay away from the greedy and industrialized American society and lived a self-sufficient life among the pure nature.

1.4 The Realistic and Naturalistic Period (1865-1914)

The period ranging from 1865 to 1914 has been regarded as the age of realism and naturalism in the literary history of the United States.

The American scene changed tremendously after the Civil War. Things seemed less romantic with the coming of the Industrial Revolution. American Realism expressed concern for the world of experience, for the commonplace, for the familiar and the low. Emphasis was put on the individual.

1.4.1 The Realistic Period (1865–1900)

The Realistic Period is characterized by true-to-life novels and short stories, which focus on presenting the reality of struggling Americans. Writers began to show life as they observed and express their own personal feelings. Their characters were more complex than in the Romantic Movement. They wrote about every-day events and every-day people. Many of their plots were unpleasant. The novel became the typical form of expression. The three dominant figures of this period are Mark Twain, William Dean Howells and Henry James.

Samuel Clemens (1835-1910), better known by his pen name of Mark Twain[6], is the most famous author of the Realistic Period and even perhaps one of the most famous of American literature in its entirety. He is considered "the true father of national literature". Twain's style, based on vigorous, realistic, colloquial American speech, gave American writers a new appreciation of their national voice.

For Twain and other American writers of the late 19th century, realism was not merely a literary technique: it was a way of speaking truth and exploding worn-out conventions. The most well-known example is Huck Finn, a poor boy who decides to follow the voice of his conscience and help a Negro slave escape to freedom, even though Huck thinks this means that he will be damned to hell for breaking the law. In deciding to save Jim, Huck grows morally beyond the bounds of his slave-owning society.

Mark Twain's other famous novels are *The Adventure of Tom Sawyer*, *The Prince and the Pauper*, *Life on the Mississippi*, and *The Mysterious Stranger*, etc.

William Dean Howells (1837-1920) was a famous critic and prolific writer. The greatest of all his works is *The Rise of Silas Lapham*. Silas Lapham is a self-made man who starts his paint business from scratch and becomes a millionaire but ends up in ruin. Although he falls and suffers, he manages to keep a greater number of people from suffering. By falling, he achieves his moral and ethical "rise".

With Twain, Henry James (1843-1916) is generally ranked as the greatest American novelist of the second half of the 19th century. Outstanding were *The American*, his masterpiece *The Portrait of a Lady* and *The Spoils of Poynton*. The earliest of his works were international novels wherein conflicts arose from relationships between Americans and Europeans. In *The American*, for example, Christopher Newman, a naive but intelligent and idealistic self-made millionaire industrialist, goes to Europe seeking a bride. When her family rejects him because he lacks an aristocratic background, he has a chance to revenge himself; in deciding not to, he demonstrates his moral superiority.

Mark Twain, William Dean Howells, and Henry James together focused on realistic portrayal of the landscape and social surfaces, brought to perfection the style native to America. But they differed in understanding of the "truth". Mark Twain and Howells had paid more attention to the life of the American; Henry James had laid more emphasis on "inner world" of man, probing the deepest parts of the psychological and moral nature of human being. Though Mark Twain and Howells had the same concern in presenting the truth of American society, they had each of them different emphases. Howells focused his discussion on the rising middle class and the way they lived, while Mark Twain preferred to have his own region and people at the forefront of his stories, which is known as "local colorism".

1.4.2 The Naturalistic Period (1900–1914)

At the end of the 19th century came a generation of writers when the impact of Darwin's evolutionary on the American thought, the influence of 19th century French literature on the American letters and the economic determinism of Karl Marx gave rise to American naturalism.

Naturalism[7] attempts to apply scientific theories to art and adds an amoral attitude to the objective presentation of life. Naturalistic writers regard human behavior as controlled by instinct, emotion, or social and economic conditions. Artistically, naturalistic writing is unpolished in language, lacking in academic skills, and clumsy in structure. Philosophically, naturalists believed that the real and true is always hidden from eyes of individual, or beyond the control. In a word, naturalism is evolved from realism when the author's tone in writing becomes less serious and less sympathetic but more ironic and pessimistic.

Stephen Crane (1871-1900) is the pioneer of American naturalistic writing. His first novel *Maggie: A Girl of the Streets* is one of the best, if not the earliest, naturalistic American novels.

A poor, self-taught worker from California, the naturalist Jack London (1876-1916) rose from the bottom of society. Jack London rose from poverty to fame by his first collection of stories, *The Son of the Wolf.* Others of his best-sellers, including *The Call of the Wild* and *The Sea-Wolf* made him the highest paid writer in the United States of his time. The autobiographical novel *Martin Eden* depicts the inner stresses of the American dream as London experienced them during his rise from obscure poverty to wealth and fame.

Theodore Dreiser(1871-1945)[8] is one of the first important writers to come from the lowest society. His novels deal with everyday life, often its tragic side. His earliest novels are *Sister Carrie* and *Jennie Gerhardt*. The 1925 work *An American Tragedy*, like London's *Martin Eden*, explores the dangers of the American dream. The novel relates the life of Clyde Griffiths, a boy of weak will and little self-awareness. He grows up in great poverty, but dreams of wealth. When his girlfriend Roberta becomes pregnant, Clyde has fallen in love with a wealthy society girl who represents success, money, and social acceptance. Clyde carefully plans to drown

Roberta on a boat trip, but at the last minute he begins to change his mind; however, she accidentally falls out of the boat. Clyde, a good swimmer, does not save her, and she drowns. Dreiser, in *An American Tragedy*, built up an overwhelming sense of tragic inevitability. *An American Tragedy* is a reflection of the dissatisfaction, envy, and despair that afflicted many poor and working people in America's competitive, success-driven society.

O Henry (1862-1910) is one of the most prolific short story writers in American literary history. He is a master of surprise ending which is termed as "O Henry's ending". A twist of plot which turns on an ironic or coincidental circumstance is typical in O Henry's stories. His best stories, familiar to Chinese readers, included *The Gift of Magi* and *Last Leave*.

1.5 The Modernist Period (1914-1939)

The era from World War I to World War II (1914-1939) is known as the Modernist Period. The social upheavals caused by two world wars, one Great Depression, and a growing void in American spiritual life created a disillusioned society.

The American Modernist Period produced writers of Modernist Period Subclasses, for example, writers of the Jazz Age, writers of the Harlem Renaissance, writers of the Lost Generation and writers of Depression-era.

1.5.1 The Jazz Age[9]

The Jazz Age describes the period during the 1920s; the years after the end of World War I, continuing through the Roaring Twenties and ending with the rise of the Great Depression. The traditional values of the previous period saw great decline. People accepted technological developments as well as new modernist trends in social behavior, arts, and culture. The Jazz Age was a golden period in American literature.

F. Scott Fitzgerald (1896-1940)[10] has been regarded as the literary spokesman of the Jazz Age. In most of his fictions, he dealt with the bankruptcy of the American dream due to the clashes between their romantic version of life and the miserable reality. His novel *The Great Gatsby* (1925) is one of the most representative literary works of this period. Gatsby's life follows a clear pattern. There is, at first, a dream, then disenchantment, and finally a sense of failure and despair.

1.5.2 Harlem Renaissance[11]

Harlem Renaissance, also known as the Black Literary Renaissance and the New Negro Movement, refers to the flowering of African American cultural and intellectual life during the 1920s and 1930s. It is described as a "spiritual coming of age" in which the black community was able to seize upon its "first chances for group expression and self-determination".

Black-owned magazines and newspapers flourished. The white literary establishment soon became fascinated with the writers of the Harlem Renaissance and began publishing them in larger numbers. But for the writers themselves, acceptance by the white world was less important, as Langston Hughes put it, than the "expression of our individual dark-skinned selves."

1.5.3 The Lost Generation

When the First World War broke out, many young Americans volunteered to take part in "the war to end wars" only to find that modern warfare was not as glorious or heroic as they thought. The term "the Lost Generation" was first used by Gertrude Stein to describe the post-World War I generation of American writers: men and women haunted by a sense of betrayal and emptiness brought about by the destructiveness of the war, especially those who lived in Paris and Europe after the First World War. The term is commonly applied to Hart Crane, Ernest Hemingway, F. Scott Fitzgerald, and others.

Ernest Hemingway(1899-1961)[12], a giant of modern literature, was the spokesman for the Lost Generation and a Nobel Prize winner. Many of his works are now considered classics of American literature. His major works include *The Sun Also Rises*, *A Farewell to Arms*, *For Whom the Bell Tolls*, and *The Old Man and the Sea.*

The Sun Also Rises is Hemingway's first true novel. It casts light on a whole generation after the First World War and the effects of the war by way of a vivid portrait of the Lost Generation. Its protagonist Jake Barnes was one representative of the Lost Generation.

The Old Man and the Sea, Hemingway's most famous allegorical novel, won him a Pulitzer Prize and a Nobel Prize in 1954. The short story is about an old Cuban fishman Santiago and his losing battle with a giant marlin. For 84 days, Santiago catches no fish, but he goes far off into gulf-stream and hooks a huge marlin, which pulls his boat three days and nights till it grows exhausted. Santiago manages to kill this marlin with the last drop of his strength and ties its body to the boat. But its blood trail attracts sharks. He fights against the endless sharks devouring the marlin's meat and leaving only the skeleton, head, and tail. Santiago in this story is a typical Hemingway coded hero. The heartbreaking loss of the marlin won by arduous struggle becomes the proof of dignity and "grace under pressure". Santiago's famous lines "a man is not made for defeat... A man can be destroyed but not defeated" are the faith of Hemingway's hero. The story highlights the honor in struggle, defeat and death and claims that pride is the source of greatness and determination.

In the general situation of Hemingway's novels, life is full of tension and battles. Though life is but a losing battle, it is a struggle man can dominate in such a sense that loss becomes dignity.

Ezra Pound (1885-1972) is a major figure of the Modernist movement in the first half of the 20th century. His significant contributions to poetry begin with his promotion of Imagism[13], a movement in poetry which derived its technique from classical Chinese and Japanese poetry. As a translator, Pound did much to introduce Chinese poetry to English-speaking audiences. For example, he helped popularize major poems of Du Fu.

1.5.4 Depression-era Literature

The 1930s were a decade of great change. Americans suffered a lot to weather such a disastrous period and their true strength was shown. From it arose John Steinbeck(1902-1968)[14], a representative figure of Depression-era literature which was frank and direct in its social criticism. Steinbeck often wrote about poor, working-class people and their struggle to lead a decent and honest life. His books are reflections of what really went on in the 1930s politically, economically and socially.

The Grapes of Wrath, considered as his masterpiece, tells the story of the Joads, a poor family from Oklahoma and their journey to California in search of a better life. Other popular novels include *The Pearl* and *East of Eden*. He was awarded the Nobel Prize in Literature in 1962.

1.6 The Contemporary Period (1939-)

The year of 1939 marked the beginning of the Contemporary Period of American Literature. The following types of novels came to public notice in the years from the end of the war through 1960s: the war novel, the southern novel, the Jewish novel, the Beat novel and the Black novel. And the period after that has been one in which American fiction is noted for its fantasy and surrealism[15], its nonfiction, science fiction, black or absurd humor, and its experimental novelistic techniques.

1.6.1 War Novel

Right after WWII, a series of young writers wrote intelligent novels showing how the pressures of war highlight men's characters. Controversial, celebrated post-WWII American writer Norman Mailer (1923-2007) first gained recognition at age 25 for his anti-war novel, *The Naked and the Dead* which was commented by *The Times* as "the best war novel to come out of the United States". By 1961, Joseph Heller (1923-1999) published his satiric war novel *Catch-22*, in which war is portrayed as an absurd exercise of madmen.

1.6.2 Literature of the Modern South

William Faulkner (1897-1962)[16]is a giant in the realm of American literature, who won the 1949 Nobel Prize. He is considered as one of the most important Southern writers. Most of Faulkner's stories are about people from a small region, Yoknapatawpha[17] County, which is actually an imaginary place based on Faulkner's childhood memory about his hometown. By his Yoknapatawpha series, Faulkner managed to show the life in Southern society. His major works include *The Sound and the Fury*, *As I Lay Dying*, *Light in August*, *Absalom, Absalom!* and *Go Down, Moses*.

1.6.3 Jewish Writers

The works of the Jewish writers at this time deal with the modern urban dweller disaffected by society but not destroyed in spirit and explore relationship between secular society and Jewish tradition.

One of the most outstanding representatives of Jewish literature is Saul Bellow (1915-2005)[18], who won the 1976 Nobel Prize. Bellow saw many flaws in modern civilization, and its ability to foster madness, materialism and misleading knowledge. His famous works include *Dangling Man*, *The Victim*, *Seize the Day*, *Henderson the Rain King*, Herzog, and *Humboldt's Gift*.

1.6.4 The Beat Generation[19]

The Beat Generation refers to a group of American writers and artists popular in the 1950s and early 1960s, whose writing expressed profound dissatisfaction with contemporary American society. They are known especially for their use of nontraditional forms and their rejection of conventional social values concerning sex, religion and the American way of life. Furthermore, many Beat writers discovered Asian literature while exploring the ideas of Zen[20]Buddhism.

In 1956, with the publication of Ginsberg's epic poem *Howl*, Beat Generation achieved broad national recognition. Kerouac's semiautobiographical *On the Road* is regarded as the best-known Beat novel.

1.6.5 Black Writers

The Harlem Renaissance changed forever the position of African American arts and literature in the United States. The writers that followed in the 1930s and 1940s found that publishers and the public were more open to African American literature.

Richard Wright (1908-1960)'s *Native Son* explores the extreme psychological pressures that drive a young urban black man to violence. It established Wright as the leading African American author of the 1940s. Ralph Ellison's (1914-1994) *The Invisible Man* is often cited as one of the great American novels of the 20th century. In this account of an unnamed young black man's search for his place in the world, Ellison criticizes that American society consciously turns a blind eye to its black members.

1.6.6 The Black Women's Literary Renaissance and Women's Voice

A variety of literary, cultural, and political developments during the 1950s and 1960s fostered what has been termed "the black women's literary renaissance" of the 1970s.

Toni Morrison (1931-2019)[21], is the first African-American writer to win a Nobel Prize in literature. Her works deal with the black experience and celebrate the black community. She also explores the relationship between individual and community, revealing how public attitudes can shape private conceptions. *Beloved* is regarded as Morrison's finest novel. Set in post-Civil War Ohio, it tells the story of Margaret Garner, a slave who escaped in 1851 with her children and, when recaptured, attempted to kill her children rather than return them to a life of slavery.

Amy Tan (1952-)[22] is an American writer of Chinese descent whose works portray the lives of Chinese-American daughters and their immigrant mothers and explore mother-daughter relationships. In 1993, Tan's adaptation of her most popular fiction work, *The Joy Luck Club* became a commercially successful film.

1.6.7 New Drama

By the end of the 19th century American drama was moving toward realism.

Eugene O'Neill(1888-1953)[23], considered as the foremost United States playwright, was awarded the Nobel Prize for literature in 1936. O Neill's *The Hairy Ape* was one of the first plays in America to introduce expressionism[24], which emphasized subjective feelings and emotions rather than a detailed or objective depiction of reality.

After WWII two playwrights emerged who would dominate dramatic activity for the next 15 years or so: Tennessee Williams and Arthur Miller.

Tennessee Williams (1911-1983), one of America's most lyrical dramatists, was good at writing about the isolated and lonely people in American society. In *The Glass Menagerie*, he created a pathetic woman, Laura, who lies in her illusion, only to be smashed to pieces by a male intruder, who is the symbol of reality.

Arthur Miller (1915-2005) definitely deserved the title of "social dramatist" since all of his works concern the conflicts of the individual within society. One of Miller's modern tragedies is *Death of a Salesman*, a tale of the life and death of the ordinary working man Willy Loman.

2. Arts

The development of the arts in America has two strong sources of inspiration: European sophistication and domestic originality.

2.1 Film

Moving pictures were not an American invention; however, they have nonetheless been the preeminent American contribution to world entertainment.

In the early 1900s, when the medium was new, many immigrants, found employment in the U.S. film industry. The exhibition of short films in theaters called nickelodeons[25], after their admission price of a nickel (five cents).

Within a few years, ambitious men like Samuel Goldwyn and the Warner Brothers had switched to the production side of the business. Soon they were the heads of a new kind of enterprise—the movie studio. The major studios were located in the Hollywood section of Los Angeles, California.

During the so-called Golden Age of Hollywood in the 1930s and 1940s, the studios were producing a total of about 400 movies a year, seen by an audience of 90 million Americans per week.

The major studios kept thousands of people on salary and they owned hundreds of theaters in cities and towns across the nation.

The number of movies being made dropped sharply, even as the average budget soared, because Hollywood wanted to offer audiences the kind of spectacle they couldn't see on television.

This blockbuster syndrome[26] has continued to affect Hollywood. Movies released today tend to be either huge successes or huge failures, depending on how well their enormous costs match up with the public taste.

2.2 Music

All musical genres are represented on the American music scene, especially jazz and rock/country music.

2.2.1 Jazz

Jazz originated in New Orleans early in the 20th century. One of the distinguishing elements of jazz was its fluidity: in live performances, the musicians would almost never play a song the same way twice but would compose variations on its notes and words. Jazz was the reigning popular American music from the 1920s through the 1940s. In the 1930s and 1940s, the most popular form of jazz was "big band swing". In the late 1940s, a new form of mostly instrumental jazz, called be-bop[27], began to attract audiences. In the 1960s, jazz musicians such as Miles Davis and John Coltrane experimented with a wide range of musical influences. Younger jazz musicians began to include the rhythms of rock and roll. Later, in the 1970s, many jazz musicians experimented with electronic instruments and created a blend of rock and jazz called fusion.

2.2.2 Rock and Country

By the early 1950s, however, jazz had lost some of its appeal to a mass audience. A new form of pop music, rock and roll, evolved from a black style known as rhythm and blues: songs with strong beats and provocative lyrics.

A challenge to rock appeared in the form of folk music. Folk music was based largely on ballads brought over from Scotland, England, and Ireland; it had been preserved in such areas as the mountains of North Carolina and West Virginia.

Bob Dylan extended the reach of folk music by writing striking new songs that addressed contemporary social problems. The division between the two camps—rock enthusiasts and folk purists—came to a head when Dylan was booed for "going electric" (accompanying himself on electric guitar) at the 1965 Newport Folk Festival. Far from being stopped, Dylan led virtually the entire folk movement into a blend of rock and folk. This was an important event, setting a pattern that holds true to this day. Rock remains the prevalent pop music of America—and much of the rest of the world—largely because it can absorb almost any other kind of music, along with new varieties of showmanship, into its strong rhythmical framework.

Like folk, country music descends from the songs brought to the United States from England, Scotland, and Ireland. The original form of country music, called "old-time" and played by string bands, can still be heard at festivals held each year in many southern states. Modern country music developed in the 1920s, roughly coinciding with a mass migration of rural people to big cities in search of work. Like many other forms of American pop music, country lends itself easily to a rock-and-roll beat, and country rock has been yet another successful music merger.

2.3 Theater

American theater is traditionally dated from the arrival of Lewis Hallam's English troupe in 1752. After the end of the Revolutionary War, the Republic witnessed a slow expansion of the dramatic arts.

Theater became a more pervasive part of American life during the early 19th century. In the second half of the 19th century, theater became both more diverse and more specialized.

The development of motion pictures changed the theatre scene. By the 1920s, theater had lost its national mass audience. The early 20th century witnessed a turn to serious drama and innovative stagecraft. During the depression, an unprecedented social and political consciousness was displayed on the stage. The oppression of workers and immigrants was publicly criticized.

The musical stage of the 20th century proved to be the country's most popular theatrical export. By the end of the 19th century the American musical stage included a number of genres. After World War I, Broadway entered a golden period. In the 1930s, dance became more closely linked to the story. Ever since the production of "West Side Story" in 1957, dance has been integral to the story.

Today's American theater might be divided into three categories. First, Broadway productions persist and many new plays are presented first in the theater district of New York City. Over the years, New York theater has developed new avenues known as "off-Broadway"[28] and "off-off Broadway". Second, many regional theaters produce some of the best new drama. Third, colleges and universities support active theater programs.

2.4 The Visual Arts

America's first well-known school of painting—the Hudson River school[29]—appeared in 1820. The Hudson River painters' directness and simplicity of vision influenced such later artists as Winslow Homer (1836-1910), who depicted rural America—the sea, the mountains, and the people who lived near them. Middle-class city life found its painter in Thomas Eakins (1844-1916).

Controversy soon became a way of life for American artists. In fact, much of American painting and sculpture since 1900 has been a series of revolts against tradition. "To hell with the artistic values," announced Robert Henri (1865-1929). He was the leader of what critics called the "ash-can" school of painting[30], after the group's portrayals of the miserable aspects of city life. Soon the ash-can artists gave way to modernists arriving from Europe—the cubists[31] and abstract painters promoted by the photographer Alfred Stieglitz (1864-1946) in New York City.

In the years after World War II, a group of young New York artists formed the first native American movement to exert major influence on foreign artists: abstract expressionism[32]. The abstract expressionists abandoned formal composition and representation of real objects to concentrate on instinctual arrangements of space and color.

Members of the next artistic generation favored a different form of abstraction: works of mixed media. They used photos, newsprint, and discarded objects in their compositions. Pop artists reproduced, with satiric care, everyday objects and images of American popular culture—Coca-Cola bottles, soup cans and comic strips.

Joyful Moment

Can You Hear Me Now?

Never criticize someone until you've walked a mile in their shoes. That way, when you criticize them, they won't be able to hear you from that far away. Plus, you'll have their shoes.

Notes

[1] Nathaniel Hawthorne 纳撒尼尔·霍桑，美国小说家，代表作有《红字》。

[2] Edgar Allan Poe 埃德加·爱伦·坡，美国诗人、小说家，是侦探小说鼻祖、恐怖小说大师，代表作《厄舍府的倒塌》和《红死病的假面具》。

[3] Walter Whitman 沃尔特·惠特曼，美国诗人，代表作有诗集《草叶集》。

[4] transcendentalism 超验主义，主张人能超越感觉和理性而直接认识真理。

[5] Ralph Waldo Emerson 拉尔夫·沃尔多·爱默生，作品有《论自然》。

[6] Mark Twain 马克·吐温，美国小说家，19 世纪后期美国现实主义文学的杰出代表，著有《哈克贝利·费恩历险记》《汤姆·索亚历险记》等。

[7] Naturalism 自然主义，主张“按照事物本来的样子去摹仿”。

[8] Theodore Dreiser 西奥多·德莱塞，美国小说家，代表作《美国悲剧》。

[9] The Jazz Age 爵士乐时代，指一战以后、经济大萧条以前约十年的时间。

[10] F. Scott Fitzgerald 弗朗西斯·斯科特·菲茨杰拉德，“迷惘的一代”的代表作家之一，代表作《了不起的盖茨比》。

[11] Harlem Renaissance 哈莱姆文艺复兴，又称黑人文艺复兴。

[12] Ernest Hemingway 欧内斯特·海明威，美国小说家，1954 年诺贝尔文学奖获得者，代表作有《老人与海》《永别了，武器》《丧钟为谁而鸣》等。

[13] Imagism 意象派，20 世纪初的文学流派，代表人物埃兹拉·庞德。

[14] John Steinbeck 约翰·斯坦贝克，美国作家，代表作《愤怒的葡萄》《珍珠》和《伊甸园以东》。

[15] surrealism 超现实主义，现代西方文艺流派，主张超越现实，超越理智。

[16] William Faulkner 威廉·福克纳，美国作家，代表作《喧嚣与骚动》。

[17] Yoknapatawpha 约克纳帕塔法郡，福克纳作品的标志，是文学史上有名的虚构地点之一，原型是他故乡所在的拉斐特郡。

[18] Saul Bellow 索尔·贝娄，美国作家，代表作有《雨王汉德逊》《赫索格》和《洪堡的礼物》等。

[19] The Beat Generation 垮掉的一代，第二次世界大战后风行于美国的文学流派，也指当时美国一群松散结合在一起的年轻诗人和作家。

[20] Zen 禅，禅宗（佛教宗派）

[21] Toni Morrison 托尼·莫里森，美国黑人女作家，代表作《宠儿》。

[22] Amy Tan 谭恩美，美籍华裔女作家，作品有《喜福会》等。
[23] Eugene O'Neill 尤金•奥尼尔，美国戏剧作家，代表作有《猿人》
[24] expressionism 表现主义
[25] nickelodeon 五分钱电影院，因入场费只需一枚五分镍币而得名
[26] blockbuster syndrome 大片综合征
[27] be-bop 比波普爵士乐，一种激进的爵士乐风格，现代爵士乐的前身。
[28] off-Broadway 外百老汇，泛指在百老汇以外纽约其他地区上演的戏剧
off-off-Broadway 外外百老汇。外百老汇也步百老汇的后尘，走上了高成本制作的道路，从而引起再度"外迁"，形成外外百老汇剧场。
[29] Hudson River school 哈得逊河画派，美国风景画派
[30] "ash-can" school of painting 垃圾箱画派，由于该画派都是写实画家，爱画贫穷、肮脏的城市，所以被讥讽为垃圾箱画派。
[31] cubists 立体派艺术家
[32] abstract expressionism 抽象表现主义，以抽象的形式表达和激起人的情感

New Words

1. **depravity** /dɪ'prævəti/ *n.* the state of being morally bad 堕落，腐化
—The boy has gone deep in depravity.
这个男孩已经罪孽极深了。
2. **obscure** /əb'skjʊə/ *adj.* of undistinguished or humble station or reputation 身份卑微的
—The president is of obscure origin.
这位总统出身卑微。
3. **coincide** /ˌkəʊən'saɪd/ *v.* to happen at the same time or during the same period of time 同时发生
—The demonstration had been carefully stage-managed to coincide with the Prime Minister's visit.
这次示威活动事先做了精心安排，正好在首相访问时进行。
4. **hymn** /hɪm/ *n.* if a film/movie, book, etc. is a hymn to something, it praises it very strongly 赞美诗；颂歌
—The hymn followed him faintly as he crossed the fields.
在跨过田野时，他还能隐约听到圣歌。
5. **conscience** /'kɒnʃəns/ *n.* the part of one's mind that tells him whether his actions are right or wrong 良心，良知
—She was afflicted with conscience.
她受良心责备。
6. **amoral** /eɪ'mɒrəl/ *adj.* not admitting of moral distinctions or judgments; neither moral nor immoral 与道德无关的，非道德范围的

—Science is completely amoral.
科学与道德无关。

7. **coincidental** /kəʊˌɪnsə'dentl/ *adj*. happening by chance; not planned 巧合，碰巧，非计划之中的
—The similarity between these two essays is too great to be coincidental.
这两篇文章雷同的地方太多，并非巧合所致。

Exercises

1. Choose the correct answer.

1) F. Scott Fitzgerald has been regarded as the literary spokesman of the _______.
A. modern time B. young American
C. Jazz Age D. neo-romanticism

2) Of the following writers, _______ is not a Nobel Prize winner.
A. Alice Walker B. Ernest Hemingway
C. William Faulkner D. Eugene O'Neill

3) _______ is considered "the true father of national literature".
A. Shakespeare B. Ernest Hemingway
C. Mark Twain D. Henry James

4) _______ is a master of surprise endings.
A. O Henry B. Theodore Dreiser
C. Jack London D. Stephen Crane

5) The era from World War I to World War II (1914-1939) is known as the ________ Period.
A. Romantic B. Modernistic
C. Jazz Age D. Great Depression

2. Decide whether the following statements are True or False.

1) *Life on the Mississippi* tells a story of Henry James's boyhood ambition to become a riverboat pilot up and down the Mississippi.
2) Optimism and positivism are strongly reflected in Hardy's writings.
3) Hemingway's major works include *The Sun Also Rises*, *A Farewell to Arms*, *For Whom the Bell Tolls*, and *The Old Man and the Sea.*
4) Naturalistic writing is polished in language, lacking in academic skills, and unwieldy in structure.
5) When the First World War broke out, many young Americans volunteered to take part in "the war to end wars" and found that modern warfare was glorious and heroic.

3. Fill in the blanks according to the passage.

1) American literature at first was naturally a________ literature.
2) American literature finds its deep root in ____________, which stresses predestination,

original sin, total depravity, and the salvation of a selected few.

3) During the so-called Golden Age of _______in the 1930s and 1940s, the studios were producing a total of about 400 movies a year, seen by an audience of 90 million Americans per week.

4) ___________ is Hemingway's first true novel.

5) As a translator, Pound helped popularize major poems of a Chinese poet ______.

4. Explain the following terms according to the passage.

1) Jazz Age

2) The Lost Generation

3) Naturalism

4) The Beat Generation

5) The Realistic Period

5. Answer the following questions according to the passage.

1) What is Harlem Renaissance and its influence?

2) Why does Rock remain the prevalent pop music of America?

3) What are the distinctive features of American Romanticism?

6. Discussion.

1) Explain how Mark Twain, William Dean Howells, and Henry James differed in understanding of the "truth".

2) Explain the theme reflected in Hemingway's *The Old Man and the Sea.*

Stay Positive

1. Don't follow the crowd, let the crowd follow you.
2. Love of beauty is taste. The creation of beauty is art.

Appendix I: Prime Ministers of the United Kingdom

Names	Party	Term
Robert Walpole 罗伯特・沃波尔	Whig	1721-1742
Spencer Compton 斯潘塞・康普顿	Whig	1742-1743
Henry Pelham 亨利・佩勒姆	Whig	1743-1754
Thomas Pelham-Holles 托马斯・佩勒姆・霍利斯	Whig	1754-1756 (1st time)
William Cavendish 威廉・卡文迪什	Whig	1756-1757
Thomas Pelham-Holles 托马斯・佩勒姆-霍利斯	Whig	1757-1762 (2nd time)
John Stuart 约翰・斯图尔特	Tory	1762-1763
George Grenville 乔治・格伦维尔	Whig	1763-1765
Charles Watson-Wentworth 查尔斯・沃森-文特沃斯	Whig	1765-1766 (1st time)
William Pitt 老威廉・皮特	Whig	1766-1768
Augustus Henry FitzRoy 奥古斯都・亨利・菲茨罗伊	Whig	1768-1770
Frederick North 腓特烈・诺斯	Tory	1770-1782
Charles Watson-Wentworth 查尔斯・沃森-文特沃斯	Whig	1782 (2nd time)
William Petty 威廉・佩蒂	Whig	1782-1783
William Cavendish-Bentinck 威廉・卡文迪许・本廷克	Whig	1783 (1st time)

continued

Names	Party	Term
William Pitt, the Younger 小威廉·皮特	Tory	1783-1801 (1st time)
Henry Addington 亨利·阿丁顿	Tory	1801-1804
William Pitt, the Younger 小威廉·皮特	Tory	1804-1806 (2nd time)
William Wyndham Grenville 威廉·温德姆·格伦维尔	Whig	1806-1807
William Cavendish-Bentinck 威廉·卡文迪许·本廷克	Whig	1807-1809 (2nd time)
Spencer Perceval 斯潘塞·帕西瓦尔	Tory	1809-1812
Charles Jenkinson 查尔斯·詹金逊	Tory	1812-1827
George Canning 乔治·坎宁	Tory	1827
Frederick John Robinson 弗雷德里克·约翰·罗宾逊	Tory	1827-1828
Arthur Wellesley 亚瑟·韦尔斯利	Tory	1828-1830 (1st time)
Charles Grey 查尔斯·格雷	Whig	1830-1834
William Lamb 威廉·兰姆	Whig	1834 (1st time)
Arthur Wellesley 亚瑟·韦尔斯利	Tory	1834 (2nd time)
Robert Peel 罗伯特·皮尔	Tory	1834-1835
William Lamb 威廉·兰姆	Whig	1835-1841 (2nd time)
Robert Peel 罗伯特·皮尔	Conservative	1841-1846
John Russell 约翰·罗素	Whig-Liberal	1846-1852 (1st time)
Edward Smith-Stanley 爱德华·史密斯-斯坦利	Conservative	1852 (1st time)

continued

Names	Party	Term
George Hamilton-Gordon 乔治·汉密尔顿-戈登	Conservative	1852-1855
Henry John Temple 亨利·约翰·坦普尔	Liberal	1855-1858 (1st time)
Edward Smith-Stanley 爱德华·史密斯-斯坦利	Conservative	1858-1859 (2nd time)
Henry John Temple 亨利·约翰·坦普尔	Liberal	1859-1865 (2nd time)
Earl Russell 约翰·罗素	Liberal	1865-1866 (2nd time)
Edward Smith-Stanley 爱德华·史密斯-斯坦利	Conservative	1866-1868 (3rd time)
Benjamin Disraeli 本杰明·迪斯雷利	Conservative	1868 (1st time)
William Ewart Gladstone 威廉·尤尔特·格莱斯顿	Liberal	1868-1874 (1st time)
Benjamin Disraeli 本杰明·迪斯雷利	Conservative	1874-1880 (2nd time)
William Ewart Gladstone 威廉·尤尔特·格莱斯顿	Liberal	1880-1885 (2nd time)
Robert Cecil 罗伯特·塞西尔	Conservative	1885-1886 (1st time)
William Ewart Gladstone 威廉·尤尔特·格莱斯顿	Liberal	1886 (3rd time)
Robert Cecil 罗伯特·塞西尔	Conservative	1886-1892 (2nd time)
William Ewart Gladstone 威廉·尤尔特·格莱斯顿	Liberal	1892-1894 (4th time)
Archibald Primrose 阿奇博尔德·普里姆罗斯	Liberal	1894-1895
Robert Cecil 罗伯特·塞西尔	Conservative	1895-1902 (3rd time)
Arthur James Balfour 亚瑟·詹姆斯·鲍尔福	Conservative	1902-1905
Henry Campbell-Bannerman 亨利·坎贝尔-班纳姆	Liberal	1905-1908

continued

Names	Party	Term
H. H. Asquith 赫伯特·亨利·阿斯奎斯	Liberal	1908-1916
David Lloyd George 戴维·劳和·乔治	Liberal	1916-1922
Andrew Bonar Law 安德鲁·博纳尔·劳	Conservative	1922-1923
Stanley Baldwin 斯坦利·鲍德温	Conservative	1923-1924 (1st time)
Ramsay Macdonald 拉姆齐·麦克唐纳	Labour	1924 (1st time)
Stanley Baldwin 斯坦利·鲍德温	Conservative	1924-1929 (2nd time)
Ramsay Macdonald 拉姆齐·麦克唐纳	Labour	1929-1935 (2nd time)
Stanley Baldwin 斯坦利·鲍德温	Conservative	1935-1937 (3rd time)
Arthur Neville Chamberlain 亚瑟·内维尔·张伯伦	Conservative	1937-1940
Winston Churchill 温斯顿·丘吉尔	Conservative	1940-1945 (1st time)
Clement Attlee 克莱门特·艾德礼	Labour	1945-1951
Winston Churchill 温斯顿·丘吉尔	Conservative	1951-1955 (2nd time)
Anthony Eden 安东尼·艾登	Conservative	1955-1957
Harold Macmillan 哈罗德·麦克米伦	Conservative	1957-1963
Alec Douglas-Home 亚历克·道格拉斯-霍姆	Conservative	1963-1964
Harold Wilson 哈罗德·威尔逊	Labour	1964-1970 (1st time)
Edward Heath 爱德华·希斯	Conservative	1970-1974
Harold Wilson 哈罗德·威尔逊	Labour	1974-1976 (2nd time)

continued

Names	Party	Term
James Callaghan 詹姆斯·卡拉汉	Labour	1976-1979
Margaret Thatcher 玛格丽特·撒切尔	Conservative	1979-1990
John Major 约翰·梅杰	Conservative	1990-1997
Tony Blair 托尼·布莱尔	Labour	1997-2007
Gordon Brown 戈登·布朗	Labour	2007-2010
David Cameron 戴维·卡梅伦	Conservative	2010-2016
Theresa May 特雷莎·梅	Conservative	2016-2019

Appendix II: Presidents of the United States

No.	President	Political Party	Term
1	George Washington 乔治 • 华盛顿		1789-1797
2	John Adams 约翰 • 亚当斯	Federalist	1797-1801
3	Thomas Jefferson 托马斯 • 杰斐逊	Democratic-Republican	1801-1809
4	James Madison 詹姆斯 • 麦迪逊	Democratic-Republican	1809-1817
5	James Monroe 詹姆斯 • 门罗	Democratic-Republican	1817-182
6	John Quincy Adams 约翰 • 昆西 • 亚当斯	Democratic-Republican	1825-1829
7	Andrew Jackson 安德鲁 • 杰克逊	Democratic	1829-1837
8	Martin Van Buren 马丁 • 范布伦	Democratic	1837-1841
9	William Henry Harrison 威廉 • 亨利 • 哈里森	Whig	1841
10	John Tyler 约翰 • 泰勒	Whig	1841-1845
11	James K. Polk 詹姆斯 • 波尔克	Democratic	1845-1849

continued

No.	President	Political Party	Term
12	Zachary Taylor 扎卡里・泰勒	Whig	1849-1850
13	Millard Fillmore 米勒德・菲尔莫尔	Whig	1850-1853
14	Franklin Pierce 富兰克林・皮尔斯	Democratic	1853-1857
15	James Buchanan 詹姆斯・布坎南	Democratic	1857-1861
16	Abraham Lincoln 亚伯拉罕・林肯	Republican	1861-1865
17	Andrew Johnson 安德鲁・约翰逊	Democratic	1865-1869
18	Ulysses S. Grant 尤利塞斯・格兰特	Republican	1869-1877
19	Rutherford B. Hayes 拉瑟富德・海斯	Republican	1877-1881
20	James A. Garfield 詹姆斯・加菲尔德	Republican	1881
21	Chester A. Arthur 切斯特・阿瑟	Republican	1881-1885
22	Grover Cleveland 格罗弗・克利夫兰	Democratic	1885-1889
23	Benjamin Harrison 本杰明・哈里森	Republican	1889-1893
24	Grover Cleveland 格罗弗・克利夫兰	Democratic	1893-1897
25	William McKinley 威廉・麦金莱	Republican	1897-1901
26	Theodore Roosevelt 西奥多・罗斯福	Republican	1901-1909

continued

No.	President	Political Party	Term
27	William Howard Taft 威廉·霍华德·塔夫脱	Republican	1909-1913
28	Woodrow Wilson 伍德罗·威尔逊	Democratic	1913-1921
29	Warren G. Harding 沃伦·哈定	Republican	1921-1923
30	Calvin Coolidge 卡尔文·柯立芝	Republican	1923-1929
31	Herbert Hoover 赫伯特·胡佛	Republican	1929-1933
32	Franklin D. Roosevelt 富兰克林·罗斯福	Democratic	1933-1945
33	Harry S. Truman 哈里·杜鲁门	Democratic	1945-1953
34	Dwight D. Eisenhower 德怀特·艾森豪威尔	Republican	1953-1961
35	John F. Kennedy 约翰·肯尼迪	Democratic	1961-1963
36	Lyndon B. Johnson 林登·约翰逊	Democratic	1963-1969
37	Richard M. Nixon 理查德·尼克松	Republican	1969-1974
38	Gerald R. Ford 杰拉尔德·福特	Republican	1974-1977
39	Jimmy Carter 吉米·卡特	Democratic	1977-1981
40	Ronald Reagan 罗纳德·里根	Republican	1981-1989

continued

No.	President	Political Party	Term
41	George Bush 乔治 • 布什	Republican	1989-1993
42	Bill Clinton 比尔 • 克林顿	Democratic	1993-2001
43	George W. Bush 乔治 • 布什	Republican	2001-2009
44	Barack Obama 贝拉克 • 奥巴马	Democratic	2009-2017
45	Donald Trump 唐纳德 • 特朗普	Republican	2017-

References

[1] Anthony Paul. A Guide to the English-Speaking World [M]. London: Longman Group Ltd., 1975.

[2] Campbell John L., Hollingsworth Joseph Rogers, Lindberg Leon N.. Governance of the American Economy [M], Cambridge: Cambridge University Press, 1991.

[3] Carroll John M., Baxter Colin F.. American Military Tradition: from Colonial Times to the Present [M]. Lanham: Rowman & Littlefield Publishers, Inc., 2007.

[4] Heidler David Stephen, Heidler Jeanne T., Coles David J.. Encyclopedia of the American Civil War: a Political, Social, and Military History [M]. New York: W.W. Norton & Co., 2002.

[5] Higham Robin D.S.. A Guide to the Sources of British Military History [M]. London: Routledge & Kegan Paul Ltd, 1972.

[6] Luvaas Jay. The Education of an Army: British Military Thought, 1815-1940 [M]. Chicago: University of Chicago Press, 1964.

[7] Mackinnon Donald, Statham June, Hales Margaret. Education in the UK: Facts and Figures [M]. London: Holder and Stoughton and the Open University, 1996.

[8] Schagrin Morton. The society and Culture of Major English-speaking Countries [M]. Beijing: Higher Education Press, 2003.

[9] Thernstrom Stephan, ed. Harvard Encyclopedia of American Ethnic Groups [M]. Cambridge: Harvard University Press, 1980.

[10] Zenfell Martha. United States on the Road [M]. Singapore: Insight Print Services (Pte) Ltd, 2005.

[11] http://atheism.about.com/

[12] http://beijing.usembassy-china.org.cn/visiual_arts.html

[13] http://classiclit.about.com/

[14] http://en.wikipedia.org/

[15] http://factfinder.census.gov/servlet/SAFFBusiness?_submenuld=business_4

[16] http://great-writers.suite101.com/

[17] http://hirr.hartsem.edu/ency/american.htm

[18] http://normanconquest.co.uk/

[19] http://projectbritain.com/

[20] http://spectator.org

[21] http://religions.pewforum.org/reports

[22] http://usa.usembassy.de/society-religion.htm

[23] http://www.army.mod.uk/
[24] http://www.army.mil/
[25] http://www.bookrags.com/
[26] http://www.america.gov/index.html
[27] http://www.associatedcontent.com/
[28] http://www.britisharmedforces.org/
[29] http://www.britainexpress.com/History/medieval/black-death.htm
[30] http://www.britannia.com/history/monarchs/mon46.html
[31] http://www.bbc.co.uk
[32] http://www.britishcouncil.org/
[33] http://www.care4america.com
[34] http://www.christiantoday.co.uk/
[35] http://www.christianitymagazine.co.uk/
[36] http://www.culture.gov.uk
[37] http://www.defense.gov/
[38] http://www.economywatch.com/world_economy/united-kingdom/
[39] http://www.ed.gov/index.jhtml
[40] http://www.educationuk.org/
[41] http://www.encyclopedia.com
[42] http://www.ensignmessage.com/
[43] http://www.gradesaver.com/
[44] http://www.great-britain.co.uk/history/roses.htm
[45] http://www.indianchild.com/the_great_depression.htm
[46] http://www.infoplease.com/
[47] http://www.kirjasto.sci.fi/
[48] http://www.learnenglish.de/culture/educationculture.html
[49] http://www.lifeintheusa.com
[50] http://www.libraryindex.com/pages/1281/International-Trade-America-s-Place-in-Glo
[51] http://www.mapsofworld.com/
[52] http://www.mediauk.com
[53] http://www.megaessays.com/
[54] http://www.military-kit.co.uk/
[55] http://www.navy.mil/swf/index.asp
[56] http://www.open.gov.uk/dfee
[57] http://www.pad.press.net
[58] http://www.poemsource.com
[59] http://www.quotationspage.com
[60] http://www.rae.org/ReligiousFreedom.html

[61] http://www.referatele.com/
[62] http://www.rickross.com/
[63] http://www.spartacus.schoolnet.co.uk/FWW.htm
[64] http://www.sparknotes.com/
[65] http://www.schoolshistory.org.uk/romaninvasion.htm
[66] http://www.statistics.gov.uk/socialtrends
[67] http://www.ukstudentlife.com/Britain.html
[68] http://www.usma.edu/
[69] http://usmilitary.about.com/
[70] http://www.warsoftheroses.com/
[71] http://www.statistics.gov.uk/instantfigures.asp
[72] http://www.washingtonpost.com/
[73] http://www.worldwariihistory.info/WWⅡ/war.html
[74] 埃塞尔·狄尔斯基. 美国制度与文化[M]. 北京：中国人民大学出版社，2006.
[75] 陈德. 新编英语国家概况[M]. 西安：西安交通大学出版社，2008.
[76] 段洁云. 英语国家社会与文化[M]. 昆明：云南大学出版社，2008.
[77] 范悦. 美国历史概况[M]. 北京：对外经济贸易大学出版社，2006.
[78] 何田. Cultural Background for English Study: Britain and Australia [M]. 北京：北京大学出版社，2001.
[79] 来安方.新编英美概况[M]. 郑州：河南人民出版社，2008.
[80] 罗选民.英美文化与社会[M]. 武汉：华中理工大学出版社，1997.
[81] 马晓宇. 新编英语国家概况[M]. 西安：西安交通大学出版社，2008.
[82] 苏立昌. 英国社会与文化[M]. 天津：南开大学出版社，2008.
[83] 王恩铭. 英语国家概况[M]. 上海：上海外语教育出版社，2009.
[84] 王九萍，张锦萍. 英美概况[M]. 西安：西安交通大学出版社，2009.
[85] 温洪瑞. 英语国家概况[M]. 北京：首都经济贸易大学出版社，2008.
[86] 吴斐. 英国社会与文化[M]. 武汉：武汉大学出版社，2003.
[87] 吴伟仁. 美国文学史及选读[M]. 北京：外语教学与研究出版社，1997.
[88] 肖惠云. 当代英国概况[M]. 上海：上海外语教育出版社，2001.
[89] 谢福之. 英语国家概况[M]. 北京：外语教学与研究出版社，2007.
[90] 徐晓晴，张红岩，王威. 英语国家社会与文化[M]. 苏州：苏州大学出版社，2008.
[91] 余志远. English-speaking Countries: A Survey [M]. 北京：外语教学与研究出版社，1996.
[92] 余志远. 英语国家概况[M]. 北京：外语教学与研究出版社，2000.
[93] 张奎武. 英美概况[M]. 长春：吉林科学技术出版社，2000.
[94] 周叔麟，C. W. Pollard, June Almes. 新编英美概况教程[M]. 北京：北京大学出版社，2008.
[95] 朱永涛，王立礼. 英语国家社会与文化入门[M]. 北京：高等教育出版社，2005.
[96] 朱永涛. Essentials of British and American Cultures [M]. 北京：外语教学与研究出版社，1995.